# FINANCIAL MANAGEMENT

# FINANCIAL MANAGEMENT

**Dr. Sudhir Gupta**

CENTRUM PRESS
NEW DELHI-110002 (INDIA)

**CENTRUM PRESS**
**H.O.:** 4360/4, Ansari Road, Daryaganj,
New Delhi-110002 (India)
Tel: 23278000, 23261597, 23255577, 23286875
**B.O.:** No. 1015, Ist Main Road, BSK IIIrd Stage,
IIIrd Phase, IIIrd Block, Bangalore-560085 (INDIA)
Tel: 080-41723429
*Email:* centrumpress@gmail.com
*Visit us at:* www.centrumpress.com

*Financial Management*



First Edition, 2011

ISBN 978-93-80921-17-4

PRINTED IN INDIA

---

*Printed at* Balaji Offset, Delhi.

# Contents

# Preface

Financial management plays a critical role in business enterprise. Without money and its successful management, a firm would not survive much less grow and prosper. In today's rapidly changing business environment, financial management is more complex than in any time in history. This makes understanding corporate finance not only important and exciting but also challenging and sometimes be wildering. Similar to other business disciplines, financial management has its own terminology, conflicting theories and varying practices. The theory and practice of financial management continue to advance at an uncommonly rapid pace in response to shifts in economic conditions. Those involved with financial management in business organization must run just to keep in place. Yet, the core principles underlying financial management have changed relatively little over time. Financial theory has added to the store of knowledge and provided needed structure, but these advances have generally been in the details. Often considerable time is required before meaningful financial developments or innovations become embedded in the fabric of finance.

The discussion made in this book will help the readers to understand and learnt about the different aspects of "Financial Management" in a most comprehensive way.

***Author***

# 1

# Introduction

## CONCEPT OF FINANCIAL MANAGEMENT

Financial management entails planning for the future of a person or a business enterprise to ensure a positive cash flow. It includes the administration and maintenance of financial assets. Besides, financial management covers the process of identifying and managing risks.

The primary concern of financial management is the assessment rather than the techniques of financial quantification. A financial manager looks at the available data to judge the performance of enterprises. Managerial finance is an interdisciplinary approach that borrows from both managerial accounting and corporate finance.

Some experts refer to financial management as the science of money management. The primary usage of this term is in the world of financing business activities. However, financial management is important at all levels of human existence because every entity needs to look after its finances.

## FINANCIAL MANAGEMENT: LEVELS

Broadly speaking, the process of financial management takes place at two levels. At the individual level, financial management involves tailoring expenses just as to the financial resources of an individual. Individuals with surplus cash or access to funding invest their money to make up for the impact of taxation and inflation. Else, they spend it on discretionary items. They need to be able to take the financial decisions that are intended to benefit them in the long run and help them achieve their financial goals. From an organizational point of view, the process of financial management is associated with financial planning and financial control. Financial planning seeks to quantify various financial resources available and plan the size and timing of expenditures. Financial control refers to monitoring cash flow. Inflow is the amount of money coming into a particular company, while outflow is a record of the expenditure being made by the company. Managing this movement of funds in relation to the budget is essential for a business.

At the corporate level, the main aim of the process of managing finances is to achieve the various goals a company sets at a given point of time. Businesses also seek to generate substantial amounts of profits, following a particular set of financial processes. Financial managers aim to boost the levels of resources at their disposal. Besides, they control the functioning on money put in by external investors. Providing investors with sufficient amount of returns on their investments is one of the goals that every company tries to achieve. Efficient financial management ensures that this becomes possible.

*Strong financial management in the business arena requires managers to be able to:*

- Interpret financial reports including income statements, Profits and Loss or P&L, cash flow statements and balance sheet statements
- Improve the allocation of working capital within business operations
- Review and fine tune financial budgeting, and revenue and cost forecasting
- Look at the funding options for business expansion, including both long and short term financing
- Review the financial health of the company or business unit using ratio analyses, such as the gearing ratio, profit per employee and weighted cost of capital

- Understand the various techniques using in project and asset valuations
- Apply critical financial decision making techniques to assess whether to proceed with an investmtn
- Understand valuations frameworks for businesses, portfolios and intangible assets.

## MANAGERIAL FINANCE

Managerial finance is the branch of the finance that concerns itself with the managerial significance of finance techniques. It is focused on assessment rather than technique.

The difference between a managerial and a technical approach can be seen in the questions one might ask of annual reports. One concerned with technique would be primarily interested in measurement. They would ask: are moneys being assigned to the right categories? Were generally accepted accounting principles GAAP followed?

*One concerned with management though would want to know what the figures mean*:

- They might compare the returns to other businesses in their industry and ask: are we performing better or worse than our peers? If so, what is the source of the problem? Do we have the same profit margins? If not why? Do we have the same expenses? Are we paying more for something than our peers?
- They may look at changes in asset balances looking for red flags that indicate problems with bill collection or bad debt.
- They will Analyse working capital to anticipate future cash flow problems.

Managerial finance is an interdisciplinary approach that borrows from both managerial accounting and corporate finance.

Sound financial management creates value and organisational agility through the allocation of scarce resources amongst competing business opportunities. It is an aid to the implementation and monitoring of business strategies and helps achieve business objectives.

## ROLE OF MANAGERIAL ACCOUNTING

Managers also need to look at how resources are allocated within an organization. They need to know what each activity costs and why. These questions require managerial accounting techniques such as activity based costing. Managers also need to anticipate future expenses. To get a better understanding of the accuracy of the budgeting process, they may use variable budgeting.

## ROLE OF CORPORATE FINANCE

Managerial finance is also interested in determining the best way to use money to improve future opportunities to earn money and minimize the impact of financial shocks.

*To accomplish these goals managerial finance uses the following techniques borrowed from Corporate finance:*

- Valuation
- Portfolio theory
- Hedging
- Capital structure

## CORPORATE FINANCE

Corporate finance is an area of finance dealing with financial decisions business enterprises make and the tools and analysis used to make these decisions. The primary goal of corporate finance is to maximize corporate value while managing the firm's financial risks. Although it is in principle different from managerial finance which studies the financial decisions of all firms, rather than corporations alone, the main concepts in the study of corporate finance are applicable to the financial problems of all kinds of firms.

The discipline can be divided into long-term and short-term decisions and techniques. Capital investment decisions are long-term choices about which projects receive investment, whether to finance that investment with equity or debt, and when or whether to pay dividends to shareholders. On the other hand, the short term decisions can be grouped under the heading "Working capital management". This subject deals with the short-term balance of current assets and current liabilities; the focus here is on managing cash, inventories, and short-term borrowing and lending.

The terms corporate finance and corporate financier are also associated with investment banking. The typical role of an investment bank is to evaluate the company's financial needs and raise the appropriate type of capital that best fits those needs.

## CAPITAL INVESTMENT DECISIONS

Capital investment decisions are long-term corporate finance decisions relating to fixed assets and capital structure.

*Decisions are based on several inter-related criteria*:

- Corporate management seeks to maximize the value of the firm by investing in projects which yield a positive net present value when valued using an appropriate discount rate.
- These projects must also be financed appropriately.
- If no such opportunities exist, maximizing shareholder value dictates that management must return excess cash to shareholders. Capital investment decisions thus comprise an investment decision, a financing decision, and a dividend decision.

### Investment Decision

Management must allocate limited resources between competing opportunities in a process known as capital budgeting. Making this capital allocation decision requires estimating the value of each opportunity or project, which is a function of the size, timing and predictability of future cash flows.

#### *Project Valuation*

In general, each project's value will be estimated using a discounted cash flow valuation, and the opportunity with the highest value, as measured by the resultant net present value will be selected. This requires estimating the size and timing of all of the incremental cash flows resulting from the project. Such future cash flows are then discounted to determine their *present value*. These present values are then summed, and this sum net of the initial investment outlay is the NPV.

The NPV is greatly affected by the discount rate. Thus, identifying the proper discount rate - often termed, the project "hurdle rate" - is critical to making an appropriate decision. The hurdle rate is the minimum acceptable return on an investment—i.e. the project appropriate discount rate. The hurdle rate should reflect the riskiness of the investment, typically measured by volatility of cash flows, and must take into account the financing mix.

Managers use models such as the CAPM or the APT to estimate a discount rate appropriate for a particular project, and use the weighted average cost of capital to reflect the financing mix selected.

In conjunction with NPV, there are several other measures used as selection criteria in corporate finance. These are visible from the DCF and include discounted payback period, IRR, Modified IRR, equivalent annuity, capital efficiency, and ROI. Alternatives to NPV include MVA/ EVA and APV.

### *Valuing Flexibility*

In many cases, for example R&D projects, a project may open paths of action to the company, but this reality will not typically be captured in a strict NPV approach. Management will therefore employ tools which place an explicit value on these options. So, whereas in a DCF valuation the most likely or average or scenario specific cash flows are discounted, here the "flexibile and staged nature" of the investment is modelled, and hence "all" potential payoffs are considered. The difference between the two valuations is the "value of flexibility" inherent in the project.

*The two most common tools are Decision Tree Analysis and Real options analysis; they may often be used interchangeably*:

- DTA values flexibility by incorporating *possible events* and consequent *management decisions*. In the decision tree, each management decision in response to an "event" generates a "branch" or "path" which the company could follow; the probabilities of each event are determined or specified by management. Once the tree is constructed:

- "All" possible events and their resultant paths are visible to management;
- Given this "knowledge" of the events that could follow, management chooses the actions corresponding to the highest value path probability weighted;
- Then, assuming rational decision making, this path is taken as representative of project value.

- ROA is usually used when the value of a project is *contingent* on the *value* of some other asset or underlying variable. Here:
  - Using financial option theory as a framework, the decision to be taken is identified as corresponding to either a call option or a put option;
  - An appropriate valuation technique is then employed - usually a variant on the Binomial options model or a bespoke simulation model, while Black Scholes type formulae are used less often
  - The "true" value of the project is then the NPV of the "most likely" scenario plus the option value.

## *Quantifying Uncertainty*

Given the uncertainty inherent in project forecasting and valuation, analysts will wish to assess the sensitivity of project NPV to the various inputs to the DCF model. In a typical sensitivity analysis the analyst will vary one key factor while holding all other inputs constant, ceteris paribus.

The sensitivity of NPV to a change in that factor is then observed, and is calculated as a"slope": ΔNPV/ Δfactor. For example, the analyst will determine NPV at various growth rates in annual revenue as specified, and then determine the sensitivity using this formula.

Often, several variables may be of interest, and their

various combinations produce a"value-surface", where NPV is then a function of several variables.

Using a related technique, analysts also run scenario based forecasts of NPV. Here, a scenario comprises a particular outcome for economy-wide,"global" factors as well as for company-specific factors. As an example, the analyst may specify specific growth scenarios, where all key inputs are adjusted so as to be consistent with the growth assumptions, and calculate the NPV for each. Note that for scenario based analysis, the various combinations of inputs must be internally consistent, whereas for the sensitivity approach these need not be so. An application of this methodology is to determine an"unbiased" NPV, where management determines a probability for each scenario - the NPV for the project is then the probability-weighted average of the various scenarios.

A further advancement is to construct stochastic or probabilistic financial models - as opposed to the traditional static and deterministic models. For this purpose, the most common method is to use Monte Carlo simulation to Analyse the project's NPV. This method was introduced to finance by David B. Hertz in 1964, although has only recently become common: today analysts are even able to run simulations in spreadsheet based DCF models, typically using an add-in, such as Crystal Ball. Using simulation, the cash flow components that are impacted by uncertainty are simulated, mathematically reflecting their"random characteristics". Here, the simulation produces several thousand random but possible outcomes, or"trials"; The output is then a histogram of project NPV, and the average NPV of the potential investment - as well as its volatility and other sensitivities - is then observed. This histogram provides information not visible from the static DCF: for example, it allows for an estimate of the probability that a project has a net present value greater than zero.

Instead of assigning three discrete values to revenue growth, and to the other relevant variables, the analyst would assign an appropriate probability distribution to each variable, and, where possible, specify the observed or supposed correlation between the variables. These distributions would then be"sampled" repeatedly - incorporating this correlation - so as to generate several thousand scenarios, with corresponding valuations, which are then used to generate the NPV histogram. The resultant statistics will be a more accurate mirror of the project's"randomness" than the variance observed under the scenario based approach.

## Financing Decision

Achieving the goals of corporate finance requires that any corporate investment be financed appropriately. Since both hurdle rate and cash flows will be affected, the financing mix can impact the valuation. Management must therefore identify the"optimal mix" of financing-the capital structure that results in maximum value.

The sources of financing will, generically, comprise some combination of debt and equity financing. Financing a project through debt results in a liability or obligation that must be serviced, thus entailing cash flow implications independent of the project's degree of success. Equity financing is less risky with respect to cash flow commitments, but results in a dilution of ownership, control and earnings. The cost of equity is also typically higher than the cost of debt and so equity financing may result in an increased hurdle rate which may offset any reduction in cash flow risk. Management must also attempt to match the financing mix to the asset being financed as closely as possible, in terms of both timing and cash flows.

One of the main theories of how firms make their financing decisions is the Pecking Order Theory, which suggests that firms avoid external financing while they have internal financing available and avoid new equity financing while they can engage in new debt financing at reasonably low interest rates. Another major theory is the Trade-Off Theory in which firms are assumed to trade-off the tax benefits of debt with the bankruptcy costs of debt when making their decisions. An emerging area in finance theory is right-financing whereby investment banks and corporations can enhance investment return and company value over time by determining the right investment objectives, policy framework, institutional structure, source of financing and expenditure framework within a given economy and under given market conditions. One last theory about this decision is the Market timing hypothesis which states that firms look for the cheaper type of financing regardless of their current levels of internal resources, debt and equity.

### Dividend Decision

Whether to issue dividends, and what amount, is calculated mainly on the basis of the company's unappropriated profit and its earning prospects for the coming year. If there are no NPV positive opportunities, i.e. projects where returns exceed the hurdle rate, then management must return excess cash to investors. These free cash flows comprise cash remaining after all business expenses have been met. This is the general case, however there are exceptions.

For example, investors in a"Growth stock", expect that the company will, almost by definition, retain earnings so as to fund growth internally. In other cases, even though an opportunity is currently NPV negative, management may consider"investment flexibility"/ potential payoffs and decide to retain cash flows.

Management must also decide on the form of the dividend distribution, generally as cash dividends or via a share buyback. Various factors may be taken into consideration: where shareholders must pay tax on dividends, firms may elect to retain earnings or to perform a stock buyback, in both cases increasing the value of shares outstanding. Alternatively, some companies will pay"dividends" from stock rather than in cash. Today, it is generally accepted that dividend policy is value neutral.

## WORKING CAPITAL MANAGEMENT

Decisions relating to working capital and short term financing are referred to as *working capital management*. These involve managing the relationship between a firm's short-term assets and its short-term liabilities. The goal of Corporate Finance is the maximization of firm value. In the context of long term, capital investment decisions, firm value is enhanced through appropriately selecting and funding NPV positive investments. These investments, in turn, have implications in terms of cash flow and cost of capital. The goal of Working capital management is therefore to ensure that the firm is able to operate, and that it has sufficient cash flow to service long term debt, and to satisfy both maturing short-term debt and upcoming operational expenses. In so doing, firm value is enhanced when, and if, the return on capital exceeds the cost of capital.

## Decision Criteria

Working capital is the amount of capital which is readily available to an organization. That is, working capital is the difference between resources in cash or readily convertible into cash and cash requirements. As a result, the decisions relating to working capital are always current, i.e. short term, decisions.

In addition to time horizon, working capital decisions differ from capital investment decisions in terms of discounting and profitability considerations; they are also "reversible" to some extent..

Working capital management decisions are therefore not taken on the same basis as long term decisions, and working capital management applies different criteria in decision making:

*The main considerations are:*

- Cash flow/ liquidity and
- Profitability/ return on capital.
  - The most widely used measure of cash flow is the net operating cycle, or cash conversion cycle. This represents the time difference between cash payment for raw materials and cash collection for sales. The cash conversion cycle indicates the firm's ability to convert its resources into cash. Because this number effectively corresponds to the time that the firm's cash is tied up in operations and unavailable for other activities, management generally aims at a low net count.
  - In this context, the most useful measure of profitability is Return on capital. The result is shown as a percentage, determined by dividing relevant income for the 12 months by capital

employed; Return on equity shows this result for the firm's shareholders. Firm value is enhanced when, and if, the return on capital, exceeds the cost of capital. ROC measures are therefore useful as a management tool, in that they link short-term policy with long-term decision making.

## Management of Working Capital

Management will use a combination of policies and techniques for the management of working capital.

*These policies aim at managing the current assets and the short term financing, such that cash flows and returns are acceptable:*

- *Cash management*: Identify the cash balance which allows for the business to meet day to day expenses, but reduces cash holding costs.
- *Inventory management*: Identify the level of inventory which allows for uninterrupted production but reduces the investment in raw materials - and minimizes reordering costs - and hence increases cash flow.
- *Debtors management*: Identify the appropriate credit policy, i.e. credit terms which will attract customers, such that any impact on cash flows and the cash conversion cycle will be offset by increased revenue and hence Return on Capital.
- *Short term financing*: Identify the appropriate source of financing, given the cash conversion cycle: the inventory is ideally financed by credit granted by the supplier; however, it may be necessary to utilize a bank loan or to "convert debtors to cash" through "factoring".

## FINANCIAL RISK MANAGEMENT

Risk management is the process of measuring risk and then developing and implementing strategies to manage that risk. Financial risk management focuses on risks that can be managed using traded financial instruments. Financial risk management will also play an important role in cash management. This area is related to corporate finance in two ways. Firstly, firm exposure to business risk is a direct result of previous Investment and Financing decisions. Secondly, both disciplines share the goal of enhancing, or preserving, firm value. All large corporations have risk management teams, and small firms practice informal, if not formal, risk management. Derivatives are the instruments most commonly used in financial risk management. Because unique derivative contracts tend to be costly to create and monitor, the most cost-effective financial risk management methods usually involve derivatives that trade on well-established financial markets. These standard derivative instruments include options, futures contracts, forward contracts, and swaps.

## RELATIONSHIP WITH OTHER AREAS IN FINANCE

### Investment Banking

Use of the term"corporate finance" varies considerably across the world. In the United States it is used to describe activities, decisions and techniques that deal with many aspects of a company's finances and capital. In the United Kingdom and Commonwealth countries, the terms"corporate finance" and"corporate financier" tend to be associated with investment banking - i.e. with transactions in which capital is raised for the corporation.

### Personal and Public Finance

Corporate finance utilizes tools from almost all areas of finance. Some of the tools developed by and for corporations have broad application to entities other than corporations, for example, to partnerships, sole proprietorships, not-for-profit organizations, governments, mutual funds, and personal wealth management. But in other cases their application is very limited outside of the corporate finance arena. Because corporations deal in quantities of money much greater than individuals, the analysis has developed into a discipline of its own. It can be differentiated from personal finance and public finance.

## EVOLUTION OF FINANCIAL MANAGEMENT

There is an assumption that inadequate financial management practices are contributors to turbulence in the small firm sector; yet there have been few investigations into the factors that influence an owner-manager's approach and the processes involved in the evolution of strategy and associated learning in this area.

A comparative static approach that is survey-based; we argue that these studies can only give limited insights. We adopt a comparative case study methodology to develop an evolutionary process view of financial management in small firms.

Despite the increased attention paid to owner-managers in the small firms sector, we know comparatively little about the process of financial management and how small firms learn and adjust strategy and decision-making in this area.

We attempt to shed some light on the process issues within small firms from qualitative evidence collected as part of a programme of case study research with entrepreneurs and owner-managers. We discuss case evidence and focus on how owner-managers reach financial management decisions, how they learn and adjust behaviour within the entrepreneurship process.

## SCOPE OF FINANCIAL MANAGEMENT

Scope of financial management is vast and important to business. It is involve in all level of management and all fields of human activities. We can prove that without good financial management, no organization can be alive.

Organization is helpful for people and wants welfare of public. But, it need fund, money and cash and for getting it, it uses techniques of financial management. So, financial management makes his place everywhere.

*We can divide financial management scope into three major parts:*

- *Financial Management in New Companies*: A new company spends large amount on production and marketing but it should ignore proper use of its fund.

Financial management's gateway is new company and if new company ignores financial management study, it means it is ignoring cash, inventory, debtors and fixed assets management. Past study reveals that big organization or companies did not trade even one year and before one year they took their baggage and became liquidated. Why? Because, given debt was demanded from these companies by creditors. By answering no, court had liquidated them.

- *Financial Management in Old Companies*: Old company can survive in long run, if it is capable to pay debt timely, to pay salary on time and to pay other daily expenses. Because old company has good reputation in financial market, so financial management's some part like working capital management is very significant. Old company should try to increase growth rate by using new techniques of financial management.
- *Financial Management in NGO*: In this material age, every work is becoming business. Only NGO are working not for profit aim. Its aim is not to earn money but here is also question of its existence. Like survive of company, NGO can live only and only after proper management of its cost and management of cost can be taught only in financial management. So, NGO are also under the scope of financial management.

  Every NGO wants to provide free services long time. Without, use the techniques of financial management, NGO starts misuse the scarce sources of public. After revealing this fact, public may reduce to donate to NGO, so NGO should be aware about financial management.

## OBJECTIVES OF FINANCIAL MANAGEMENT

### PROVIDE SUPPORT FOR DECISION MAKING

Financial management provides managers with the

information and knowledge they need to support operational decisions and to understand the financial implications of decisions before they are made.

It also enables managers to monitor their decisions for any potential financial implications and for lessons to be learned from experience, and to adapt or react as needed.

## TIMELY, RELEVANT, RELIABLE FINANCIAL AND NON-FINANCIAL INFORMATION

Financial management gives managers the information that either forms the basis for calculating financial information, or is used for management control and accountability purposes.

## MANAGE RISKS

Financial management enables an organization to identify, assess and consider the financial consequences of events that could compromise its ability to achieve its goals and objectives and/or result in significant loss of resources.

Financial management is an important component of risk management and needs to be considered with the full range of business risks, such as operational and strategic risks as well as social, legal, political and environmental risks.

## USE RESOURCES EFFICIENTLY, EFFECTIVELY AND ECONOMICALLY

Financial management is necessary to ensure that an organization has enough resources to carry out its operations, and that it uses these resources with due regard to economy, efficiency and effectiveness.

## STRENGTHEN ACCOUNTABILITY

Financial management is essential for an organization to understand and demonstrate how it has used the financial resources entrusted to it and what it has accomplished with them.

## PROVIDE A SUPPORTIVE CONTROL ENVIRONMENT

Financial management contributes to promoting an organizational climate that fosters the achievement of financial management objectives - a climate that includes commitment from senior management, shared values and ethics, communication and organizational learning.

## COMPLY WITH AUTHORITIES AND SAFEGUARD ASSETS

Financial management is essential to ensuring that an organization carries out its transactions in accordance with applicable legislation, regulations and executive orders; that spending limits are observed; and that transactions are authorized. It also provides an organization with a system of controls for assets, liabilities, revenues and expenditures. These controls help to protect against fraud, financial negligence, violation of financial rules or principles and losses of assets or public money.

# AGENCY PROBLEMS AND GOAL CONFLICTS

## INTRODUCTION

The importance of establishing goals for financial regulators is recognized by the Basel Committee on Banking Supervision.

*The first sentence of the Committee's first principle states*:

- An effective system of banking supervision will have clear responsibilities and objectives for each agency involved in the supervision of banking organizations.

*The Core Principle goes on to state the following*:

- Each such agency should possess operational independence and adequate resources. A suitable legal framework for banking supervision is also necessary, including provisions relating to authorisation of banking organisations and their ongoing supervision; powers to address compliance with laws as well as safety and soundness concerns; and legal protection for supervisors. Arrangements for sharing information between supervisors and protecting the confidentiality of such information should be in place.

Effective design of a regulatory system to ensure financial stability typically includes specification of a set of regulations to ensure that institutions operate in a safe and sound manner, a system of prudential supervision of depository institutions either vested in the central bank or some other regulator, and a system of safety nets in the form of a lender of last resort function coupled with either an explicit or implicit deposit insurance plan.

However, the regulatory systems can often be plagued by agency problems and potential goal conflicts, especially since regulations and financial structures dynamically evolve over time, which may interfere with the objectives of ensuring safety and soundness.1 Clearly, regulatory design and agency problems have been important contributors to financial crises in the U.S., such as the collapse of the Ohio state deposit insurance fund, and more recently the collapse of the Rhode Island credit union insurance funds, not to mention the problems that contributed to the collapse of the FSLIC. Similar issues have been equally important in the rest of the world as well.2 Witness the many incidents of financial crises that have occurred in even the last few years – often at great costs to taxpayers. Because of the importance of a sound, well-functioning financial system to achieving economic growth and improving societal welfare through the promotion of efficient allocation of resources, the potential for goal conflicts and agency problems to arise should be considered in designing a financial regulatory and supervisory system. Moreover, an effective design would consider not only current issues but also be incentive compatible and timeconsistent to address new problems as they arise.

The Economic and Financial Committee of the European Union recently concluded that "...the existing regulatory and supervisory arrangements in Europe provide a coherent and flexible basis for safeguarding financial stability, but recommended that their practical functioning needs enhancement." Furthermore, the Committee put forward the general principle that "...private institutions should be involved as much as possible in both crisis prevention and, if this fails, in crisis management. Each financial institution is responsible for its own safety and soundness. If financial losses occur, the firm's shareholders should bear the costs and its management should suffer the consequences."3 While such pronouncements sound good, without also providing explicit mechanisms detailing how the private sector will be involved, little has been accomplished, especially if the loss control incentives of the regulators and financial institutions are misaligned.

It has been widely recognized both in the US and elsewhere that goal conflicts and agency problems exist which may frustrate the effective functioning of these loss control arrangements. Without more explicit consideration of these issues in designing a financial regulatory structure, it may be difficult to assure that, should a crisis arise, it will be handled efficiently or that the public will be adequately protected from losses.

Employing the framework in Wall and Eisenbeis, first discusses the nature of these conflicts and then considers whether the structure being put in place for the European Monetary Union raises special considerations that have not yet been addressed and may impact the ability to achieve the objectives put forth by the Basel Committee. In particular, there is an attempt to isolate key features of the "new" system that may be vulnerable to conflicts or problems. In the process, the experience of the US is relied upon to the extent that there are relevant parallels that may provide useful insights as to the potential vulnerabilities in the European design.

The nature of the goal and agency conflicts, the turns to ways that they typically are resolved in a democratic system. Finally, turn to design features that would help mitigate the problems and their application to the European Monetary Union.

## AGENCY PROBLEMS AND GOAL CONFLICTS

The issues surrounding the appropriate way to structure financial regulatory agencies and how to apportion their responsibilities are long standing but are seldom dealt with in a systematic way before a crisis arises. In the United States, Congress tends to address financial regulatory problems in a sequential and evolving way. It usually responds to weakness or design flaws exposed by financial crises or emerging competitive inequities spawned by innovations of financial institutions designed to take advantage of regulatory arbitrage.4 When problems appear, Congress often puts regulatory solutions in place in a piecemeal fashion without regard to secondary consequences of subsequent market responses.

But more important for this discussion, while at least temporarily solving one problem, the solutions may result in conflicts and imprecise or overlapping mandates to different regulatory bodies that carry with them another set of problems. For example, a staff report of the U.S. Senate Committee on Governmental Affairs notes that "Where several agencies are involved i n a particular regulatory function there is the possibility of omissions, inconsistencies and conflicting policy."

Horvitz stresses the importance of this problem to financial services by pointing out that Congress has assigned multiple goals to the financial service regulators. Each of the three major federal banking agencies – the Office of the Comptroller of the Currency, the Federal Reserve System and Federal Deposit Insurance Corporation has a different mix of goals. The OCC, for example, charters and regulates national banks. The FDIC provides federal deposit insurance and supervises state chartered banks that aren't members of the Federal Reserve System and certain thrift institutions. The Federal Reserve not only conducts monetary policy but also serves as the lender-of-lastresort and the supervisor of both state chartered member banks and bank holding companies. Because of this differing mix of responsibilities and goals, policies may be applied or implemented differently and jurisdictional conflicts arise between the regulatory agencies over the form, substance, and implementation of regulations.

One clear example of such a goal conflict existed many years ago between the US banking agencies' safety and soundness responsibilities and their requirement to enforce the securities laws when applied to banks. The banking agencies long perceived that providing disclosures to investors of the financial condition of a bank might in some instances trigger a run on the bank to the detriment of depositors and result in potential losses to the deposit insurance fund. This problem was particularly critical to the FDIC that perceived its primary mission to protect the deposit insurance fund, even if it came at the expense of shareholders.

For this reason, the FDIC resisted for many years the disclosure of financial information - even a basic income statement - out of fear that accurate information might trigger a run on financial intuitions it was responsible for, even if the information was relevant to investors. It wasn't until the bank holding company form of organization became the dominant form of banking organization, whose disclosure requirements were administered by the SEC, New York Stock Exchange, other securities exchanges and not the banking agencies, that financial institutions were required to expand their financial disclosures. Of course now, we would regard such information as not only relevant to investors, but also important to achieving market discipline, which was an anathema in earlier regulatory regimes.

An additional layer of potential conflicts among the regulators exists beyond just those at the federal level because each of the 51 states not only charter banks and thrift institutions but also promulgate rules and regulations governing their operations and activities within their home states. They also provide overlapping supervision of these institutions. State and federal regulations are not necessarily harmonized and can be conflicting. For example, there is currently a dispute brewing between many state regulators and the OCC who has pre-empted state banking agency enforcement actions for national banks as well as the application of state laws pertaining to mortgage lender/broker licensing laws, escrow account laws, credit score disclosure laws, and antipredatory lending laws by national banks.5 As a result, many larger institutions, especially those with significant multi-state operations are now opting for national over state charters. The resulting loss of constituents – that is, institutions to supervise and regulate by state banking regulators not only threatens the agencies' raison d'etra but also depletes their financial base. State regulators typically rely upon examination fees for their funding, a feature of regulatory design that is also fraught with potential conflicts of interest. This trend away from state charters is clearly an example of regulatory arbitrage.

More generally, in the financial regulatory arena, there are several affected parties with stakes in the outcome. These include the Congress and other legislative bodies, the public, regulated and non-regulated financial institutions, shareholders and financial institution customers, and the regulatory agencies themselves. Each of these different parties interact with each other in a dynamically evolving economy in a dialectical process described by Kane. There are many examples where conflicts arise from agency problems, such as the case where the FSLIC used the provision of tax benefits to induce acquirers to take over failed S&Ls. These inducements may have helped protect the FSLIC fund, but shifted risk to the US taxpayer who ultimately ended up paying over 150 billion dollars to resolve the thrift crisis in the late 70s and early 1980s. It has also been emphasised how the assignment of different and possibly conflicting goals to regulatory agencies may lead to problems. In many cases the conflicts can be resolved i n a consistent fashion in the public arena only by congressional action or compromise between the agencies. When goal conflicts are resolved external to the agencies, this is termed external conflict resolution.

In some cases, these conflicts could be reduced or eliminated by assigning jurisdiction for the conflicting goals to a single agency. However, in most important instances, assigning jurisdiction to a single agency does not eliminate the conflict, rather, it merely transforms the way that the conflicts are resolved, as was the case with the conflict described earlier for the FDIC between the interest of the insurance fund and the interests of investors. Resolving goal conflicts administratively means that the decision will be conditioned by agency's perception and interpretation of the primacy of its responsibilities and mandates. And the resulting outcomes may not necessarily reflect those that would arise if the conflicts were resolved in the political arena. When the resolution process is de facto delegated to a single agency to solve, this process is called internal conflict resolution.

While the concerns about financial regulatory structure noted by Horvitz have long existed, the problem has become more acute in recent years. Financial firms have used advances in information processing and financial technology to exploit legal loopholes and to offer ever more products that are functionally equivalent to those offered by differently regulated financial services firms. The result has been that competing institutions offering essentially identical products are subject to different rules, regulations, and regulatory burdens that differentially impact firms' profits and competitiveness in markets. To exploit these differences, institutions now routinely seek the most favourable regulatory climate in which to operate for the products they offer. As a consequence, policies adopted by one regulator intended to achieve a specific public policy goal often have the unintended consequence of shifting market shares either to financial services firms regulated by another agency with different goals or to unregulated firms who perceive a competitive advantage and enter the market.

The range of policy areas with possible goals that may be subject to possible conflicts includes: consumer protection, monetary policy, community development, investor protection, market transparency, safety and soundness, ensuring the safety net, reducing systemic risk, and antitrust. The potential problems associated with conflicting regulatory goals are almost certain to increase whenever financial innovations arise to arbitrage regulations or financial modernization legislation is passed to modify the legal barriers separating different types of financial services firms. The question is to how best resolve the conflicts.

## A FRAMEWORK FOR OPTIMAL RESOLUTION OF AGENCY AND GOAL CONFLICTS

At the highest level, design of optimal policies to resolve

conflicting policy goals requires policymakers to have information on the trade-offs among the available alternatives to achieve their policy goals. Selection of the best combination of policies and methods for their implementation depends on social preferences and requires knowledge of and the ability to measure utility that is aggregated across all of the individuals in society. Because the aggregate social welfare function depends on preferences of the members of society, its parameters are surely not known nor are they directly observable. In the absence of knowledge of the social welfare function, revealed preference exercised through the political process can be used as an indirect mechanism to infer the appropriate goal tradeoffs. To this end a presumption of a representative democracy is that the elected members of the legislature are a microcosm of society whose views and preferences reflect those of society at large. But since voters cannot directly control their legislator's actions, the elected official is essentially the voters' agent.7 Moreover, these representatives are able to listen to and balance competing special interests. This process reveals preferences for different policy outcomes. For this reason, legislators are better suited to make policy judgments than is a bureaucratic agency, for example, which often has a narrower set of goals and priorities. Because the legislature is explicitly structured so as to reflect society's views and preferences, it could be argued that all goal conflicts should be resolved by the legislature.

But the myriad of issues and lack of time makes reliance upon the legislature to essentially micromanage disputes among competing interests in a timely fashion in financial markets infeasible. One option would be for parties with special interests in particular regulatory outcomes to appeal to the legislature each time there is need for a new regulatory policy or a change in regulation. The legislature would then be faced with two costly choices. One would be to attempt ex ante to gather information and write legislation that covers all contingencies— a task that would generally be prohibitively costly and difficult, and another would be to plan regularly to write new legislation to cover changing circumstances.

The alternative would be to legislate a general framework for regulatory decision making and delegates, subject to judicial oversight, to regulatory agencies the responsibility to make case by case decisions and to write specific regulations to achieve specified policy objectives.

This, of course, is the option most often selected by the US Congress. For example, in passing the Bank Holding Company Amendments of 1970, there was great debate over what activities would and would not be permitted to banking organizations through the holding company form. In the end, instead of putting forth a laundry list of permissible activities, it listed several activities that presumptively would be permissible and then delegated to the Board of Governors of the Federal Reserve System the authority to decide what activities would be permissible. The Congress also specified the criteria that the Board would use – that permissible activities would be "... so closely related to banking or managing or controlling banks as to be a proper incident thereto..."8 This delegation to the Board has resulted in new activities being authorized over time and emphasises how delegation to an agency can work. There has been little need for the US congress to intervene in the authorization of new banking activities. Having said this, some criticism has been levied that the Board has not been pro-active enough in authorizing new activities in a timely fashion.

Agency problems also arise within legislative bodies because of the need to conserve members' time, which is the scarce resource. The committee system, with oversight responsibility over related sets of issues, not only economizes on time through specialization but also creates the potential for members of the oversight and funding committees to obtain control rents from regulatory agencies and their constituencies. Members who are particularly interested in a set of economic goals may be able to exercise substantial influence over an agency's choice of priorities. Indeed, these members may be able to induce the agency to establish priorities among the goals in cases where there is almost no chance the full legislature would agree to such priorities.

This ability to influence agencies provides a further incentive for the committee writing legislation to delegate goal conflicts to a regulatory agency especially when that agency will be subject to the committee's jurisdiction in the future. Blinder offers another reason for delegation of more decisions to government agencies, related to the fact that agencies tend to have longer time horizons than legislators.9 US congressmen for example, must stand for election every two years, and thus need to demonstrate to their constituents that they have been productive on their behalf before the next election.

By definition, this means that they prefer solutions to problems that generate immediately perceivable results or that avoid imposing short term costs on their constituents. In contrast, those regulators who serve at the pleasure of the President likely will have the option of staying in their positions for at least four years, while other regulatory appointees, such as the Comptroller of the Currency serve six year terms and members of the Board of Governors of the Federal Reserve serve fourteen year terms.

These longer term serving regulators can afford to take a longer view when assessing regulatory alternatives and this might result in more socially desirable decision making.

*Regulatory agencies play two important roles in setting public policy*:

- They provide legislative bodies with information about the set of efficient policies, and
- They implement the resolution of conflicting goals delegated to them.

One consideration is the relative efficiency of different agency structures in producing information. If economies of scope exist in gathering information across different types of financial services, especially when institutions are headquartered in one locality but operate across borders, then internalizing goal conflicts may enhance the efficiency of information production. Alternatively, there may be diseconomies of scope such that information is more efficiently produced by agencies that specialize in particular problems or industries. This issue may be especially important in situations where regulation is decentralized, as in the EMU, but there is great need for information sharing across jurisdictions when institutions operate across borders.

## POTENTIAL AGENCY PROBLEMS AND GOAL CONFLICTS

There are many areas where the potential for agency problems and goal conflicts may arise within the structure of the regulation of financial institutions within the EMU.

*Faced with these conflicts, authorities are faced with three choices*:

- Rely upon legislation to hardwire the choices and tradeoffs.
- Assign the resolution of conflicts to a single agency and rely upon internal resolution of conflicts by the agency itself.
- Assign conflicting goals to different regulatory agencies so that conflict resolution is externalized and ultimately left to the political process.

The EU did not have the luxury of a clean slate as far as banking supervisory structure is concerned. While the EU did create a central bank, existing financial systems and legal/regulatory structures have been too different to permit the creation of a single banking regulatory agency. Thus, in practice, the choice of goal conflict resolution had to rely upon quasi-legislative solutions. In this case the European Commission, which is the body formally charged with originating and drafting legislative proposals to the Council and the European Parliament, delegated through directives to individual member countries and their respective regulatory and supervisory agencies the responsibility to design their own regimes.

The intent of the European Union was to create a single market for goods and services, including financial services to foster economic growth and to enhance consumer welfare through increased competition. Under the agreements, a so-called "single passport" was agreed to which allowed any financial institution chartered in one member country to operate freely in other member countries. However, having established this principle, the question then was how to shape the regulatory structure? Historical practice had been to rely upon the host country to regulate how firms doing business within its borders would conduct their business.

The problem with this in the EU was the concern that the host country would potentially structure regulation in ways that would disadvantage the foreign firms in competing with domestic institutions. But this would be inconsistent with the single market objective, and this was made more imperative with the introduction of the EURO. The alternative selected was to rely upon the home country to provide regulation, supervision and deposit insurance for the depository institutions that they chartered. Furthermore, over the longer run, regulatory competition would likely come into play facilitating the evolution of a single market.

Individual country self interest in promoting and their institutions would also be an inducement to compete via deregulation of financial services. Countries offering more attractive charter options or accommodative regulatory regimes would expect to see their institutions gain market share in the EU. The logical consequence of allowing home country regulation would, as the result of regulatory competition, be a less regulated and homogeneous market place.

One consequence of leaving regulation and supervision to the home country is that the member countries in the EU have adopted different structures for financial institution supervision and regulation. Some have split supervision and regulation just as to function while others have consolidated supervision and regulation into a single agency. In some instances the central bank is involved and in other countries it is not. Hence, if faced with the same supervisory or regulatory issue, agencies with different mix of functions will potentially choose different sets of policy tradeoffs depending upon their mix of responsibilities and their individual statutory mandates. Some will face external resolution while others will be faced with internal resolution of conflicts.

Policies will also differ across countries to the extent that internal goal conflict resolution is required as compared with external goal resolution. These differing tradeoffs will result in different policies and will set up many opportunities for individual institutions to pit the countries' agencies against each other and will foster regulatory arbitrage on the part of financial institutions to seek a competitive advantage. Relying upon regulatory competition to level the playing field carries with it the risk of a race to the bottom and more lax supervision as far as safety and soundness is concerned. The EU has attempted to address this problem by setting minimum supervisory standards to be universally applicable through directives and agreements. In effect, the attempt is at least to set a lower bound as far as safety and soundness risks are concerned.

One of the more important of these directives sets policy towards capital adequacy through the Capital Adequacy Directive, which led to the Basel I capital standards for EU supervisors to follow. Basel I has now been refined by the Basel Bank Supervisors Committee now known as Basel II. Unfortunately, concentration of supervisory efforts on capital standards substitutes supervisory judgment for marketbased risk weights to determine if an institution has sufficient capital. Wall and Eisenbeis argue that this focus is misplaced and misdirects supervisory attention from prompt corrective action and least cost resolution of troubled institution.

While the EU has attempted to set minimum regulatory standards and promote cooperation and information sharing among the individual country supervisors, there is no EU-wide supervisor responsible for resolving the failures of institutions, and hence any goal conflicts that may arise should a major institution experience financial difficulty must rely upon external resolution of those conflicts. With no national supervisor to make the goal tradeoffs, it will likely be left to the European Commission or some similar body to resolve conflicts as they arise.

The kinds of conflicts and implications for financial stability are significant and may become more so as the EU evolves. The financial system will become more integrated and more countries with different economic and financial systems at different stages of development are joining the EU. The remainder will focus on three critical areas where the goal conflicts are likely to be most important: the design of deposit insurance system, the apportionment of supervisory responsibilities between home and host country regulators, and the structure of bankruptcy resolution in the event that institutions get into financial difficulties.

## Structure of Deposit Insurance Within the EMU

The desired structure for deposit insurance in the EU was sketched out in the EU's Deposit Guarantee Directive that went into effect in 1995. The DGD endorses a decentralized approach to deposit insurance, despite the fact that depository institutions are authorized to operate within any of the member countries, and delegates to the member countries the responsibility to provide coverage to the depositors in the banks headquartered within the country. Additionally, it is the responsibility of the home country's central bank to serve as the lender of last resort in cases that don't involve EUwide systemic risk issues. The broad-based systemic lender of last resort function is left to the European Central Bank. In effect, the system bifurcates the responsibilities for controlling banking risk between the micro-risk associated with the operation of single institutions from the macro-risk associated with contagion risk or risk that spreads from one institution to another regardless of where the institutions are headquartered.

The DGD specifies the general features that an acceptable deposit insurance system should have. The most specific features being that the system should provide deposit insurance coverage of 20 thousand Euros, should exclude coverage of inter-bank deposits, and may exclude other liabilities at the discretion of the national government. Co-insurance of liabilities is permitted but not required. Coverage of depositors in branches in countries other than the home country is the responsibility of the home country. Interestingly, there is a provision that permits the branches of a multinational bank to opt to provide top coverage up to those branch depositors through the host country's deposit insurance plan, when that coverage would be "better" than that provided by the home country's plan. Finally, it is also instructive in terms of what deposit insurance features are not prescribed.

These include funding of the plans, pricing of coverage, who should operate the plan how troubled institutions should be handled, what too-big-to-fail policies might or might not be pursued, or how conflicts would be resolved where two deposit insurance funds might be affected by failure of an institution with top up coverage.

In establishing the minimal requirements for deposit insurance plans, the attempt was obviously to balance the fact that some EU members already had deposit insurance plans in place and generally, most of the key provisions and features of there programs were different. There was no one obviously optimal structure for deposit insurance plans, and presumably the best that could be hoped for was that the plans would be harmonized over time. The potential for cross-boarder conflicts appeared minimal since there were few truly multinational institutions in the EU. As might be expected, those plans that were put in place in order to comply with the DGD varied substantially from those already in place. Finally, responsibility for supervision and risk monitoring is apportioned differently across the system and within the different countries.

Going forward, however, the patchwork set of deposit insurance plans, when coupled with the bifurcated approach to controlling systemic risk, seems fraught with the potential for agency and conflicts of interest problems.

*These arise from several sources including*:

- Uncertainties about the funding of the deposit insurance plans,
- Differences in deposit insurance coverage and pricing of coverage,
- Reliance upon the home country, as opposed to host country responsibility, should institutions get into financial difficulties,

- Differences in treatment with respect to the lender-of-last-resort function,
- Differences in approaches to bankruptcy and priority of claims in troubled institutions and
- Differences in EMU vs non-EMU participants.

Based upon the long history within the United States with multiple decentralized deposit insurance plans and a fragmented bank regulatory and supervisory structure, there is a very great risk that the system being put in place in the EU will be fraught with conflicts and regulatory competition and that will not be robust to financial crises.

Much of the difficulty flows from a fundamental misunderstanding of the role of deposit insurance, the nature of the guarantees being given, and the relationship between deposit insurance systems and the central bank's lender of last resort function in controlling systemic risk.

## TIME VALUE OF MONEY

The time value of money is the value of money figuring in a given amount of interest earned over a given amount of time.

For example, 100 dollars of today's money invested for one year and earning 5 Per cent interest will be worth 105 dollars after one year. Therefore, 100 dollars paid now or 105 dollars paid exactly one year from now both have the same value to the recipient who assumes 5 Per cent interest; using time value of money terminology, 100 dollars invested for one year at 5 Per cent interest has a *future value* of 105 dollars. This notion dates at least to Martín de Azpilcueta of the School of Salamanca.

The method also allows the valuation of a likely stream of income in the future, in such a way that the annual incomes are discounted and then added together, thus providing a lump-sum "present value" of the entire income stream.

All of the standard calculations for time value of money derive from the most basic algebraic expression for the present value of a future sum, "discounted" to the present by an amount equal to the time value of money. For example, a sum of *FV* to be received in one year is discounted to give a sum of *PV* at present:

$$PV = FV - r \cdot PV = FV/(1+r).$$

*Some standard calculations based on the time value of money are*:

- Present value the current worth of a future sum of money or stream of cash flows given a specified rate of return. Future cash flows are discounted at the discount rate, and the higher the discount rate, the lower the present value of the future cash flows. Determining the appropriate discount rate is the key to properly valuing future cash flows, whether they be earnings or obligations.
- Present value of an annuity An annuity is a series of equal payments or receipts that occur at evenly spaced intervals. Leases and rental payments are examples. The payments or receipts occur at the end of each period for an ordinary annuity while they occur at the beginning of each period for an annuity due.
- Present value of a perpetuity is an infinite and constant stream of identical cash flows.
- Future value is the value of an asset or cash at a specified date in the future that is equivalent in value to a specified sum today.
- Future value of an annuity is the future value of a stream of payments, assuming the payments are invested at a given rate of interest.

## CALCULATIONS

The solutions may be found using the formulas, a financial calculator or a spreadsheet. The formulas are programmed into most financial calculators and several spreadsheet functions.

The formula may also be rearranged to determine one of the other unknowns. In the case of the standard annuity formula, however, there is no closed-form algebraic solution for the interest rate. These equations are frequently combined for particular uses.

For example, bonds can be readily priced using these equations. A typical coupon bond is composed of two types of payments: a stream of coupon payments similar to an annuity, and a lump-sum return of capital at the end of the bond's maturity - that is, a future payment.

The two formulas can be combined to determine the present value of the bond.An important note is that the interest rate $i$ is the interest rate for the relevant period. For an annuity that makes one payment per year, $i$ will be the annual interest rate.

For an income or payment stream with a different payment schedule, the interest rate must be converted into the relevant periodic interest rate.

For example, a monthly rate for a mortgage with monthly payments requires that the interest rate be divided by 12 The rate of return in the calculations can be either the variable solved for, or a predefined variable that measures a discount rate, interest, inflation, rate of return, cost of equity, cost of debt or any number of other analogous concepts.

The choice of the appropriate rate is critical to the exercise, and the use of an incorrect discount rate will make the results meaningless.

For calculations involving annuities, you must decide whether the payments are made at the end of each period or at the beginning of each period. If you are using a financial calculator or a spreadsheet, you can usually set it for either calculation.

The following formulas are for an ordinary annuity. If you want the answer for the Present Value of an annuity due simply multiply the PV of an ordinary annuity by $(1 + i)$.

## FORMULA

### Present Value of a Future Sum

The present value formula is the core formula for the time value of money; each of the other formulae is derived from this formula. For example, the annuity formula is the sum of a series of present value calculations.

*The present value (PV) formula has four variables, each of which can be solved for:*

$$PV = \frac{FV}{(1+i)^n}$$

- PV is the value at time=0
- FV is the value at time=n
- i is the rate at which the amount will be compounded each period
- n is the number of periods

The cumulative present value of future cash flows can be calculated by summing the contributions of $FV_t$, the value of cash flow at time=t

$$PV = \sum_{t=0}^{n} \frac{FV}{(1+i)^t}$$

Note that this series can be summed for a given value of n, or when n is $\infty$. This is a very general formula, which leads to several important special cases.

**Present Value of an Annuity for n Payment Periods**

In this case the cash flow values remain the same throughout the n periods.

*The present value of an annuity formula has four variables, each of which can be solved for:*

$$PV(A) = \frac{A}{i} \cdot \left[1 - \frac{1}{(1+i)^n}\right]$$

- PV(A) is the value of the annuity at time=0
- A is the value of the individual payments in each compounding period
- i equals the interest rate that would be compounded for each period of time
- n is the number of payment periods.

To get the PV of an annuity due, multiply the equation by (1 + *i*).

**Present Value of a Growing Annuity**

In this case each cash flow grows by a factor of (1+g). Similar to the formula for an annuity, the present value of a growing annuity (PVGA) uses the same variables with the addition of *g* as the rate of growth of the annuity (A is the annuity payment in the first period). This is a calculation that is rarely provided for on financial calculators.

Where i '" g:

$$PV = \frac{A}{(i-g)}\left[1 - \left(\frac{1-g}{1+i}\right)^n\right]$$

To get the PV of a growing annuity due, multiply the equation by (1 + *i*).

*Where i = g*:

$$PV = \frac{A * n}{1+i}$$

**Present Value of a Perpetuity**

When $n \to \infty$, the PV of a perpetuity (a perpetual annuity) formula becomes simple division.

$$PV(P) = \frac{A}{i}$$

**Present Value of a Growing Perpetuity**

When the perpetual annuity payment grows at a fixed rate (g) the value is theoretically determined just as to the following formula. In practice, there are few securities with precise characteristics, and the application of this valuation approach is subject to various qualifications and modifications. Most importantly, it is rare to find a growing perpetual annuity with fixed rates of growth and true perpetual cash flow generation. Despite these qualifications, the general approach may be used in valuations of real estate, equities, and other assets.

$$PVGP = \frac{A}{(i-g)}$$

This is the well known Gordon Growth model used for stock valuation.

**Future Value of a Present Sum**

The future value (FV) formula is similar and uses the same variables.

$$FV = PV.(1+i)^n$$

## Future Value of an Annuity

*The future value of an annuity (FVA) formula has four variables, each of which can be solved for:*

$$FV(A) = A.\frac{(1+i)^n - 1}{i}$$

- *FV(A)* is the value of the annuity at time = *n*
- *A* is the value of the individual payments in each compounding period
- *i* is the interest rate that would be compounded for each period of time
- *n* is the number of payment periods

## Future Value of a Growing Annuity

*The future value of a growing annuity (FVA) formula has five variables, each of which can be solved for:*

*Where* $i \neq g$:

$$FV(A) = A.\frac{(1+i)^n - (1+g)^n}{i - g}$$

*Where* $i = g$:

$$FV(A) = A.n(1+i)^{n-1}$$

- *FV(A)* is the value of the annuity at time = *n*
- *A* is the value of initial payment paid at time 1
- *i* is the interest rate that would be compounded for each period of time
- *g* is the growing rate that would be compounded for each period of time
- *n* is the number of payment periods

## DERIVATIONS

### Annuity Derivation

The formula for the present value of a regular stream of future payments is derived from a sum of the formula for future value of a single future payment where C is the payment amount and *n* the period.

*A single payment C at future time m has the following future value at future time n:*

$$FV = C(1+i)^{n-m}$$

Summing over all payments from time 1 to time n, then reversing the order of terms and substituting $k = n - m$:

$$FVA = \sum_{m=1}^{n} C(1+i)^{n-m} = \sum_{k=0}^{n-1} C(1+i)^{k}$$

Note that this is a geometric series, with the initial value being $a = C$, the multiplicative factor being $1 + i$, with $n$ terms. Applying the formula for geometric series, we get

$$FVA = \frac{C(1-(1+i)^{n})}{1-(1+i)} = \frac{C((1+i)^{n}-1)}{i}$$

The present value of the annuity (PVA) is obtained by simply dividing by $(1 + i)^n$:

$$PVA = \frac{FVA}{(1+i)^{n}} = \frac{C}{i}\left(1 - \frac{1}{(1+i)^{n}}\right)$$

Another simple and intuitive way to derive the future value of an annuity is to consider an endowment, whose interest is paid as the annuity, and whose principal remains constant. The principal of this hypothetical endowment can be computed as that whose interest equals the annuity payment amount:

$$\text{Principal} \times i = C$$

$$\text{Principal} = C/\,i + \text{goal}$$

Note that no money enters or leaves the combined system of endowment principal + accumulated annuity payments, and thus the future value of this system can be computed simply via the future value formula:

$$FV = PV(1 + i)^n$$

Initially, before any payments, the present value of the system is just the endowment principal ($PV = C/\,i$). At the end, the future value is the endowment principal plus the future value of the total annuity payments ($FV = C/\,i + FVA$). Plugging this back into the equation:

$$\frac{C}{i} + FVA = \frac{C}{i}(1+i)^{n}$$

$$FAV = \frac{C}{i}\left[(1+i)^{n} - 1\right]$$

## Perpetuity Derivation

Without showing the formal derivation here, the perpetuity formula is derived from the annuity formula. Specifically, the term:

$$\left(1-\frac{1}{(1+i)^n}\right)$$

can be seen to approach the value of 1 as n grows larger. At infinity, it is equal to 1, leaving

$$\frac{C}{i}$$

as the only term remaining.

## DIFFERENTIAL EQUATIONS

Ordinary and partial differential equations —equations involving derivatives and one variables are ubiquitous in more advanced treatments of financial mathematics.

While time value of money can be understood without using the framework of differential equations, the added sophistication sheds additional light on time value, and provides a simple introduction before considering more complicated and less familiar situations. This exposition follows.

The fundamental change that the differential equation perspective brings is that, rather than computing a *number* one computes a *function*. This function may then be Analysed – how does its value change over time – or compared with other functions.

*Formally, the statement that "value decreases over time" is given by defining the linear differential operator L as:*

$$L := -\partial_t + r(t).$$

This states that values decreases (–) over time ($\partial_t$) at the discount rate ($r(t)$).

*Applied to a function it yields:*

$$Lf = -\partial_t f(t) + r(t)f(t).$$

For an instrument whose payment stream is described by $f(t)$, the value $V(t)$ satisfies the inhomogeneous first-order ODE $LV = f$ this encodes the fact that when any cash flow occurs, the value of the instrument changes by the value of the cash flow. The standard technique tool in the analysis of ODEs is the use of Green's functions, from which other solutions can be built.

In terms of time value of money, the Green's function is the value of a bond paying \$1 at a single point in time $u$ – the value of any other stream of cash flows can then be obtained by taking combinations of this basic cash flow. In mathematical terms, this instantaneous cash flow is modeled as a delta function $\delta_u(t) := \delta(t - u)$.

The Green's function for the value at time $t$ of a \$1 cash flow at time $u$ is,

$$b(t;u) := H(u-t).\exp\left(-\int_t^u r(v)dv\right)$$

where $H$ is the Heaviside step function – the notation ";$u$" is to emphasize that $u$ is a *parameter* (fixed in any instance – the time when the cash flow will occur), while $t$ is a *variable* (time). In other words, future cash flows are exponentially discounted (exp) by the sum (integral, $\int$ ) of the future discount rates ( $\int_t^u$ for future, $r(v)$ for discount rates), while past cash flows are worth 0 ($H(u - t) = 1$ if $t < u$,0 if $t > u$), because they have already occurred. Note that the value *at* the moment of a cash flow is not well-defined – there is a discontinuity at that point, and one can use a convention (assume cash flows have already occurred, or not already occurred), or simply not define the value at that point.

In case the discount rate is constant, $r(v) \equiv r$ this simplifies to where $(u - t)$ is "time remaining until cash flow".

$$b(t;u) = H(u-t).e^{-(u-t)r} = \begin{cases} e^{-(u-t)r} & t < u \\ 0 & t > u, \end{cases}$$

Thus for a stream of cash flows $f(u)$ ending by time $T$ (which can be set to $T = +\infty$ for no time horizon) the value at time $t$, $V(t;T)$ is given by combining the values of these individual cash flows:

$$V(t;T) = \int_t^T f(u)b(t;u)du.$$

This formalizes time value of money to future values of cash flows with varying discount rates, and is the basis of many formulas in financial mathematics, such as the Black–Scholes formula with varying interest rates.

## BOND VALUATION

Bond valuation is the process of determining the fair price of a bond. As with any security or capital investment, the theoretical fair value of a bond is the present value of the stream of cash flows it is expected to generate.

Hence, the value of a bond is determined by discounting the bond's expected cash flows to the present using the appropriate discount rate. Determining this rate in practice - i.e. "pricing" the bond - is done with reference to other instruments. Once the price or value has been calculated, the sensitivity of the price can then be estimated; the various yields, which relate the price of the bond to its coupons, can also be determined.

When the bond includes embedded options, the valuation is more specialized and combines option pricing with the cash flow based approach. Depending on the option as embedded, the option price as calculated is either added to or subtracted from the price of the "straight" portion. This total is then the value of the bond; the various yields can then be calculated for the total price.

### CONCEPT

The fair price of a straight bond is determined by discounting its expected cash flows at the appropriate discount rate. The formula applied is as follows:

### Present Value Relationship

- *Cash flows*:
  - The periodic coupon payments C, each of which is made n times every year
  - The par or face value F, which is payable at maturity of the bond after T years. In some of the bonds, their Maturity Redemption Price

might be more than par value, in this case the F is actually the Redemption Price.

- *Discount rate*: The required yield or rate of return r
  - r is the market interest rate for bonds with similar terms and risk ratings
  - m is the number of coupons to be paid over the remaining lifetime of the bond, i.e. n times T.
  - u is (1 + r) i.e. an interest accumulation factor over one coupon period

$$\text{Bond Price} = P_c = \sum_{t=1}^{m} \frac{C}{u^t} + \frac{F}{(1+r)T}.$$

Since the price is the present value of the cash flows, there is an inverse relationship between price and discount rate: the higher the discount rate the lower the value of the bond.

## Clean and Dirty Price

When the bond is not valued precisely on a coupon date, the present value relationship, will incorporate accrued interest: i.e. any interest due to the owner of the bond since the previous coupon date. The price of a bond which includes this accrued interest is known as the "dirty price"; the "clean price" is the price excluding any interest that has accrued. The value returned by the formula is thus the dirty price.

Clean prices are generally more stable over time than dirty prices. This is because clean prices change for economic reasons whereas dirty prices change day to day depending on where the current date is in relation to the coupon dates, in addition to any economic reasons. It is market practice to quote bonds on a clean-price basis. When a bond settles the accrued interest is added to the value based on the clean price to reflect the full market value.

## BOND PRICING

The present value relationship reflects the theoretical approach to determining the value of a bond. In practice though, the bond's price is determined with reference to other, more liquid instruments. The two main approaches are as follows:

### Relative Price Approach

Under this approach, the bond will be priced relative to a benchmark, usually a government security. Here, the yield to maturity on the bond is determined based on the bond's Credit rating relative to a government security with similar maturity or duration.

The better the quality of the bond, the smaller the spread between its required return and the YTM of the benchmark.

### Arbitrage-free Pricing Approach

Under this approach, the bond price will reflect its arbitrage-free price. Here, each cash flow is separately discounted at the same rate as a zero-coupon bond corresponding to the coupon date, and of equivalent credit worthiness. Here, in general, we apply the rational pricing logic relating to "Assets with identical cash flows".

*In detail*:

- The bond's coupon dates and coupon amounts are known with certainty. Therefore
- Some multiple (or fraction) of zero-coupon bonds, each corresponding to the bond's coupon dates, can be specified so as to produce identical cash flows to the bond. Thus
- The bond price today must be equal to the sum of each of its cash flows discounted at the discount rate implied by the value of the corresponding ZCB. Were this not the case,
- The abitrageur could finance his purchase of whichever of the bond or the sum of the various government securities was cheaper, by short selling the other, and meeting his cash flow commitments using the coupons or maturing zeroes as appropriate. Then
- His "risk free", arbitrage profit would be the difference between the two values.

## YIELD AND PRICE RELATIONSHIPS

Once the price or value has been calculated, various yields - which relate the price of the bond to its coupons - can then be determined.

### Yield to Maturity

The yield to maturity is the discount rate which returns the market price of the bond; it is identical to r in the equation. YTM is thus the internal rate of return of an investment in the bond made at the observed price. Since YTM can be used to price a bond, bond prices are often quoted in terms of YTM.

*To achieve a return equal to YTM, i.e. where it is the required return on the bond, the bond owner must:*

- Buy the bond at price $P_0$,
- Hold the bond until maturity, and
- Redeem the bond at par.

### Coupon Yield

The coupon yield is simply the coupon payment (C) as a percentage of the face value (F).

$$\text{Coupon yield} = C/F$$

Coupon yield is also called nominal yield.

### Current Yield

The current yield is simply the coupon payment (C) as a percentage of the (*current*) bond price (P).

$$\text{Current yield} = C/P_0.$$

### Relationship

The concept of current yield is closely related to other bond concepts, including yield to maturity, and coupon yield.

*The relationship between yield to maturity and the coupon rate is as follows:*

- When a bond sells at a discount, YTM > current yield > coupon yield.
- When a bond sells at a premium, coupon yield > current yield > YTM.
- When a bond sells at par, YTM = current yield = coupon yield amt

## PRICE SENSITIVITY

The sensitivity of a bond's market price to interest rate movements is measured by its duration, and, additionally, by its convexity.

Duration is a linear measure of how the price of a bond changes in response to interest rate changes. It is approximately equal to the percentage change in price for a given change in yield, and may be thought of as the elasticity of the bond's price with respect to interest rates. For example, for small interest rate changes, the duration is the approximate percentage by which the value of the bond will fall for a 1% per annum increase in market interest rate. So a 15-year bond with a duration of 7 would fall approximately 7% in value if the interest rate increased by 1% per annum.

Convexity is a measure of the "curvature" of price changes, and is thus a complement to duration. The necessity for this additional measure arises since duration is a linear measure, whereas, in reality, as interest rates change, the price is a convex function of interest rates. Continuing the example, for a more accurate estimate of sensitivity, the convexity score would be added to the value of 7 for duration.

## EXTENSIONS: MORE SOPHISTICATED BOND PRICING MODELS

- Bond pricing under CIR model
- Bond pricing under Hull-White model
- Bond pricing under HJM framework
- Bond pricing under Chen model

## STOCK VALUATION

*Valuing stocks involves four basic issues*:

- The characteristics of the stock as a financial security
- The financial and business prospects of the issuer of the stock
- The relative valuation of the particular stock versus other stocks, and
- The valuation of financial securities in general and the stock market in particular.

"Stock pickers" focus on the characteristics of the particular stock as a financial security and the financial and business prospects of the particular issuer. They believe that they should value the stock and Analyse the prospects for the issuer independent of market and economic changes. With their focus on individual securities, they believe that they are"buying companies" that will prosper over a longer period of time and reward investors because of their success. Value investors try to buy"good companies at cheap prices" when these companies are out of favour with other less disciplined and more faddish investors.

Growth investors strive to find companies with business strategies and products that will allow them to achieve high levels of growth. Both value and growth investors try to ignore the future path of the market or economy. They are confident that the prospects for the individual securities they are buying will overwhelm over factors and do not try to"time the market". If they cannot find individual stocks that are attractive, they might leave some monies in cash. This really reflects their ability to find attractive investment ideas rather than a call on the market.

"Sector rotators" focus on the relative valuation of a stock compared to other stocks and the overall prospects for the stock market in general. They assess the relative valuation of individual stocks and move between stocks and industry groups when they are cheap by comparison using historical standards. They also assess the the overall valuation of the market using aggregate data on earnings, price and other historical accounting measures and compare these to historical norms. Another valuation yardstick is a comparison to other financial assets, such as bonds and money market securities. Much emphasis is given to the relative levels of bond and money market yields and the market dividend yield.

The stage of the economic cycle is important, as stock industry groups have differential performance over the course of a market and economic cycle. If their valuation measures suggest that the market is expensive, they sell stocks and raise cash to defend their portfolios from a potential market setback.

The average investment manager combines stock picking and sector rotation, maintaining her portfolio reasonably similar to her index benchmark and other managers. This type of manager will make industry and security"bets" in their portfolio weightings, moving into defensive stocks and cash in overvalued markets and weighting stocks and industries that are relatively attractive.

## FUNDAMENTAL VALUATION TECHNIQUES

Fundamental valuation of equity securities relies on financial analysis of historical financial data and an assessment of the business prospects of an issuer. The historical data demonstrates the"track record" of the company and its management. The assessment of the business prospects of an issuer involves a study of the conditions and environment under which a company operates.

The financial analysis of the company examines trends in its profitably, efficiency in employing capital, financial capability and other factors that the analyst consideres important. These are assessed by calculating the applicable financial ratios and patterns of sales and profit growth. Important ratios would include: gross and net margin, sales and inventory turnover, financial and operating leverage, interest coverage, current and quick ratios. Valuation yardsticks would include price/earnings, earnings yield, dividend yield and return on equity.

A basic assessment of a company's business prospects includes a review of all public information available on a company and third party research reports.

A more"in depth" review would include interviews of senior management of the company, both telephone and in person, and even discussions of the company's prospects with suppliers, regulators and even competitors' personnel.

## MARKET VALUE ADDED

Market Value Added is the difference between the current market value of a firm and the capital contributed by investors. If MVA is positive, the firm has added value. If it is negative, the firm has destroyed value. The amount of value added needs to be greater than the firm's investors could have achieved investing in the market portfolio, adjusted for the leverage of the firm relative to the market.

*The formula for MVA is:*
*where:*

- MVA is market value added
- V is the market value of the firm, including the value of the firm's equity and debt
- K is the capital invested in the firm

MVA is the present value of a series of EVA values. MVA is economically equivalent to the traditional NPV measure of worth for evaluating an after-tax cash flow profile of a project if the cost of capital is used for discounting.

# 2

# Funds

## MUTUAL FUND

A mutual fund is a professionally managed type of collective investment plan that pools money from many investors and invests typically in investment securities (stocks, bonds, short-term money market instruments, other mutual funds, other securities, and/or commodities such as precious metals).

The mutual fund will have a fund manager that trades (buys and sells) the fund's investments in accordance with the fund's investment objective. In the U.S., a fund registered with the Securities and Exchange Commission (SEC) under both SEC and Internal Revenue Service (IRS) rules must distribute nearly all of its net income and net realized gains from the sale of securities (if any) to its investors at least annually. Most funds are overseen by a board of directors or trustees (if the U.S. fund is organized as a trust as they commonly are) which is charged with ensuring the fund is managed appropriately by its investment adviser and other service organizations and vendors, all in the best interests of the fund's investors.

Since 1940 in the U.S., with the passage of the Investment Company Act of 1940 (the '40 Act) and the Investment Advisers Act of 1940, there have been three basic types of registered investment companies: open-end funds (or mutual funds), unit investment trusts (UITs); and closed-end funds. Other types of funds that have gained in popularity are exchange traded funds (ETFs) and hedge funds. Similar types of funds also operate in Canada, however, in the rest of the world, *mutual fund* is used as a generic term for various types of collective investment vehicles, such as unit trusts, open-ended investment companies (OEICs), unitized insurance funds, undertakings for collective investments in transferable securities (UCITS, pronounced "YOU-sits") and SICAVs.

## USAGE, INVESTMENT OBJECTIVES

Since the Investment Company Act of 1940, a mutual fund is one of three basic types of investment companies available in the United States.

Mutual funds may invest in many kinds of securities (subject to its investment objective as set forth in the fund's prospectus, which is the legal document under SEC laws which offers the funds for sale and contains a wealth of information about the fund). The most common securities purchased are "cash" or money market instruments, stocks, bonds, other mutual fund shares, and more exotic instruments such as senior loans and derivatives like forwards, futures, options and swaps. Some funds' investment objectives (and or its name) define the type of investments in which the fund invests.

For example, the fund's objective might state "...the fund will seek capital appreciation by investing primarily in listed equity securities (stocks) of U.S. companies with any market capitalization range."

This would be "stock" fund or a "domestic/US stock" fund since it stated U.S. companies. A fund may invest primarily in the shares of a particular industry or market sector, such as technology, utilities or financial services. These are known as specialty or sector funds. Bond funds can vary just as to risk (e.g., high-yield junk bonds or investment-grade corporate bonds), type of issuers (e.g., government agencies, corporations, or municipalities), or maturity of the bonds (short- or long-term). Both stock and bond funds can invest in primarily U.S. securities (domestic funds), both U.S. and foreign securities (global funds), or primarily foreign securities (international funds).

Since fund names in the past may not have provided a prospective investor a good indication of the type of fund it was, the SEC issued a rule under the '40 Act which aims to better align fund names with the primary types of investments in which the fund invests, commonly called the "name rule".

Thus, under this rule, a fund must invest under normal circumstances in at least 80% of the securities referenced in it's name. for example, the "ABC New Jersey Tax Free Bond Fund" would generally have to invest, under normal circumstances, at least 80% of its assets in tax-exempt bonds issued by the state of New Jersey and its political subdivisions. Some fund names are not associated with specific securities so the name rule has less relevance in those situations.

For example, the "ABC Freedom Fund" is such that its name does not imply a specific investment style or objective. Lastly, an index fund strives to match the performance of a particular market index, such as the S&P 500 Index. In such a fund, the fund would invest in securities and likely specific derivates such as S&P 500 stock index futures in order to most closely match the performance of that index.

Most mutual funds' investment portfolios are continually monitored by one or more employees within the sponsoring investment adviser or management company, typically called a portfolio manager and their assistants, who invest the funds assets in accordance with its investment objective and trade securities in relation to any net inflows or outflows of investor capital (if applicable), as well as the ongoing performance of investments appropriate for the fund. A mutual fund is advised by the investment adviser under an advisory contract which generally is subject to renewal annually.

Mutual funds are subject to a special set of regulatory, accounting, and tax rules. In the U.S., unlike most other types of business entities, they are not taxed on their income as long as they distribute 90% of it to their shareholders and the funds meet certain diversification requirements in the Internal Revenue Code. Also, the type of income they earn is often unchanged as it passes through to the shareholders. Mutual fund distributions of tax-free municipal bond income are tax-free to the shareholder.

Taxable distributions can be either ordinary income or capital gains, depending on how the fund earned those distributions. Net losses are not distributed or passed through to fund investors.

## NET ASSET VALUE

The *net asset value,* or NAV, is the current market value of a fund's holdings, minus the fund's liabilities, that is usually expressed as a per-share amount. For most funds, the NAV is determined daily, after the close of trading on some specified financial exchange, but some funds update their NAV multiple times during the trading day.

The public offering price, or POP, is the NAV plus a sales charge. Open-end funds sell shares at the POP and redeem shares at the NAV, and so process orders only after the NAV is determined. Closed-end funds (the shares of which are traded by investors) may trade at a higher or lower price than their NAV; this is known as a *premium* or *discount,* respectively. If a fund is divided into multiple classes of shares, each class will typically have its own NAV, reflecting differences in fees and expenses paid by the different classes.

Some mutual funds own securities which are not regularly traded on any formal exchange. These may be shares in very small or bankrupt companies; they may be derivatives; or they may be private investments in unregistered financial instruments (such as stock in a non-public company). In the absence of a public market for these securities, it is the responsibility of the fund manager to form an estimate of their value when computing the NAV. How much of a fund's assets may be invested in such securities is stated in the fund's prospectus.

The price per share, or NAV (net asset value), is calculated by dividing the fund's assets minus liabilities by the number of shares outstanding. This is usually calculated at the end of every trading day.

## AVERAGE ANNUAL RETURN

US mutual funds use SEC form N-1A to report the average annual compounded rates of return for 1-year, 5-year and 10-year periods as the"average annual total return" for each fund.

*The following formula is used*:

$$P(1+T)n = ERV$$

*Where*:

P = a hypothetical initial payment of $1,000.

T = average annual total return.

n = number of years.

ERV = ending redeemable value of a hypothetical $1,000 payment made at the beginning of the 1–, 5–, or 10-year periods at the end of the 1–, 5–, or 10–year periods (or fractional portion).

## TURNOVER

Turnover is a measure of the fund's securities transactions, usually calculated over a year's time, and usually expressed as a percentage of net asset value.

This value is usually calculated as the value of all transactions (buying, selling) divided by 2 divided by the fund's total holdings; i.e., the fund counts one security sold and another one bought as one"turnover". Thus turnover measures the replacement of holdings.

In Canada, under NI 81–106 (required disclosure for investment funds) turnover ratio is calculated based on the lesser of purchases or sales divided by the average size of the portfolio (including cash).

## EXPENSES AND EXPENSE RATIOS

Mutual funds bear expenses similar to other companies. The fee structure of a mutual fund can be divided into two or three main components: management fee, non-management expense, and 12b–1/non–12b–1 fees. All expenses are expressed as a percentage of the average daily net assets of the fund.

### Management Fees

The management fee for the fund is usually synonymous with the contractual investment advisory fee charged for the management of a fund's investments. However, as many fund companies include administrative fees in the advisory fee component, when attempting to compare the total management expenses of different funds, it is helpful to define management fee as equal to the contractual advisory fee plus the contractual administrator fee. This"levels the playing field" when comparing management fee components across multiple funds.

Contractual advisory fees may be structured as"flat-rate" fees, i.e., a single fee charged to the fund, regardless of the asset size of the fund. However, many funds have contractual fees which include breakpoints so that as the value of a fund's assets increases, the advisory fee paid decreases. Another way in which the advisory fees remain competitive is by structuring the fee so that it is based on the value of all of the assets of a group or a complex of funds rather than those of a single fund.

### Non-management Expenses

Apart from the management fee, there are certain non-management expenses which most funds must pay. Some of the more significant (in terms of amount) non-management expenses are: transfer agent expenses custodian expense (the fund's assets are kept in custody by a bank which charges a custody fee), legal/audit expense, fund accounting expense, registration expense (the SEC charges a registration fee when funds file registration statements with it), board of directors/ trustees expense (the members of the board who oversee the fund are usually paid a fee for their time spent at meetings), and printing and postage expense (incurred when printing and delivering shareholder reports).

### 12b–1/Non–12b–1 Service Fees

In the United States, 12b–1 service fees/shareholder servicing fees are contractual fees which a fund may charge to cover the marketing expenses of the fund. Non–12b–1 service fees are marketing/shareholder servicing fees which do not fall under SEC rule 12b–1. While funds do not have to charge the full contractual 12b–1 fee, they often do. When investing in a front-end load or no-load fund, the 12b–1 fees for the fund are usually.250% (or 25 basis points).

The 12b–1 fees for back-end and level-load share classes are usually between 50 and 75 basis points but may be as much as 100 basis points. While funds are often marketed as "no-load" funds, this does not mean they do not charge a distribution expense through a different mechanism. It is expected that a fund listed on an online brokerage site will be paying for the "shelf-space" in a different manner even if not directly through a 12b–1 fee.

### Investor Fees and Expenses

Fees and expenses borne by the investor vary based on the arrangement made with the investor's broker. Sales loads (or contingent deferred sales loads (CDSL)) are included in the fund's total expense ratio (TER) because they pass through the statement of operations for the fund.

Additionally, funds may charge early redemption fees to discourage investors from swapping money into and out of the fund quickly, which may force the fund to make bad trades to obtain the necessary liquidity. For example, Fidelity Diversified International Fund (FDIVX) charges a 10 Per cent fee on money removed from the fund in less than 30 days.

### Brokerage Commissions

An additional expense which does not pass through the fund's income statement (statement of operations) and cannot be controlled by the investor is brokerage commissions. Brokerage commissions are incorporated into the price of securities bought and sold and, thus, are a component of the gain or loss on investments. They are a true, real cost of investing though.

The amount of commissions incurred by the fund and are reported usually 4 months after the fund's fiscal year end in the "statement of additional information" which is legally part of the prospectus, but is usually available only upon request or by going to the SEC's or fund's website. Brokerage commissions, usually charged when securities are purchased and again when sold) are directly related to portfolio turnover which is a measure of trading volume/velocity (portfolio turnover refers to the number of times the fund's assets are bought and sold over the course of a year). Usually, higher rate of portfolio turnover (trading) generates higher brokerage commissions.

The advisors of mutual fund companies are required to achieve "best execution" through brokerage arrangements so that the commissions charged to the fund will not be excessive as well as also attaining the best possible price upon buying or selling.

## TYPES OF MUTUAL FUNDS

### Open-end Fund, Forms of Organization, Other Funds

The term *mutual fund* is the common name for what is classified as an open-end investment company by the SEC. Being open-ended means that, at the end of every day, the fund continually issues new shares to investors buying into the fund and must stand ready to buy back shares from investors redeeming their shares at the then current net asset value per share.

Mutual funds must be structured as corporations or trusts, such as business trusts, and any corporation or trust will be classified by the SEC as an investment company if it issues securities and primarily invests in non-government securities.

An investment company will be classified by the SEC as an open-end investment company if they do not issue undivided interests in specified securities (the defining characteristic of unit investment trusts or UITs) and if they issue redeemable securities. Registered investment companies that are not UITs or open-end investment companies are closed-end funds.

Closed-end funds are like open end except they are more like a company which sells its shares a single time to the public under an initial public offering or "IPO".

Subsequently, the fund's shares trade with buyers and sellers of shares in the secondary market at a market-determined price (which is likely not equal to net asset value) such as on the New York or American Stock Exchange. Except for some special transactions, the fund cannot continue to grow in size by attracting more investor capital like an open-end fund may.

## Exchange-traded Funds

A relatively recent innovation, the exchange-traded fund or ETF, is often structured as an open-end investment company. ETFs combine characteristics of both mutual funds and closed-end funds.

ETFs are traded throughout the day on a stock exchange, just like closed-end funds, but at prices generally approximating the ETF's net asset value. Most ETFs are index funds and track stock market indexes. Shares are issued or redeemed by institutional investors in large blocks.

Most investors purchase and sell shares through brokers in market transactions. Because the institutional investors normally purchase and redeem in in kind transactions, ETFs are more efficient than traditional mutual funds (which are continuously issuing and redeeming securities and, to effect such transactions, continually buying and selling securities and maintaining liquidity positions) and therefore tend to have lower expenses.

Exchange-traded funds are also valuable for foreign investors who are often able to buy and sell securities traded on a stock market, but who, for regulatory reasons, are limited in their ability to participate in traditional U.S. mutual funds.

## Equity Funds

Equity funds, which consist mainly of stock investments, are the most common type of mutual fund. Equity funds hold 50 Per cent of all amounts invested in mutual funds in the United States. Often equity funds focus investments on particular strategies and certain types of issuers.

### *Capitalization*

Fund managers and other investment professionals have varying definitions of mid-cap, and large-cap ranges.

*The following ranges are used by Russell Indexes:*

- Russell Microcap Index – micro-cap ($54.8 – 539.5 million)
- Russell 2000 Index – small-cap ($182.6 million – 1.8 billion)

- Russell Midcap Index – mid-cap ($1.8 – 13.7 billion)
- Russell 1000 Index – large-cap ($1.8 – 386.9 billion)

### *Growth vs. Value*

Another distinction is made between growth funds, which invest in stocks of companies that have the potential for large capital gains, and value funds, which concentrate on stocks that are undervalued. Value stocks have historically produced higher returns; however, financial theory states this is compensation for their greater risk.

Growth funds tend not to pay regular dividends. Income funds tend to be more conservative investments, with a focus on stocks that pay dividends. A balanced fund may use a combination of strategies, typically including some level of investment in bonds, to stay more conservative when it comes to risk, yet aim for some growth.

### *Index Funds Versus Active Management*

An index fund maintains investments in companies that are part of major stock (or bond) indexes, such as the S&P 500, while an actively managed fund attempts to outperform a relevant index through superior stock-picking techniques. The assets of an index fund are managed to closely approximate the performance of a particular published index. Since the composition of an index changes infrequently, an index fund manager makes fewer trades, on average, than does an active fund manager.

For this reason, index funds generally have lower trading expenses than actively managed funds, and typically incur fewer short-term capital gains which must be passed on to shareholders. Additionally, index funds do not incur expenses to pay for selection of individual stocks (proprietary selection techniques, research, etc.) and deciding when to buy, hold or sell individual holdings. Instead, a fairly simple computer model can identify whatever changes are needed to bring the fund back into agreement with its target index.

Certain empirical evidence seems to emphasise that mutual funds do not beat the market and actively managed mutual funds under-perform other broad-based portfolios with similar characteristics. One study found that nearly 1,500 U.S. mutual funds under-performed the market in approximately half of the years between 1962 and 1992. Moreover, funds that performed well in the past are not able to beat the market again in the future.

## Bond Funds

Bond funds account for 18% of mutual fund assets. Types of bond funds include term funds, which have a fixed set of time (short-, medium-, or long-term) before they mature. Municipal bond funds generally have lower returns, but have tax advantages and lower risk. High-yield bond funds invest in corporate bonds, including high-yield or junk bonds. With the potential for high yield, these bonds also come with greater risk.

## Money Market Funds

Money market funds hold 26% of mutual fund assets in the United States. Money market funds entail the least risk, as well as lower rates of return. Unlike certificates of deposit (CDs), money market shares are liquid and redeemable at any time.

## Funds of Funds

Funds of funds (FoF) are mutual funds which invest in other mutual funds (i.e., they are funds composed of other funds). The funds at the underlying level are often funds which an investor can invest in individually, though they may be 'institutional' class shares that may not be within reach of an individual shareholder).

A fund of funds will typically charge a much lower management fee than that of a fund investing in direct securities because it is considered a fee charged for asset allocation services which is presumably less demanding than active direct securities research and management.

The fees charged at the underlying fund level are a real cost or drag on performance but do not pass through the FoF's income statement (statement of operations), but are usually disclosed in the fund's annual report, prospectus, or statement of additional information. FoF's will often have a higher overall/combined expense ratio than that of a regular fund. The FoF should be evaluated on the combination of the fund-level expenses and underlying fund expenses, as these both reduce the return to the investor.

Most FoFs invest in affiliated funds (i.e., mutual funds managed by the same advisor), although some invest in unaffilated funds (those managed by other advisors) or both.

The cost associated with investing in an unaffiliated underlying fund may be higher than investing in an affiliated underlying because of the investment management research involved in investing in fund advised by a different advisor. Recently, FoFs have been classified into those that are actively managed (in which the investment advisor reallocates frequently among the underlying funds in order to adjust to changing market conditions) and those that are passively managed (the investment advisor allocates assets on the basis of on an allocation model which is rebalanced on a regular basis).

The design of FoFs is structured in such a way as to provide a ready mix of mutual funds for investors who are unable to or unwilling to determine their own asset allocation model. Fund companies such as TIAA-CREF, American Century Investments, Vanguard, and Fidelity have also entered this market to provide investors with these options and take the "guess work" out of selecting funds.

The allocation mixes usually vary by the time the investor would like to retire: 2020, 2030, 2050, etc. The more distant the target retirement date, the more aggressive the asset mix.

## Hedge Funds

Hedge funds in the United States are pooled investment funds with loose, if any, SEC regulation, unlike mutual funds. Some hedge fund managers are required to register with SEC as investment advisers under the Investment Advisers Act of 1940.

The Act does not require an adviser to follow or avoid any particular investment strategies, nor does it require or prohibit specific investments. Hedge funds typically charge a management fee of 1% or more, plus a "performance fee" of 20% of the hedge fund's profit. There may be a "lock-up" period, during which an investor cannot cash in shares. A variation of the hedge strategy is the 130–30 fund for individual investors.

## MUTUAL FUNDS VS. OTHER INVESTMENTS

Mutual funds offer several advantages over investing in individual stocks. For example, the transaction costs are divided among all the mutual fund shareholders, which allows for cost-effective diversification. Investors may also benefit by having a third party (professional fund managers) apply expertise and dedicate time to manage and research investment options, although there is dispute over whether professional fund managers can, on average, outperform simple index funds that mimic public indexes.

Yet, the Wall Street Journal reported that separately managed accounts (SMA or SMAs) performed better than mutual funds in 22 of 25 categories from 2006 to 2008. This included beating mutual funds performance in 2008, a tough year in which the global stock market lost US$21 trillion in value. In the story, Morningstar, Inc said SMAs outperformed mutual funds in 25 of 36 stock and bond market categories. Whether actively managed or passively indexed, mutual funds are not immune to risks. They share the same risks associated with the investments made. If the fund invests primarily in stocks, it is usually subject to the same ups and downs and risks as the stock market.

### Share Classes

Many mutual funds offer more than one class of shares. For example, you may have seen a fund that offers "Class A" and "Class B" shares. Each class will invest in the same pool (or investment portfolio) of securities and will have the same investment objectives and policies. But each class will have different shareholder services and/or distribution arrangements with different fees and expenses.

These differences are supposed to reflect different costs involved in servicing investors in various classes; for example, one class may be sold through brokers with a front-end load, and another class may be sold direct to the public with no load but a "12b–1 fee" included in the class's expenses (sometimes referred to as "Class C" shares). Still a third class might have a minimum investment of $10,000,000 and be available only to financial institutions (a so-called "institutional" share class).

In some cases, by aggregating regular investments made by many individuals, a retirement plan (such as a 401(k) plan) may qualify to purchase "institutional" shares (and gain the benefit of their typically lower expense ratios) even though no members of the plan would qualify individually. As a result, each class will likely have different performance results.

A multi-class structure offers investors the ability to select a fee and expense structure that is most appropriate for their investment goals (including the length of time that they expect to remain invested in the fund).

## Load and Expenses

A front-end load or sales charge is a commission paid to a broker by a mutual fund when shares are purchased, taken as a percentage of funds invested.

The value of the investment is reduced by the amount of the load. Some funds have a deferred sales charge or back-end load. In this type of fund an investor pays no sales charge when purchasing shares, but will pay a commission out of the proceeds when shares are redeemed depending on how long they are held. Another derivative structure is a level-load fund, in which no sales charge is paid when buying the fund, but a back-end load may be charged if the shares purchased are sold within a year.

Load funds are sold through financial intermediaries such as brokers, financial planners, and other types of registered representatives who charge a commission for their services. Shares of front-end load funds are frequently eligible for breakpoints (i.e., a reduction in the commission paid) based on a number of variables. These include other accounts in the same fund family held by the investor or various family members, or committing to buy more of the fund within a set period of time in return for a lower commission "today".

It is possible to buy many mutual funds without paying a sales charge. These are called no-load funds. In addition to being available from the fund company itself, no-load funds may be sold by some discount brokers for a flat transaction fee or even no fee at all. (This does not necessarily mean that the broker is not compensated for the transaction; in such cases, the fund may pay brokers' commissions out of "distribution and marketing" expenses rather than a specific sales charge. The purchaser is therefore paying the fee indirectly through the fund's expenses deducted from profits.)

No-load funds include both index funds and actively managed funds. The largest mutual fund families selling no-load index funds are Vanguard and Fidelity, though there are a number of smaller mutual fund families with no-load funds as well. Expense ratios in some no-load index funds are less than 0.2% per year versus the typical actively managed fund's expense ratio of about 1.5% per year. Load funds usually have even higher expense ratios when the load is considered.

The expense ratio is the anticipated annual cost to the investor of holding shares of the fund. For example, on a $100,000 investment, an expense ratio of 0.2% means $200 of annual expense, while a 1.5% expense ratio would result in $1,500 of annual expense. These expenses are before any sales commissions paid to purchase the mutual fund.

Many fee-only financial advisors strongly suggest no-load funds such as index funds. If the advisor is not of the fee-only type but is instead compensated by commissions, the advisor may have a conflict of interest in selling high-commission load funds.

## SOURCES OF LONG TERM FUNDS

Long-term sources or funds are required to create production facilities through purchases of fixed assets such as plant,machinery,land,building,furniture,e.t.c. Investments in these assets represent that part of firm's capital which is blocked on a permanent or fixed basis and is called fixed capital.

*The long-term sources of finance are*:

- *Ownership securities*: These securities represents shares. Share are the most common form of raising long-term funds from the market.Every company,except a company limited by a guarantee,has a statutory right to issue shares. The capital of a company is divided into a number of equal parts called shares.
  - *Equity shares*: Represents the owner's capital in a company.The holders of these shares have full control over the working of the company and have voting rights.Equity shareholders are paid dividends from the remaining income of a company. The rate of dividend depends upon the profit of the company.
  - *Preference Shares*: As the name suggests,these shares have certain preferences. There is a preference for payment of dividend.they have fixed rate of dividend,but they don't have any voting rights and control over the management of a company.
- *Creditorship securities*: It is also known as debt-capital,and it represnts debenture and bondsThe use of such securities along with shares in financing of a business generally tends to reduce the cost of capital and helps to improve the earnings of the shareholders.
  - *Debentures or Bonds*: A debenture is an acknowledgement of debt.It is a form of loan on which a company has to pay a fixed amount of interest to debenture-holders.they are the creditors of the company. There are many type of debentures i.e. unsecured, secured, registered, reedemable. irredeemable, convertible, zero coupon bonds,deep discount bonds,e.t.c.
- *Loan financing*: A business can also finance through

loans from specialised financial institutions and development banks or from commercial banks.

- *Internal financing:* A new company can raise funds only through external sources,such as shares, debentures, loans,public deposits,e.t.c. But an existing firm which needs finaance for it's future growth and expansion can generate funds through retained earnings.
- Public deposits.

## EQUITY SHARES

Equity is the term commonly used to describe the ordinary share capital of a business. Ordinary shares in the equity capital of a business entitle the holders to all distributed profits after the holders of debentures and preference shares have been paid.

## ORDINARY ( EQUITY) SHARES

Ordinary shares are issued to the owners of a company. The ordinary shares of UK companies typically have a nominal or'face' value (usually something like £1 or 5Op, but shares with a nominal value of 1p, 2p or 2Sp are not uncommon).

However, it is important to understand that the market value of a company's shares has little (if any) relationship to their nominal or face value.

The market value of a company's shares is determined by the price another investor is prepared to pay for them. In the case of publicly-quoted companies, this is reflected in the market value of the ordinary shares traded on the stock exchange (the"share price").

In the case of privately-owned companies, where there is unlikely to be much trading in shares, market value is often determined when the business is sold or when a minority shareholding is valued for taxation purposes.

In your studies, you may also come across"Deferred ordinary shares". These are a form of ordinary shares, which are entitled to a dividend only after a certain date or only if profits rise a certain amount. Voting rights might also differ from those attached to other ordinary shares.

## WHY MIGHT A COMPANY ISSUE ORDINARY SHARES?

*A new issue of shares might be made for several reasons:*

- *The company might want to raise more cash*: For example might be needed for the expansion of a company's operations. If, for example, a company with 500,000 ordinary shares in issue decides to issue 125,000 new shares to raise cash, should it offer the new shares to existing shareholders, or should it sell them to new shareholders instead? Where a company sells the new shares to existing shareholders in proportion to their existing shareholding in the company, this is known as a"rights issue".
- *The company might want to issue new shares partly to raise cash but more importantly to'float' its shares on a stock market*: When a UK company is floated, it must make available a minimum proportion of its shares to the general investing public.
- *The company might issue new shares to the shareholders of another company, inorder to take it over*: There are many examples of businesses that use their high share price as a way of making an offer for other businesses. The shareholders of the target business being acquired received shares in the buying business and perhaps also some cash.

## SOURCES OF EQUITY FINANCE

*There are three main methods of raising equity:*

1. *Retained profits*: i.e. retaining profits, rather than paying them out as dividends. This is the most important source of equity
2. *Rights issues*: i.e. an issue of new shares. After retained profits, rights issues are the next most important source
3. *New issues of shares to the public*: i.e. an issue of new shares to new shareholders. In total in the UK, this is the least important source of equity finance

## EQUITY INVESTMENTS

Equity investments generally refers to the buying and holding of shares of stock on a stock market by individuals and firms in anticipation of income from dividends and capital gain as the value of the stock rises.

It also sometimes refers to the acquisition of equity (ownership) participation in a private (unlisted) company or a startup (a company being created or newly created).

When the investment is in infant companies, it is referred to as venture capital investing and is generally understood to be higher risk than investment in listed going-concern situations.

The equities held by private individuals are often held via mutual funds or other forms of pooled investment vehicle, many of which have quoted prices that are listed in financial newspapers or magazines; the mutual funds are typically managed by prominent fund management firms (e.g. Schroders, Fidelity Investments or the Vanguard Group). Such holdings allow individual investors to obtain the diversification of the fund(s) and to obtain the skill of the professional fund managers in charge of the fund(s).

An alternative, usually employed by large private investors and pension funds, is to hold shares directly; in the institutional environment many clients who own portfolios have what are called segregated funds as opposed to, or in addition to, the pooled e.g. mutual fund alternative.

A calculation can be made to assess whether an equity is over or underpriced compared with a long-term government bond. This is called the Yield Gap or Yield Ratio. It is the ratio of the dividend yield of an equity and that of the long-term bond.

## ACCOUNTING

In financial accounting, it is the owners' interest on the assets of the enterprise after deducting all its liabilities. It appears on the balance sheet/ Statement of Financial Position, one of the four primary financial statements.

Ownership equity includes both tangible and intangible items (such as brand names and reputation/ goodwill).

*Accounts listed under ownership equity include:*

- Prefetred stock
- Share capital, common stock
- Capital surplus
- Stock options
- Retained earnings
- Treasury stock
- Reserve (accountings)

## Book Value

*The book value of equity will change in the case of the following events:*

- Changes in the firm's assets relative to its liabilities. For example, a profitable firm receives more cash for its products than the cost at which it produced these goods, and so in the act of making a profit it is increasing its assets.
- Depreciation. Equity will decrease, for example, when machinery depreciates, which is registered as a decline in the value of the asset, and on the liabilities side of the firm's balance sheet as a decrease in shareholders' equity.
- Issue of new equity in which the firm obtains new capital increases the total shareholders' equity.
- Share repurchases, in which a firm gives back money to its investors, reducing on the asset side its financial assets, and on the liability side the shareholders' equity. For practical purposes (except for its tax consequences), share repurchasing is similar to a dividend payment, as both consist of the firm giving money back to investors. Rather than giving money to all shareholders immediately in the form of a dividend payment, a share repurchase reduces the number of shares (increases the size of each share) in future income and distributions.
- Dividends paid out to preferred stock owners are considered an expense to be subtracted from net income (from the point of view of the common share owners).

- *Other reasons*: Assets and liabilities can change without any effect being measured in the Income Statement under certain circumstances; for example, changes in accounting rules may be applied retroactively. Sometimes assets bought and held in other countries get translated back into the reporting currency at different exchange rates, resulting in a changed value.

## SHAREHOLDERS' EQUITY

When the owners are shareholders, the interest can be called shareholders' equity; the accounting remains the same, and it is ownership equity spread out among shareholders. If all shareholders are in one and the same class, they share equally in ownership equity from all perspectives. However, shareholders may allow different priority ranking among themselves by the use of share classes, and options. This complicates both analysis for stock valuation, and accounting.

The individual investor is interested not only in the total changes to equity, but also in the increase/ decrease in the value of his own personal share of the equity.

*This reconciliation of equity should be done both in total and on a per share basis*:

- Equity (beg. of year)
- + net income inter net money you gained
- – dividends how much money you gained or lost so far
- +/– gain/loss from changes to the number of shares outstanding.more or less
- = Equity (end of year) if you get more money during the year or less or not anything

## MARKET VALUE OF SHARES

In the stock market, market price per share does not correspond to the equity per share calculated in the accounting statements. Stock valuations, often much higher, are based on other considerations related to the business' operating cashflow, profits and future prospects; some factors are derived from the accounting statements. Thus, there is little or no correlation between the equity seen in financial statements and the stock valuation of the business.

## REAL ESTATE EQUITY

Individuals can also use market valuations to calculate equity in real estate. An owner refers to his or her equity in a property as the difference between the market price of a property and the liability attached to the property (mortgage or home equity loan).

## PREFERENCE SHARES

Capital stock which provides a specific dividend that is paid before any dividends are paid to common stock holders, and which takes precedence over common stock in the event of a liquidation. Like common stock, preference shares represent partial ownership in a company, although preferred stock shareholders do not enjoy any of the voting rights of common stockholders. Also unlike common stock, preference shares pay a fixed dividend that does not fluctuate, although the company does not have to pay this dividend if it lacks the financial ability to do so.

The main benefit to owning preference shares are that the investor has a greater claim on the company's assets than common stockholders. Preferred shareholders always receive their dividends first and, in the event the company goes bankrupt, preferred shareholders are paid off before common stockholders. In general, there are four different types of preferred stock: cumulative preferred, non-cumulative, participating, and convertible. also called preferred stock.

## ADVANTAGES

- *You are assured of a dividend*: If you own ordinary shares, you are not automatically entitled to a dividend every year. The dividend will be paid only if the company makes a profit and declares a dividend. This is not the case with preference shares. A preference shareholder is entitled to a dividend every year. What happens if the company doesn't have the money to pay dividends on preference shares in a particular year? The dividend is then added to the next year's dividend. If the company can't pay it the next year as well, the dividend keeps getting added until the company *can* pay. These are known as cumulative preference shares. Some preference shares are non-cumulative — if the company can't pay the dividend for one particular year, the dividend for that year lapses.

- *They get priority over ordinary shares*: Ordinary shareholders get a dividend only after the cumulative preference shareholders get theirs. Preference shareholders are given a preference over the rest. That's why it is called a preference share.
- *Preference shares are safer*: In case the company is wound up and its assets (land, buildings, offices, machinery, furniture, etc) are being sold, the money that comes from this sale is given to the shareholders. After all, shareholders invest in a business and own a portion of it. Preference shareholders' get the money first. Their accounts are settled before that of the ordinary shareholders, who are the last to get paid.

## DISADVANTAGES

- *They are not easily available*: Usually, preference shares are most commonly issued by companies to institutions. That means, it is out of the reach of the retail investor. For example, banks and financial institutions may want to invest in a company but do not want to bother with the hassles of fluctuating share prices. In that case, they would prefer to invest in a company's preference shares. Companies, on the other hand, may need money but are unwilling to take a loan. So they will issue preference shares. The banks and financial institutions will buy the shares and the company gets the money it needs. This will appear in the company's balance sheet as'capital' and not as debt (which is what would have happened if they had taken a loan).

- *They are not traded on the stock exchange*: The big disadvantage of preference shares, of course, is the fact that they aren't traded on the markets. This means they are not'liquid' assets; there's little scope for the price of these shares to move up or down. On the other hand, ordinary or equity shares are traded in the markets and their prices go up and down depending on supply and demand for the stock. But, that does not mean the investor is stuck with his shares. After a fixed period, a preference shareholder can sell his/ her preference shares back to the company. You can't do that with ordinary shares. You will have to sell your shares to any other buyer in the stock market. You can only sell your shares back to the company if the company announces a buyback offer.

## DEBENTURES

A Debenture is a long-term Debt Instrument, which is not backed by Collaterals. Debentures are unsecured debt backed by the creditworthiness and reputation of the Debenture issuer and documented by an agreement called an indenture. It is issued usually by large, financially strong companies with excellent bond ratings. One example of debenture is an unsecured bond.

A Debenture is a long-term Debt Instrument issued by governments and big institutions for the purpose of raising funds. The Debenture has some similarities with Bonds but the terms and conditions of securitization of Debentures are different from that of a Bond. A Debenture is regarded as an unsecured investment because there are no pledges (guarantee) or liens available on particular assets. Nonetheless, a Debenture is backed by all the assets which have not been pledged otherwise. Normally, Debentures are referred to as freely negotiable Debt Instruments. The Debenture holder functions as a lender to the issuer of the Debenture. In return, a specific rate of interest is paid to the Debenture holder by the Debenture issuer similar to the case of a loan. In practice, the differentiation between a Debenture and a Bond is not observed every time. In some cases, Bonds are also termed as Debentures and vice-versa. If a bankruptcy occurs, Debenture holders are treated as general creditors.

The Debenture issuer has a substantial advantage from issuing a Debenture because the particular assets are kept without any encumbrances so that the option is open for issuing them in future for financing purposes.

## DEBENTURES HOLDERS

In financial terms, a debenture is a freely transferable commodity, one that government institutions as well as big companies use to generate or amass funds.

It is similar to a bond. The distinction, however, lies in the fact that the terms and conditions of the contract are different. A debenture is not considered as safe or secure, in the sense that the issuer makes no promise on any specific property or asset. However, the conditions in the contract itself protect a debenture. If there is a bankruptcy, the holders become creditors. Debenture holders can transfer them, whenever they wish to do so. Another benefit is that their property or other assets are not tied up as collateral, leaving them open for other transactions.

Over the years in the UK, leading companies have used debentures to raise money and fund sports and leisure events. A famous example would be The All England Lawn Tennis and Croquet Club, who in, as early as 1920 issued debentures, which generated very little in the way of interest.

However, the holders had the privilege and luxury of being able to watch the world famous tennis action, right there in the thick of things at centre court. Another example are the debenture holders of The Royal Albert Hall, they become members of that prestigious association. They sit in box seating of their own, from where they get to watch all the performances that take place there. Other associations that have followed suite are world famous stadiums such as

Wembley, Millenium, and Twickenham. Top clubs like Arsenal and the Nottinghamshire County Cricket Club have been issuing debentures hoping to increase their ability to raise capitol.

These organizations issue debentures every five years. Therefore, current holders must reinvest, in order to maintain their privileges.

## DEBENTURES AGREEMENTS

Debenture agreements, or debenture contracts, are issued by governments worldwide as notes that express some degree of financial obligation. These agreements express a financial obligation on the part of the issuing government.

### Features of Debentures Agreements

Debentures agreements have a number of essential characteristics. There is not collateral in a debenture agreement meaning that the holder is not required to secure the debenture against his own property. A debenture agreement is typically supported by an indenture. Returns from the debenture contracts may vary. These variations are subject to the issuer of the agreement.

### Debentures Agreements in Corporate Sector

The debentures in the corporate world involve neither mortgages nor exchanges of properties and assets. The entire transaction is based on trust between the parties.

### Nature of Debentures Agreements

Debenture agreements have a long term period. The rate of interest that is offered the holder of the bond remains the same throughout the duration of the agreement. Debenture agreements are known as fixed income securities.

### Providers of Debentures Agreements

The major providers of the debenture agreements are business enterprises. Any business enterprise, regardless of its size, may deal in these agreements.

## Important Aspects of Debentures Agreements

The most important aspect of a debenture agreement is the fact that the general credit of the issuer is the only thing that is attached to it. The properties of the issuer are not a part of the agreement. The credibility or the reputation of the issuer is an important aspect of an agreement.

## DEBENTURE RATES

Unlike bonds or loans taken from banks, debentures appear to be something which are less concrete as the entire transaction is completed in good faith. The holder has to, and usually relies on the issuer being worthy enough of paying back when the fixed date arrives. It is an important method of generating revenue or financial income.

The debentures could be considered to be specially creditable and backed up by assets if the organization issuing them pledges property worth exactly the same as the amount quoted in the proposal. All the activities are performed keeping in mind the fact that holders need to be provided with a certain amount of assurance.

There are other factors however, which may tilt the scale in favour of the issuer. If it is found that the issuer has a clean chit regarding its treatment of the clients, past and present, as well as a uninterrupted flow of income, then the said party stands to issue debentures. It need not put its assets on the firing line itself. The condition of exchange of property then becomes as good as null and void. The holders of debentures of that company in the given circumstances, are then entitled to the property that has been kept out of the contract; a default and they would be able to lay claim to the property, not pledged by the issuer.

Nowadays debentures are a significant amount of debts or outstanding dues in the corporate sector. The cue seems to have been taken up by governments all around, or bodies affiliated to it. They have also started issuing debentures. The example of treasury securities would be worth mentioning, in this regard. Debentures could be purchased by investors from brokers entrusted with selling them.

The debentures, being sold could be priced at say, a denomination, ranging from $1000 to $10000. The price level is calculated, based on the aspect of maturity. The agreements are done with the benefit of securing the interests of the bondholders. The entire arrangement is made with an eye to maintain a status quo as much as possible.

## EXCHANGEABLE DEBENTURES

Exchangeable debentures are an intriguing as well as beguiling proposition because of their nature. They are an extremely crucial part of the investment terminology. It is said that they bear an uncanny resemblance to Convertibles. However there is an exception though. The said type of debenture could be transformed. It may be transformed as par the personal choices of the issuer himself. They may be translated into a common stock.

The resultant beneficiaries could be the subsidiary, or an affiliate of the user himself. There are different definitions of a Convertible Debenture.

The Convertible Debentures are ones which could be changed or converted, when the holder decides to do so. It could be transformed into preferably, a common stock, at a ratio fixed as par the indenture.

The ratio is open to adjustments, especially when stock dividends are taken into consideration. A situation otherwise would mean that the worth of converting the debt into securities would amount to less than what the debenture would have been if it would have matured.

The Law Encyclopedia states that, a Convertible Subordinate is subject to previous debts or rather, their repayment, of and by a particular organization. They may, however be converted into yet other forms of securities.. With Exchangeable Debentures, the issuer has the freedom to swap a Convertible Debenture with it.

There is the option of having the same rates. Organizations employ it when the urgent need to obtain equity capital,or else avail a lower tax rate. Some companies prefer to take advantage of both situations, or a subsequent change in them.

## BANK DEBENTURES

A Bank Debenture is an acknowledgment of debt issued by a bank and it is a legitimate form of investment. The maximum number of banks issue Bank Debentures and the trading of Bank Debentures is also done in principal stock exchanges. Basically, a bank issues Bank Debentures as an acknowledgment of debt. Nevertheless, Bank Debentures should not be mixed up or mistaken with Bank Guarantees or Letters of Credit.

They are examples of private and confidential notes and they are not publicly traded. When a bank issues Bank Debentures, the Bank Debentureholder becomes creditors for the bank.

In return, the bank pays interest at a fixed and predetermined rate to the Debentureholder. Bank Debenture is a form of debt security instrument. Hence, the Bank Debentureholder does not hold any voting rights. Since Bank Debentures are more risky compared to Bank Loans (loans given to banks), the rate of return in case of a Bank Debenture is also high compared to a Bank Loan.

The banks issue Bank Debentures just as to the rules and regulations or in conformance to the law for the purpose of raising funds and the credit extension can either be long term or medium term. For issuing Bank Debentures, a bank has to file an application to the competent authority. The bank has to submit the application duly completed in a specified form along with the necessary documents mentioned in the application form.

The application for issuing Bank Debentures shall receive approval if the competent authority does not have any objections with that application. For receiving the approval, the Banks have to wait for a certain period of time from the date of submission of the application. Unfortunately, there are many fraudulent organizations who gives assurances of higher returns in a short time period. They provide "Bank Guarantees" which have been issued by prime banks (the 100 leading banks) and declare that value would be manifolded by multiple numbers of trading. This is termed as a "roll Programme".

The objective of this kind of a scam is to get the money of the investor sent to a foreign bank on which the swindler has control or dominance. The money of the swindled person is then utilized by the fraudulent organization or it is used for money laundering.

## CORPORATION DEBENTURE

Corporation debenture is an unsecured loan offered by an individual to a company. The company pays a high rate of interest to the money-lenders and there is no collateral offered for the debenture. If something like a bankruptcy occurs or any kind of financial crisis, the bondholders are given priority over the debenture holders, in terms of payments. Debentures are always different from stocks and bonds, but basically, all these three are different forms of investment. Corporation debentures are usually offered in issues under an indenture which is a document that sets the term of the exchange.

A debenture may be called as a bearer instrument, because whoever is carrying the document, is entitled to get the money, even if the person is not the original creditor. All the coupons of interest payments on the credit remains attached with the debenture and these are necessary for the final payments on the term maturity.

### Comparison between Stock and Corporation Debentures

Anyone investing in stocks, becomes one of the owners of the company and becomes a partner in the company's loss or gains. The investor automatically becomes related with the company's financial graph. But debentures are more secured investment as payments with high interest rates are guaranteed. The company is bound to pay interest on the borrowed money and once the debenture matures, all the borrowed money is returned. So, this is understandable that, it is the interest which one gains from the debentures.

### Comparison between Bonds and Corporation Debentures

Bonds are more secured mode of investment than

debentures and the investor needs to consider this fact. Debenture and bonds are similar as in both of these investment forms, interest and value is guaranteed, but in case of liquidation, bond holders receive the payment first. Debenture holders have no collateral, which they can claim from the company, in case bankruptcy takes place. To compensate such losses high interest rates are paid to them.

## GOVERNMENT DEBENTURES

Government debentures are unsecured loans offered by an individual to the government. Without paying any collateral for the debenture, government pays a high rate of interest to the money-lenders. Debentures are also called fixed interest or debt securities. It is a source of regular income.

Government debentures generally come as long term or short term debentures. The security term generally consists of twelve months to five years, but these can be sold in the secondary market. There is also tax relief on the income from government debentures and because of this, they are always in demand. Debentures are always different from stocks and bonds, but basically, all three are different forms of investment. The difference is the varying risk factors and returns reflected by the higher risks and corresponding higher returns of the debentures.

When buying a stock, he/she becomes one of the owners of the company and faces "floating" fortunes, related to the company's financial graph. Debentures are a more secured investment as payments with high interest rates are guaranteed. The government is bound to pay interest on the borrowed money and once the debenture matures, the borrowed money is returned. It is actually the interest which is gained from government debentures. Government debentures and government bonds are similar, but bonds carry more security than debentures.

In both of these investments, interest and value is guaranteed, but in case of liquidation, bond holders receive the payment first. Debenture holders have no collateral which they can claim from a company in case of bankruptcy. To compensate such losses, high interest rates are paid. Bondholders have the collateral and are more secure.

## SUBORDINATED DEBENTURES

A Subordinated debenture (also known as subordinated loan, subordinated bond, subordinated debt or junior debt) is debt which ranks after other debts should a company fall into receivership or be closed. Such debt is referred to as subordinate, because the debt providers (the lenders) have subordinate status in relationship to the normal debt. Subordinated debenture has a lower priority than other bonds of the issuer in case of liquidation during bankruptcy government tax authorities and senior debt holders in the hierarchy of creditors.

Because subordinated debenture is repayable after other debts have been paid, they are more risky for the lender of the money. It is unsecured and has lesser priority than that of an additional debt claim on the same asset. A typical example for this would be when a promoter of a company invests money in the form of debt, rather than in the form of stock. In the case of liquidation (e.g. the company winds up its affairs and dissolves) the promoter would be paid just before stockholders assuming there are assets to distribute after all other liabilities and debts have been paid. Subordinated debentures typically have a higher rate of return than senior debt due to the increased inherent risk.

Major shareholders and parent companies are most likely to provide subordinated loans, as an outside party providing such a loan would normally want compensation for the extra risk. Subordinated debentures usually have a lower credit rating than senior bonds. Here are a couple examples for subordinated debentures. First of all, the main example of subordinated debenture can be found in bonds issued by banks. Subordinated debenture is issued by most large banking corporations in the U.S. periodically. It is believed that subordinated notes are risk-sensitive.

That is, subordinated debenture holders have claims on bank assets after senior debt holders and they lack the upside gain enjoyed by shareholders. This status of subordinated debenture makes it perfect for experimenting on the significance of market discipline. This can be accomplished in two separate ways. First, a simple look at secondary market prices of subordinated debenture would suffice. Second, one can have a look at issue price of these bonds initially in the primarymarkets. Subordinated debentures also enjoy a higher discount in the secondary market because of the higher interest they provide to the debenture holder. However, it is important to keep in mind that you should not expect payment from a subordinated debenture before other corporate debts have been satisfied.

### Subordinated Debenture and Stocks

When somebody decides to invest in stocks, he or she becomes one of the owners and thus, becomes a shareholder of the good and bad times of the company. The investor faces uncertain fortunes related to the company's financial graph. So this explains the amount of risk related to stock-investments. But debentures are more secured investment, as payments with high interest rates are guaranteed. The company is bound to pay interest on the borrowed money, and once the debenture matures, all the borrowed money is returned. In other words, the investors gain interest as income from the debentures.

Subordinated debenture and bonds Subordinated debenture and bonds are similar, but bonds carry more security than debentures. In both of these investment forms, interest and value is guaranteed, but in case of liquidation, bond holders receive the payment first, followed by the senior bonds, and only after that comes the subordinated debenture holders, who have no collateral which they can claim from the company in case bankruptcy takes place. To compensate for the possibility of such losses, high interest rates are paid to the subordinated debenture holders.

## CONVERTIBLE DEBENTURES

A Convertible Debenture is a type of Debenture or

commercial loan that gives the choice to the lender to take stock or shares in the company, as an alternative to taking the repayment of a loan. Usually, Convertible Debenture is any form of Debenture which can be converted into some other kind of security. Convertible Debentures can be converted into shares or Common Stocks. The Convertible Debenture's market price should not fall below its intrinsic value. The intrinsic value is calculated by multiplying the number of shares converted at face value with the current market price of common stock. Usually, Convertible Debentures offer more safety to the investor compared to Common Shares or Preference Shares. In the case of Convertible Debentures, Short Selling can be done, and by short selling, the market value of a stock comes down. This lets the Convertible Debentureholder make a claim for additional stocks with the help of more Short Selling. This is termed as death spiral financing.

Convertible Debentures are suitable for investors who look for potential increases in asset value (appreciation) compared to that yielded by Bonds, and more earnings than Common Stocks provide. In this era of Online communication, it is possible to obtain large amounts of information regarding Convertible Debentures. Before initiating any substantial investment, it is prudent to seek suggestions of the financial experts who have a deep knowledge of Convertible Debentures. Before conversion of Convertible Debentures into Common Stocks or shares, it is prudent to have clear insight related to the potential changes in earnings and the relative gains.

*Convertible Debentures can usually be categorized into the following types:*

- Secured Convertible Debentures
- Convertible Senior Debentures
- Unsecured Convertible Debentures
- Subordinated Convertible Debentures
- Senior Secured Convertible Debentures

Convertible Debentures are suitable for investors who look for potential increases in asset value (appreciation) compared to that yielded by Bonds, and more earnings than

Common Stocks provide. In this era of Online communication, it is possible to obtain large amounts of information regarding Convertible Debentures. Before initiating any substantial investment, it is prudent to seek suggestions of the financial experts who have a deep knowledge of Convertible Debentures. Before conversion of Convertible Debentures into Common Stocks or shares, it is prudent to have clear insight related to the potential changes in earnings and the relative gains.

*Convertible Debentures can usually be categorized into the following types*:

- Secured Convertible Debentures
- Convertible Senior Debentures
- Unsecured Convertible Debentures
- Subordinated Convertible Debentures
- Senior Secured Convertible Debentures

## PUBLIC DEPOSITS

Public deposits are an important source of financing the medium-term and long-term requirements of a company. The term 'public deposit' implies any money received by a company through the deposits or loans collected from the public. The public includes the general public, employees and shareholders of the company but excludes the money received in the form of shares and debentures.

*In India, this method of raising finance has gained a lot of importance because of the several advantages relating to public deposits*:

- It is an easier method of mobilising funds, especially during periods of credit squeeze.
- The administrative cost of deposits for the company is lower than that involved in the issue of shares and debentures.The procedure of inviting public deposits is also simpler and involve lesser formalities.
- The rate of interest payable by the company on public deposits is lower than the interest on loans from banks and other financial institutions. Such an interest is a tax deductible expense.

- It helps the company to borrow funds from a larger segment of public and thus reduces the dependence of the company upon financial institutions.
- It also enables the company to create contact with a large number of investors.
- It ensures the availability of funds for a longer duration and provides flexibility to the financial structure of the company. There is no risk of over-capitalisation and the deposits can be repaid when they are not required.
- There is no dilution of shareholders' control as the depositors have no voting rights and cannot interfere with the internal management of the company.

*But this mode of financing through public deposits has its own limitations*:

- As the public deposits are more likely to be affected by the uncertain conditions in the economy, the depositors response may vary accordingly. They may also tend to withdraw their deposits if the company is not performing well.
- Public deposits with the companies may cause a diversion of resources into non-priority and undesirable areas.
- Professional investors may not like to invest in such deposits as there is no or less chance for capital appreciation.
- As public deposits are unsecured, the depositors may have to bear the risk of loss of money in the event of failure of the company.
- Their widespread use restricts the growth of a healthy capital market.They also tend to distort the interest rate pattern of the economy and may result in the dearth of sound industrial securities.

## REGULATING PUBLIC DEPOSITS

The public deposits are regulated by the provisions of the Companies Act and the Companies (Acceptance of Deposit) Rules,1975.

*The following amounts are not included in the expression 'deposits':*

- Any amount received from the Central Government or a State Government, local authority, foreign Government, any foreign citizen or authority or any other source whose repayment is guaranteed by the Central Government or a State Government
- Any amount received as a loan from any banking company, State Bank of India or its subsidiaries,a nationalised bank or co-operative bank
- Any amount received as a loan from any of the notified financial institutions
- Any amount received by a company from any other company
- Any amount received from an employee of the company by way of security deposit
- Any amount received by way of security or as an advance from any purchasing,selling or other agents in the course of or for the purposes of the business of the company
- Any amount received by way of subscriptions to any shares, stock, bonds or debenture pending the allotment of such shares,etc.,and calls in advance on shares
- Any amount received in trust or any amount in transit
- Any amount received from directors of the company or from its shareholders by a private company
- Any amount of unsecured loans brought in by the promoters in pursuance of stipulations of financial institutions or loans provided by the promoters themselves and/or by their relatives but not by their friends and business associates.

Under the Companies Act and the rules framed thereunder, the invitation and acceptance of deposits by companies is subjected to the following conditions:

- Companies are not permitted to raise unlimited amounts of fund through public deposits. The aggregate of all outstanding deposits cannot exceed certain prescribed percentage of the paid up capital and free reserves of the company.

- Invitations of deposits by a company can be made only by means of an advertisement specifying the financial position,management structure and other particulars relating to a company. A company which has defaulted in repayment of deposit or interest thereon is prohibited from inviting deposits.
- The depositors shall fill the application form supplied by the company. The company in return issues a deposit receipt which is an acknowledgement of debt by the company.The terms and conditions of the deposit are printed on the back of the receipt.The company shall maintain a register of deposits containing the prescribed particulars and file returns of deposits duly certified by their auditor with a Registrar on or before 30th June of every year.
- The interest to be allowed on such deposits by the company must be in accordance with the rate fixed by the Government. The rate of interest on deposits also varies depending upon the period of deposit and the reputation of the company.

The Companies (Amendment) Act,2000 has inserted certain new sections, in order to protect the interests of small depositors. The expression 'small depositor' means "a depositor who has deposited (in a financial year) a sum not exceeding twenty thousand rupees in a company and includes his successors,nominees and legal representatives". In case of any default by the company in paying back to them, it shall inform the Company Law Board within sixty days from the date of default. The Company Law Board will then direct the company to repay to small depositors within a period of thirty days from the date of receipt of intimation of default. On failure to comply with the orders of the Board, the company and its directors shall be punishable with imprisonment and payment of daily fine during the period in which such non-compliance continues. However,if such a defaulting company wants to invite deposits from small depositors,it shall state the complete nature of default in all its future advertisements and application form.

Besides, the Reserve Bank of India issues directives from time to time for regulating public deposits. These are aimed at safeguarding the interest of the public and to give them a feeling of security in investing in the public deposits.

*These regulations pertain to*:

- The ratio of deposits to the paid-up capital and free reserves of the company
- The maximum duration of the deposits
- Obligation to invest a specified percentage of the deposit in a current or other account with a scheduled bank free from any charge or lien,or in approved securities which shall be used only for the repayment of deposits
- The filing of periodical returns with the RBI, giving the required information about public deposits/loans as well as furnishing of certain specified information on its financial position and working.

# 3

# Capital Budgeting

## AN OVERVIEW

A *capital expenditure* is an outlay of cash for a project that is expected to produce a cash inflow over a period of time exceeding one year.

Examples of projects include investments in property, plant, and equipment, research and development projects, large advertising campaigns, or any other project that requires a capital expenditure and generates a future cash flow.

Because capital expenditures can be very large and have a significant impact on the financial performance of the firm, great importance is placed on project selection. This process is called capital budgeting.

## CRITERIA FOR CAPITAL BUDGETING DECISIONS

Potentially, there is a wide array of criteria for selecting projects. Some shareholders may want the firm to select projects that will show immediate surges in cash inflow, others may want to emphasize long-term growth with little importance on short-term performance. Viewed in this way, it would be quite difficult to satisfy the differing interests of all the shareholders. Fortunately, there is a solution.

The goal of the firm is to maximize present shareholder value. This goal implies that projects should be undertaken that result in a positive *net present value,* that is, the present value of the expected cash inflow less the present value of the required capital expenditures. Using net present value (NPV) as a measure, capital budgeting involves selecting those projects that increase the value of the firm because they have a positive NPV. The timing and growth rate of the incoming cash flow is important only to the extent of its impact on NPV.

Using NPV as the criterion by which to select projects assumes efficient capital markets so that the firm has access to whatever capital is needed to pursue the positive NPV projects. In situations where this is not the case, there may be capital rationing and the capital budgeting process becomes more complex.

Note that it is not the responsibility of the firm to decide whether to please particular groups of shareholders who prefer longer or shorter term results. Once the firm has selected the projects to maximize its net present value, it is up to the individual shareholders to use the capital markets to borrow or lend in order to move the exact timing of their own cash inflows forward or backward.

This idea is crucial in the principal-agent relationship that exists between shareholders and corporate managers. Even though each may have their own individual preferences, the common goal is that of maximizing the present value of the corporation.

## ALTERNATIVE RULES FOR CAPITAL BUDGETING

While net present value is the rule that always maximizes shareholder value, some firms use other criteria for their capital budgeting decisions.

*such as*:

- Internal Rate of Return (IRR)
- Profitability Index
- Payback Period
- Return on Book Value

In some cases, the investment decisions resulting from the IRR and profitability index methods agree with those of NPV. Decisions made using the payback period and return on book value methods usually are suboptimal from the standpoint of maximizing shareholder value.

## CAPITAL BUDGETING PROCESS

*The process is designed to help policy makers:*

- Capital asset inventory
- Capital improvement plan
- Long-term financial analysis
- Capital budget

## CAPITAL ASSET INVENTORY

The monitoring of capital assets allows the state to keep track of, and locate if need be, all land, infrastructure, buildings, and equipment owned by the state. The Department of Administration is required by statute (IC 4–13–1–20) to provide for the periodic inspection, appraisal, and inventory of all of the state's real and personal property, and require reports from state agencies concerning the real and personal property in their custody.

The Auditor of State needs financial information relating to the state's real and personal property for financial reporting purposes. Therefore, the Department of Administration and the Auditor's Office have an agreement whereas the Auditor will collect asset information through the cooperation of all state agencies.

The Indiana Department of Administration, to fulfill its statutory requirements in IC 4–13–1–20 regarding personal property and IC 4–20.5–6–3 regarding real property, may monitor capital asset inventory recording and reporting and may correspond with the agencies, the Auditor of State, and State Board of Accounts, to ensure compliance. Agency officials are ultimately responsible for the accountability and security of all assets.

## REPORTING CAPITAL ASSETS

Each state agency is to report to the Auditor of State any additions (purchases), retirements or changes (traded-in, surplus, transferred, etc.) each quarter. The additions, changes, and retirements are to be reported on the Capital Asset Inventory form (State Form 39598 (R2/9–89). If you have nothing to report, a signed letter with your agency number must be submitted saying you have no action. The information needed and instructions on reporting follow.

## What to Report

*Capital assets are any*:

- Land
- Infrastructure
- Buildings
- Improvements Other than Buildings
- Construction in Progress
- Capital assets that are purchased, transferred from another agency, donated, etc. for the states use.

Improvements and repairs, which allow an asset to continue to be used during its originally established useful life, are expensed and not capitalized. Improvements and repairs, which extend the useful life of an asset, are called preservation costs.

These preservation costs will be capitalized for all capital assets with the exception of infrastructure. Additions and improvements, which increase the capacity or efficiency of the asset, will also be capitalized for all assets.

The only items to be reported to the Auditor for inclusion in the State's inventory are assets with a cost of $20,000 or more. Agencies are responsible for maintaining a manual or automated asset control system for all assets costing more than $500.

*The asset information to be maintained by the agencies should include the following*:

- Asset Tag Number
- Acquisition Date
- Asset Description
- Acquisition Cost
- Fund Number Purchased From
- Serial Number
- If purchased with federal funds, the name of the federal grant that was used.
- Location of asset within agency.

The agencies should also include the assets costing more than $20,000 in their own asset control systems in addition to reporting them to the Auditor of State. For auditing purposes, agencies must also maintain a record of all additions and retirements to their asset control system. The $500 limit is a minimum requirement. Since agencies are responsible for accountability and security of all assets, they may choose to lower this limit and to include on their system other items deemed to be necessary.

## When to Report

In accordance with the Auditor of State's capital asset policy, a capital asset report must be submitted by every state agency quarterly. A master listing of each agency's active assets will be sent to the agencies in the months of October, January, April and July. To have an asset included on the master listing, the capital asset inventory form must be received by October 5th, January 5th, April 5th, and by the date established by the Auditor's Office for the fiscal year end cutoff.

## Additions to Report

For items to be reported to the Auditor's office and added to the master listing, the Capital Asset Inventory form needs to be completed.

The top portion of this form MUST always be completed. Also include the year below the quarter dates. Any asset costing $500 or more must be tagged but the only items required to be included in the Auditor of State's inventory are those with a cost of $20,000 or more. All fields on the form must be completed for an addition. If an asset does not have a serial number, that field should be left blank. Group all your assets per location and round the asset cost to the nearest whole dollar. The name and telephone number of the person submitting the form must be included on the form.

## Changes to Report

Changes are any change to existing information on the

inventory other than "retirements." The top portion of the report always be completed for any change. The name and telephone number of the person submitting the form must be included on the form.

The only information to be put on a change is the Prefix Number, Asset Number, Sub Number, and the field(s) to be changed. Asset record information can be changed but the Prefix Number, Asset Number and Sub Number cannot be changed. Incorrect Prefix, Asset or Sub Number must be retired under the incorrect number and added under the correct.

## Retirements to Report

Retirements are any existing items on the state inventory that are no longer used, sold, given to surplus, etc. Retirements include items scrapped, abandoned, or traded.

The top portion of the report MUST always be completed for any retirement. All fields are required to be completed for a retirement. The name and telephone number of the person submitting the form must be included on the form. If any information is missing or completed incorrectly, the report will be returned for correction.

## Capital Leases

If a lease of equipment or real property qualifies as a "capital lease", the asset should not be added to their asset control system until all lease payments have been made and the agency receives title to the asset.

## Miscellaneous Information

- All reports must be typed or neatly written.
- The top portion must be fully completed for any additions, changes, and retirements.
- Do not use " " in place of information.
- All locations for adds should be grouped together. Retirements do not need to be grouped by location.
- Any asset may be tagged by an agency but only those meeting the requirements are to be reported to the

state. Assets at the minimum level of $500 must be tagged. Assets should be tagged upon receipt. Tags may be purchased through Label Tech, 1100 East Seymour St., Muncie, IN 47302. Phone: (765) 747–1234 or 1–800–359–2155.

- No asset is to be reported to the Auditor of State which does not meet the requirement of costing at least $20,000.
- If there are no capital assets to report in a particular quarter, a signed letter must be submitted saying you have no action to report unless otherwise arranged with the Auditor's office.
- If an asset is being transferred from one agency to another, the agency receiving the asset will add the asset and the other agency will retire the asset. The agency receiving the asset should assign a new asset number to the asset. The acquisition date for the asset stays the same as the original agency had for the acquisition date. The fund number for the asset becomes the fund number the new agency uses for its assets. The cost for the asset should be the original cost of the asset.
- Reports not filled out just as to these instructions will be sent back for corrections.
- For evidence of proper disposition of assets, State Form 13812 should be completed and filed with State Surplus Property Section.
- Obtain a Capital Police report for assets that are stolen.

## Report Instructions

*This report must be typed or neatly written*:

- Circle the quarter for the report and write in the year.
- Type or write your agency name.
- Type or write your agency number (only three digits).
- Check only one category (Add, Change, or Retirement).
- Fill in fields with asset information.

## CAPITAL ASSET MASTER LISTING

The Auditor's office will send a Capital Asset Master Listing quarterly. Upon receipt of the listing it should be reviewed to ensure the activity reported has been included. If activity has not been included, determine if you reported the activity in time to be included. If you have, contact the Auditor's office to determine that they received your activity report and plan to enter the activity. If you submit your activity electronically by cartridge or disk, you will get an edit list that contains your transactions as well as any error messages. Any activity that shows an error message will need to be resubmitted on another disk or cartridge or through Inventory Forms. Do not resubmit the activity that did not contain errors.

## PHYSICAL INVENTORY

Once a year a physical inventory is to be taken and compared to the master listing and the agency's listing of assets from their asset control system. The physical inventory helps ensure the asset inventory is accurate and that assets have not left the agency without authorization. It also helps identify unused or obsolete assets. Evidence that a physical inventory was taken is to be maintained.

## DISPOSITION OF SURPLUS PROPERTY

The Department of Administration establishes guidelines and requirements relating to the disposition of agency assets. The following is a summary of those guidelines and requirements.

*Generally, surplus property may be disposed of in one of the following ways:*

- May be transferred to State Surplus.
- May be transferred or sold to another state agency.
- May be traded-in on purchased equipment.
- May be junked when no other disposition is efficient or economical.
- May be sold at a public auction or sealed bid.
- May be sold to local units of government by sealed bid.

These guidelines are to be followed whether the assets are above $20,000 and reported to the Auditor of State or whether they are accounted for on the agencies asset control systems.

The State Surplus Property. The Department of Administration is to be informed whenever state property of any kind is no longer useful to the agency. State Form 13812 is used for this notification.

### Transfer to State Surplus

To transfer assets to state surplus, complete and submit State Form 13812. When Surplus Property returns the pink and goldenrod copy you may take the assets with the goldenrod copy to State Surplus.

### Transfer to Another State Agency

To transfer assets to another agency complete State Form 13812. Submit the form to State Surplus along with a letter stating you are taking the items off your inventory and a letter from the receiving agency stating they are putting the items on their inventory. The assets can be transferred after you receive the pink copy of the form.

### Trade-Ins

Trade-in of surplus property is part of the procurement process.

The Procurement Division of the Department of Administration must know about possible trade-ins. Surplus property form 13812 is to be filed with State Surplus Property. Requisitions for sealed competitive bids and non-bid procurements (including quotes) are to include the price without trade-in, the trade-in value, and the price with trade-in.

### Disposal of Junk Property

An agency may junk property once permission has been received from State Surplus Property. Prior to disposal, the agency should contact the Recycling Programme Manager in the Operations Division of the Department of Administration to see if the item may be recycled.

### Sale

Contact State Surplus Property if you have any items that may warrant being sold through auction or sealed bids.

## ASSETS PURCHASED WITH FEDERAL FUNDS

Title of equipment purchased by an agency with federal funds, in whole or in part, vests with the State. The agency is to use, manage, and dispose of the asset in accordance with State laws, rules, and procedures.

The asset shall be used by the agency in the Programme or project for which it was acquired for as long as needed, whether or not the project or Programme continues to be supported by federal funds. Property records must be kept in compliance with state rules. In addition, the records must include the percentage of federal participation in the cost of the asset, the location, use and condition of the asset, and ultimate disposition data including the date of disposal and any sales price. Agencies should supplement the Auditor of State's Capital Asset Inventory system with the additional federal requirements. Records showing proper disposition of the asset should be maintained at least three years from date of disposition.

## CAPITAL IMPROVEMENT PLAN

A Capital Improvement Plan (Programme), or CIP, is a short-range plan, usually four to six years, which identifies capital projects and equipment purchases, provides a planning schedule and identifies options for financing the plan. Essentially, the plan provides a link between a municipality, school district, parks and recreation department and/or other local government entity and a comprehensive and strategic plans and the entity's annual budget.

## BENEFITS

*A CIP provides many benefits including*:

- Allows for a systematic evaluation of all potential projects at the same time.

- The ability to stabilize debt and consolidate projects to reduce borrowing costs.
- Serve as a public relations and economic development tool.
- A focus on preserving a governmental entity's infrastructure while ensuring the efficient use of public funds.
- An opportunity to foster cooperation among departments and an ability to inform other units of government of the entity's priorities. For example, it is not uncommon for a large city or county to incorporate into its CIP the capital needs of a school district, parks and recreation department and/or some other public service structure.

## FEATURES

*The CIP typically includes the following information*:

- A listing of the capital projects or equipment to be purchased.
- The projects ranked in order of preference.
- The plan for financing the projects.
- A timetable for the construction or completion of the project.
- Justification for the project.

## OVERALL PROCESS

Prior to undertaking the development of the CIP, the government entity will want to define the criteria for what kind of projects or equipment are to be included and organize a process for developing the plan.

What is defined as a capital project or capital purchase may vary from city to county to district to state depending on the size of the local government provisioning the plan. Generally, they will be tangible items that have a life expectancy greater than one year.

A local government will also need to forecast where it believes it will face future demands and growth, which will involve an inventory of existing facilities, infrastructure and equipment. In addition, a local government will want to develop basic policies for implementing the plan. Because the CIP includes financing issues, the municipality may want to seek advice from their financial advisor and/or bond counsel. A review of the municipality's current finances is also vital.

Once the CIP is finalized, the local government is required to hold a public hearing before the plan is adopted by a city council, a board of regents and/or a bond review commission.

## SPECIFIC STEPS

- Establish a Capital Planning Committee with Bylaws
- Take Inventory of Existing Capital Assets
- Evaluate Previously Approved, Unimplemented or Incomplete Projects
- Assess Financial Capacity
- Solicit, Compile and Evaluate New Project Requests
- Prioritize Projects
- Develop a Financing Plan
- Adopt a Capital Improvements Programme
- Monitor and Manage Approved Projects within the CIP
- Update Existing/Ongoing Capital Programs

## FINANCIAL ANALYSIS

Financial analysis (also referred to as financial statement analysis or accounting analysis) refers to an assessment of the viability, stability and profitability of a business, sub-business or project. It is performed by professionals who prepare reports using ratios that make use of information taken from financial statements and other reports. These reports are usually presented to top management as one of their bases in making business decisions.

*Based on these reports, management may*:

- Continue or discontinue its main operation or part of its business;
- Make or purchase certain materials in the manufacture of its product;
- Acquire or rent/lease certain machineries and equipment in the production of its goods;

- Issue stocks or negotiate for a bank loan to increase its working capital;
- Make decisions regarding investing or lending capital;
- Other decisions that allow management to make an informed selection on various alternatives in the conduct of its business.

## GOALS

*Financial analysts often assess the firm's:*

- *Profitability*: Its ability to earn income and sustain growth in both short-term and long-term. A company's degree of profitability is usually based on the income statement, which reports on the company's results of operations;
- *Solvency*: Its ability to pay its obligation to creditors and other third parties in the long-term; 3. Liquidity - its ability to maintain positive cash flow, while satisfying immediate obligations;
- Both 2 and 3 are based on the company's balance sheet, which indicates the financial condition of a business as of a given point in time.
- *Stability*: The firm's ability to remain in business in the long run, without having to sustain significant losses in the conduct of its business. Assessing a company's stability requires the use of both the income statement and the balance sheet, as well as other financial and non-financial indicators.

## METHODS

*Financial analysts often compare financial ratios (of solvency, profitability, growth, etc.)*:

- *Past Performance*: Across historical time periods for the same firm (the last 5 years for example),
- *Future Performance*: Using historical figures and certain mathematical and statistical techniques, including present and future values, This extrapolation method is the main source of errors in financial analysis as past statistics can be poor predictors of future prospects.

- *Comparative Performance*: Comparison between similar firms.

These ratios are calculated by dividing a (group of) account balance(s), taken from the balance sheet and/ or the income statement, by another, for example:

n/ equity = return on equity

Net income/ total assets = return on assets

Stock price/ earnings per share = P/E-ratio

Comparing financial ratios is merely one way of conducting financial analysis.

*Financial ratios face several theoretical challenges*:

- They say little about the firm's prospects in an absolute sense. Their insights about relative performance require a reference point from other time periods or similar firms.
- One ratio holds little meaning. As indicators, ratios can be logically interpreted in at least two ways. One can partially overcome this problem by combining several related ratios to paint a more comprehensive picture of the firm's performance.
- Seasonal factors may prevent year-end values from being representative. A ratio's values may be distorted as account balances change from the beginning to the end of an accounting period. Use average values for such accounts whenever possible.
- Financial ratios are no more objective than the accounting methods employed. Changes in accounting policies or choices can yield drastically different ratio values.
- They fail to account for exogenous factors like investor behaviour that are not based upon economic fundamentals of the firm or the general economy (fundamental analysis).

Financial analysts can also use percentage analysis which involves reducing a series of figures as a percentage of some base amount.

For example, a group of items can be expressed as a percentage of net income. When proportionate changes in the same figure over a given time period expressed as a percentage is know as horizontal analysis. Vertical or common-size analysis, reduces all items on a statement to a"common size" as a percentage of some base value which assists in comparability with other companies of different sizes.

Another method is comparative analysis. This provides a better way to determine trends. Comparative analysis presents the same information for two or more time periods and is presented side-by-side to allow for easy analysis.

## PROJECT SELECTION

Every project begins with a proposal, but not every proposal can or should become a project. In a world of limited resources, choices have to be made. Not every project has viability. And, amongst those that do, limited resources (people, time, money and equipment), must be applied judiciously.

The goal of the project selection process is to Analyse project viability, and to approve or reject project proposals based on established criteria, following a set of structured steps and checkpoints.

## PROJECT ESTIMATION

### INTRODUCTION

The CS/10,000 project estimation tool suite allows you to generate, manage, and validate estimates of effort for a wide variety of projects. The estimation method uses proprietary AI technology to provide both task and effort based estimation for your project.

#### Estimation

*Traditionally, the accuracy of structured estimation methods such as function point analysis or COCOMO (line of code estimation) has been limited by two factors*:

1. The number and types of parameters that can be evaluated and
2. The assignment of company specific input values.

In CS/10,000 these complex issues have been addressed by a patented expert system/neural network based AI system. The CS/10,000 Project Estimator processes information from a large number of sources to create a meaningful estimate for your project. It evaluates the project plan, project requirements, information about your working environment, and even different aspects of your corporate culture. On the basis of historical project data, the estimator also tunes input parameters to your specific environment - automatically. You are shielded from the intricacies of the AI system behind a user friendly interface that guides you every step of the way. Easy to use and highly accurate compared to other structured methods, the CS/10,000 estimation module contains all the tools that you need to effectively manage and document the entire estimation life cycle.

## Validation

The CS/10,000 estimation tool set includes a reconciliation facility that assists you in validating all results generated by the estimator. The Estimation Reconciliator compares actual project effort with estimated effort on a task by task basis to provide a detailed report of method accuracy.

The results of this tool help you determine if the estimator requires further tuning. The Estimation Reconciliator also benchmarks and validates estimation results to ensure that your analysis is reliable and accurate.

## Optimizing

CS/10,000 is extremely flexible in terms of fine tuning estimation parameters to your specific mode of operation. System parameters can be tuned manually or by the neural network based Estimation Configurator. Each distinct tuning process should be based on the data from a group of similar historical projects. The results can then be used to estimate similar future projects. Multiple sets of tuning parameters can be created and stored in separate configuration files. When you are ready to estimate a project, you can choose to apply the system default configuration or a user defined configuration, whichever provides a better fit to your current project. The CS/10,000 Project Estimation tool suite offers the project analyst a powerful and sophisticated estimation method, a suite of tools to Analyse and validate results, and full control to configure system parameters for optimal results.

## Getting Started

The CS/10,000 Project Estimator will automatically generate an accurate estimate of the duration of your project in person months, based on the parameters of your particular project. To achieve this, the Project Estimator asks you a series of questions about your project. CS/10,000 will then take your answers, and use its proprietary expert system and neural network links to provide an accurate estimate of the length of time needed to complete the project. CS/10,000's neural network has been pre-trained, using estimates from numerous successful Client/Server projects.

## Preparing the Project Plan

The best way to let the Project Estimator assist you with your project estimation is to generate a customised project plan using the Task Advisor. To optimize results make certain that the Project Plan contains the actual set of task groups that will be assigned to the project team. If your project is based on the Superproject template and the Task Advisor Questionnaire has not been completed, the entire methodology of CS/10,000 will be estimated. Extraneous task groups, which will lead to higher estimates, can be easily removed with the Cut function of the Methodology Configurator. If, on the other hand, the Estimation Advisor is applied to a project based on the Empty Template, and no task groups have been added manually, the estimator will return an estimate of 0 Person Months. When task groups are added to a project that are not part of the standard CS/10,000 methodology it is necessary to configure an initial set of estimation parameters manually.

## Running the Project Estimator with System Default Parameters

Once you have run the expert system and customised the

methodology for your project, simply click on the Estimation Advisor button, which is located on CS/10,000's Command Centre.

This takes you into the Estimation Advisor, which prompts you for the answers the system needs to estimate your project at the task group level. The more questions you answer, the more accurate the estimate will be. This will invoke the CS/10,000 proprietary expert system and neural network to accurately estimate your project.

## What if Scenarios

In the beginning of a project we may not be sure how answering the questions (System Requirement Analysis) will affect our task list and subsequently affect our estimate. Test estimates can be produced to give us an idea of what effect different scenarios have on our estimate. Multiple estimation versions for a project can be stored by clicking on the Save button in the View Project Estimates window. The ability to track how various project parameters effect your estimate provides you with the means to optimize the planning and scheduling of your project before major financial commitments are made.

## Viewing Estimation Results

The Project Estimation window displays the estimated time in person months that a project is expected to take. This screen appears as a result of running the Estimation Advisor expert system and neural network. If you wish to view a preexisting estimate for the current project, choose the Project Estimator option from the Tools menu item on the main menu.

## Estimation Units—Project Effort

*The total estimate is calculated in person months, which can easily be converted to other units of effort using the following conversion factors:*

- 22 Person Days/Person Month
- 8 Person Hours/Person Day
- 176 Person Hours/Person Month

These time units represent project effort, rather than project duration. Project effort represents the absolute number of time units that need to be expended to complete a project. Project duration, on the other hand, is a measure of the length of time in calendar units between the beginning of a project and the end of a project.

Actual project duration can be calculated from project effort by taking into consideration such company dependent factors as the total number of resources assigned to the project, how many hours per day each resource can work on the project, resource attendance, holidays, etc.

To give a simple example of such a conversion, consider a CS/10,000 project estimate of 2 person months for a project to which 10 people have been assigned. 2 person months converts to 2*176 = 352 person hours.

For a 10 person team, this result divides into 35.2 hours per person. If each of the team members effectively works 5 full hours on the project per day, the project will take about 7 full work days to complete.

If the project begins on a Thursday, and team members are not scheduled to work on the weekend, the actual project duration will be 9 calendar days.

### Updating the CS/10,000 Project Plan

By clicking on the Save command bottom of the View Project Estimates screen, the Save Project Estimates screen will appear. In this screen you have the option of saving the estimate as well as updating the task list of your current project with the estimated hours that are currently displayed. Only the questions and answers of the estimate which was generated last are available for viewing.

### Effort Levels

If you selected "Update Project Tasks" in this screen, the task group estimates will be divided among the tasks based on the effort levels you entered on the project plan. If you do not wish to enter your own effort levels, CS/10,000 will use the system defaults, which have already been tested against numerous successful client/server and networking projects. Effort levels are based on a relative distribution factor - they determine how much of the task group estimate will be distributed to each individual task. The mathematical formula to calculate the hours estimate for each task in a task group based on the effort level for each task is:

Task Hours Estimate = Group Hours Estimate * (Task Effort Level/Group Effort

Effort levels are entered or modified in the timesheets or taskgrid. When creating a project template for an organization, it would be useful to save a particular effort level configuration as part of the template.

The Update Project Tasks function of the Save Project Estimates window reads the effort level assigned to each task in the task grid and distributes the Task Group estimate among the tasks of the group accordingly. The value assigned to the Estimated Hours field of each task in the project plan is also automatically assigned to the Remaining Hours field.

## Automate Scheduling

After the estimated hours field of each task of the CS/ 10,000 project plan has been populated with the results from the estimator, it is a simple matter to transfer this information to the corresponding scheduled hours field.

As soon as a resource is scheduled to a task, the scheduled hours field for the resource is automatically updated with the estimated hours value for that task. If the resource is assigned to the task group header of the task, the resource is automatically scheduled to each task underlying the task group header just as to the estimated hours for each of the tasks. This method provides a very quick way to schedule resources and hours to tasks.

## Generate a Preliminary Cost Estimate

Once scheduling data has been added, the Costing Manager can pull in the scheduled hours to automatically calculate a cost estimate for the project. Thus in a short amount of time it is possible to generate not only a time estimate for a project, but also to schedule resources and generate a cost estimate. This is possible due to the integrated nature of the CS/10,000 project design management modules.

## ESTIMATION RECONCILIATION

Once you have completed your successful client/server and networking system, you can use CS/10,000's Estimation Reconciliator to validate the result of the estimation process.

### Why Reconciliation?

The completed project may significantly differ from the planned tasks and projected conditions upon which the initial estimate was based. The initial estimate must be adjusted to account for these differences if a meaningful comparison between the estimate and the actual project effort is be established. The purpose of the Reconciliation Advisor is to recalculate the estimated effort using the actual statistics and results from the completed project. The Reconciliation Advisor gathers actual project data through a question and answer process similar to that used when the system requirements were gathered for the initial estimate. The questions differ only in that the past tense is used: "Did the application replace a mission critical or line of business process?" instead of " Does the application replace a mission critical or line of business process?".

### Preparing the Project Plan

To reconcile the actual duration of your project with the results from the estimator it is necessary for the Reconciliator to calculate the actual duration of a completed project. The actual duration is calculated from the total number of actual hours that have been entered for each task of the current project plan. Before reconciling an estimation result, make certain that all tasks of the project to be reconciled have been completed, and that the actual hours have been entered for each task. Actual hours can be entered into the CS/10,000 timesheet or task grid; the Reconciliator will pull the scheduling data from either module.

## Reconciliating Your Projects

To begin the reconciliation process, simply select Project Estimate Reconciliation from the Advisor menu. This will take you into the Project Estimate Reconciliation Advisor. Answer the questions of the Advisor based on the actual statistics and results from the completed project, after the fact. The Report command invokes the CS/10,000 proprietary expert system and neural network. This button when you have answered as many questions as you can in the Project Estimate Reconciliation Advisor. The artificially intelligent advisor will use your answers to the questions to generate its best estimate for your project, which you can then compare against the actual time the project took.

Once you have reconciled your project, you can then decide whether or not to use the project to train the neural network, so that it becomes increasingly tuned to your environment and to your particular style of corporate management. If the estimate and the actual hours are remarkably different, you may wish to pay particular attention as to why this occurred, and you may wish to save the project as a separate configuration so that it can be used as the estimator template for similar projects in the future.

## Viewing Results

The Project Estimate Reconciliation window displays both the actual number of person months the project took to complete, and also the reconciled estimate. This screen can be reached by pressing the Report button from the Project Estimate Reconciliation Advisor.

The Actual and Estimated checkboxes are used to toggle between details on the actual project, which are taken from the actual hours on the timesheets or task grid, and the estimate you have just run on the completed project. A comparison between the two shows you how accurately the CS/10,000 Project Estimator is estimating your projects.

If the Actual option is checked, the total amount of effort that the project actually required, in person months, is listed in the Total Effort box.

Actual phase totals are calculated for the Define, Plan, Prototype, and Implement phases. The buttons for each of the four phases of a project to view the task group breakdown for that phase, which indicates how long each task group took to complete. This information is displayed in person days, as the Task Group Effort, with the percentage displayed in the"Percentage of this phase" box.

If the Estimate option is checked, the Total Effort box lists the total estimated effort of the project. The estimate is based on the parameters of the completed project and was calculated by the Estimation Reconciliator.

The estimation results from the Estimation Reconciliator will be used by the Estimation Configurator when you are ready to tune the neural network.

As for the actuals, estimates by phase are calculated for the Define, Plan, Prototype, and Implement phases. The buttons for each of the four phases of a project to view the task group breakdown for that phase, which lists the CS/10,000 estimate of how much effort each task is estimated to require for completion. This information is displayed in person days, as the Task Group Effort, with the percentage displayed in the"Percentage of this phase" box.

## ESTIMATION CONFIGURATION

### The CS/10,000 Neural Network

After about 5 projects have been completed, you should consider tuning the neural net. Although it is technically possible to tune the neural network with fewer projects, a group of five gives the system a sufficiently wide range of historical data to evaluate. Before project data can participate in tuning, it must be reconciliated. Reconciliation will provide the Estimation Configurator with the accurate historical estimation data that is needed for precise tuning.

### Rule Groups and Weights

To gain an understanding of the tuning process, it is necessary to be familiar with the concept of rule groups and weights. Each task group of the CS/10,000 methodology, as well as any task groups that have been configured manually, is associated with a set of rule groups. Rule groups are factors that influence a task group. The degree to which individual rule groups influence a task group is expressed numerically by the weight assigned to the rule group.

In the course of the tuning process the neural network will adjust the weights that are associated with the rule groups in order to align estimation results more closely to actual effort. Tuning is a safe and reliable process - it is not possible to overtrain the neural network. A complete set of tuned estimation parameters can be stored in CS/10,000 as a user defined estimation configuration. Multiple configurations can be created and stored for the estimation of many different types of projects.

Projects developed under disparate development conditions should not be tuned as a group because a distinct configuration, or set of estimation parameters, may be appropriate for each. For example, if an organization has two IS departments which differ significantly in terms of the complexity of their technologies, employee skill levels, and style of management you may wish to use a different set of tuning parameters for each of the departments.

Estimation configurations can also be modified and tuned on a task group by task group basis. You have the ability to manually change default rule groups that are associated with a task group as well as adjust the degree to which the weights of the rule groups will be tuned.

### Effort Factors

You influence the current weights of a task group's rule group by specifying a new minimum, medium, and maximum effort factor for the task group. The effort factors represent the range of effort, in person days, that the task group is judged to require for completion. You can even train the estimator to recognize and estimate any task group that you have created yourself. To accomplish this you first need to link a set of appropriate rule groups to the task group. You must then assign a minimum, medium, and maximum effort factor. After all associations have been made, new as well as modified task groups are automatically tuned by the neural network.

## Using the Project Estimation Configurator

Choose the Estimation Configurator item from the Tools menu, to configure the estimator and fine-tune the estimator to your organization's environment.

*There are four configuration operations*:

1. Tune the project estimator
2. View the estimator configurations
3. Add task groups to the estimator, and
4. Modify task groups in the estimator.

## Tuning the Project Estimator

By choosing the Tune the Project Estimator option, the Estimation Configurator will use your past project history to automatically train the estimator to your environment. You must select a configuration to tune.

A configuration contains all the parameters necessary to estimate a project. CSCL Project Estimation Configuration is the configuration shipped with CS/10,000. Next, you must select the projects with which you want to train the neural network.

It is recommended that you tune the estimator with a minimum of five projects and that the selected projects are representative of your corporation's development environment. You may choose any grouping of projects you have completed in CS/10,000 and use them to teach the neural net.

## Viewing the Estimation Configurations

The Project Estimator Configuration window is opened by choosing View the Estimator Configurations in the Project Estimation Configurator. After specifying which configuration to view the Project Estimator Configuration window will appear. This window displays the neural network rule groups and their weighting for each task group in the methodology.

Review the task groupings for each project phase by clicking on the phase button (Define, Plan, Prototype or Implement) to populate the task group and rule group listboxes with the appropriate data.

*Task Groups listbox*: The task groups for each project phase are displayed in this list. Click on any of the task groups for that phase to view the rule groups which influence how that task group is estimated.

## Add Task Groups to the Estimator

The Project Estimator maintains a list of tasks it knows how to estimate. If you have added your own tasks to the CS/10,000 methodology, choose this option to add your new tasks to the list. This enables the task groups you added to be automatically estimated.

Simply select a task group from the available list, and CS/10,000 will guide you through linking it to the data that the neural net uses to make predictions.

You can either let the Estimation Configurator automatically link the new task groups to default rule groups or you can perform a manual link. Each rule group represents an aspect of the project that influences the task effort, for example, Project Size, Project Politics, Management Skills to name just a few.

Next, you must assign a minimum, medium and maximum effort level to the task group. An effort level is the amount of person days required to complete the task or task group. Now you are ready to add the new task groups to the estimator.

## Modify Task Groups in the Estimator

The advanced feature of CS/10,000's Project Estimator is that it allows you to modify the way the expert system and neural net estimate task groups.

Essentially, selecting this option from the Project Estimation Configurator allows you to tune the estimation parameters for any task group manually.

Select the task group you wish to modify. The rule groups

that are linked to that task will be displayed. The rule groups relate to the questions you answered in the Project Estimation Advisor. They indicate at a high level which questions will affect how the Estimator predicts the time it will take to complete this task group.

CS/10,000 then guides you through the steps to alter any of the rule groups that are linked to the task group. When you change which rule groups are linked to the selected task group, you are prompted to enter your own estimates on the effort required to complete the task group. These steps will automatically tune the estimator for the selected task group.

### Selecting an Estimation Configuration

If your corporation is estimating projects over multiple departments, CS/10,000 allows you to save your estimation parameters as separate configurations for each department, to allow for differing management styles across the corporation. A configuration is the set of data the neural net uses to make predictions.

Simply choose the default configuration to tune the estimator, then save that estimation as a new name. This estimate configuration can then be used to estimate subsequent, similar projects. The default configuration can never be altered, so that you may always revert to using the system defaults to estimate your projects.

When you wish to use a particular estimate configuration for estimating a project, select Estimation Configuration from the Options menu.

This will provide you with a list of all the current configurations available in the system. Simply select the configuration you wish to use. The data for the chosen configuration will then be used to estimate your current project.

## CASH FLOW

Cash flow (also"cashflow") refers to the movement of cash into or out of a business, a project, or a financial product. It is usually measured during a specified, finite period of time.

*Measurement of cash flow can be used*:

- To determine a project's rate of return or value. The time of cash flows into and out of projects are used as inputs in financial models such as internal rate of return, and net present value.
- To determine problems with a business's liquidity. Being profitable does not necessarily mean being liquid. A company can fail because of a shortage of cash, even while profitable.
- As an alternate measure of a business's profits when it is believed that accrual accounting concepts do not represent economic realities. For example, a company may be notionally profitable but generating little operational cash (as may be the case for a company that barters its products rather than selling for cash). In such a case, the company may be deriving additional operating cash by issuing shares, or raising additional debt finance.
- Cash flow can be used to evaluate the'quality' of Income generated by accrual accounting. When Net Income is composed of large non-cash items it is considered low quality.
- To evaluate the risks within a financial product. E.g. matching cash requirements, evaluating default risk, re-investment requirements, etc.

Cash flow is a generic term used differently depending on the context. It may be defined by users for their own purposes. It can refer to actual past flows, or to projected future flows.

It can refer to the total of all the flows involved or to only a subset of those flows. Subset terms include'net cash flow', operating cash flow and free cash flow.

## STATEMENT OF CASH FLOW IN A BUSINESS'S FINANCIALS

The (total) net cash flow of a company over a period (typically a quarter or a full year) is equal to the change in cash balance over this period: positive if the cash balance increases (more cash becomes available), negative if the cash balance decreases.

*The total net cash flow is the sum of cash flows that are classified in three areas*:

1. *Operational cash flows*: Cash received or expended as a result of the company's internal business activities. It includes cash earnings plus changes to working capital. Over the medium term this must be net positive if the company is to remain solvent.
2. *Investment cash flows*: Cash received from the sale of long-life assets, or spent on capital expenditure (investments, acquisitions and long-life assets).
3. *Financing cash flows*: Cash received from the issue of debt and equity, or paid out as dividends, share repurchases or debt repayments.

## WAYS COMPANIES CAN AUGMENT REPORTED CASH FLOW

*Common methods include*:

- *Sales*: Sell the receivables to a factor for instant cash. (leading)
- *Inventory*: Don't pay your suppliers for an additional few weeks at period end. (lagging)
- *Sales Commissions*: Management can form a separate (but unrelated) company and act as its agent. The book of business can then be purchased quarterly as an investment.
- *Wages*: Remunerate with stock options.
- *Maintenance*: Contract with the predecessor company that you prepay five years worth for them to continue doing the work
- *Equipment Leases*: Buy it
- *Rent*: Buy the property.
- *Oil Exploration costs*: Replace reserves by buying another company's.
- *Research & Development*: Wait for the product to be proven by a start-up lab; then buy the lab.

- *Consulting Fees:* Pay in shares from treasury since usually to related parties
- *Interest* - Issue convertible debt where the conversion rate changes with the unpaid interest.
- *Taxes:* Buy shelf companies with TaxLoss CarryForward's. Or gussy up the purchase by buying a lab or O&G explore co. with the same TLCF.

## EXAMPLES

| Description | Amount ($) | totals ($) |
|---|---|---|
| Cash flow from operations | | +10 |
| Sales (paid in cash) | +30 | |
| Materials | -10 | |
| Labor | -10 | |
| Cash flow from financing | | +40 |
| Incoming loan | +50 | |
| Loan repayment | -5 | |
| Taxes | -5 | |
| Cash flow from investments | | -10 |
| Purchased capital | -10 | |
| Total | | +40 |

The net cash flow only provides a limited amount of information. Compare, for example, the cash flows over three years of two companies:

| | Company A | | | Company B | | |
|---|---|---|---|---|---|---|
| | Year 1 | Year 2 | year 3 | Year 1 | Year 2 | year 3 |
| Cash flow from operations | +20M | +21M | +22M | +10M | +11M | +12M |
| Cash flow from financing | +5M | +5M | +5M | +5M | +5M | +5M |
| Cash flow from investment | -15M | -15M | -15M | 0M | 0M | 0M |
| Net cash flow | +10M | +11M | +12M | +15M | +16M | +17M |

Company B has a higher yearly cash flow. However, Company A is actually earning more cash by its core activities and has already spent 45M in long term investments, of which the revenues will only show up after three years.

## CASH FLOW STATEMENT

Cash flow statement may provide considerable information about what is really happening in a business beyond that contained in either the income statement or the balance sheet.

Analyzing this statement should not present an intimidating task, instead it will quickly become obvious that the benefits of understanding the sources and uses of a company's cash far outweigh the costs of undertaking some very straightforward analyses.

*Who cares about a Cash Flow Statement?*

- Executives want to know if the cash generated by the company will be sufficient to fund their expansion strategy
- Stockholders want to know if the firm is generating enough cash to pay dividends
- Suppliers want to know if their customers will be able to pay if offered credit
- Investors want to evaluate future growth potential
- Employees are interested in the overall viability of their employer as indicated by its ability to fund its operations

### Format of the Cash Flow Statement

- *The cash flow statement is divided into three parts*:
  - *Cash flow from operating activities*: shows the results of cash inflows and outflows related to the fundamental operations of the basic line or lines of business in which the company engages. *Example*: Cash receipts from the sale of goods or services and cash outflows for purchasing inventory and paying rent and taxes.)
  - *Cash flow from investing activities*: associated with purchases and sales of non-current assets

*Example*: building and equipment purchases or sales of investments or subsidiaries.

- *Cash flow from financing activities*: associated with financing the firm

  *Example*: selling and paying off bonds and issuing stock and paying dividends

- *Exceptions*:
  - Short-term marketable securities are treated as long-term investments and appear in cash flow from investing activities
  - Short-term debt is treated as long-term debt and appears in cash flow from financing activities
  - Although dividends are handled as a cash outflow in the cash flow from financing activities part, interest payments are considered an operating outflow, despite the fact that both are payments to outsiders for using their money.
- *Example of a Statement of Cash Flow*: Notice how it separates the three different cash flow activities:

| **Statement of Cash Flows** | |
|---|---|
| Cash Flow from Operating Activities | |
| Net Income | XXX,XXX |
| Adjustments to reconcile net income to net | |
| cash provided by operating activities: | |
| Depreciation and amortization | XX,XXX |
| Changes in other accounts affecting operations: | |
| (Increase)/decrease in accounts receivable | X,XXX |
| (Increase)/decrease in inventories | X,XXX |
| (Increase)/decrease in prepaid expenses | X,XXX |
| Increase/(decrease) in accounts payable | X,XXX |
| Increase/(decrease) in taxes payable | X,XXX |
| Net cash provided by operating activities | XXX,XXX |
| Cash Flow from Investing Activities | |
| Capital expenditures | (XXX,XXX) |
| Proceeds from sales of equipment | XX,XXX |
| Proceeds from sales of investments | XX,XXX |

| | |
|---|---|
| Investments in subsidiary | (XXX,XXX) |
| Net cash provided by investing activities | (XXX,XXX) |
| Cash Flow from Financing Activities | |
| Payments of long-term debt | (XX,XXX) |
| Proceeds from issuance of long-term debt | XX,XXX |
| Proceeds from issuance of common stock | XXX,XXX |
| Dividends paid | (XX,XXX) |
| Purchase of treasury stock | (XX,XXX) |
| Net cash provided by financing activities | (XX,XXX) |
| Increase (Decrease) in Cash | XX,XXX |

- *Operating Activities*:
  - The cash flow from operating activities part of a cash flow statement can be presented using the direct format or the indirect format. The bottom line is the same, but the two begin at different points. Companies are free to use either format.
  - *Direct method*: shows how much cash came in for sales and how much cash went out for inventory and other operating expenditures.
  - *Indirect method*: starts with net income as a figure that summarizes most of the cash transactions for operating activities in a firm. However, net income also includes transactions that ere not cash, so we must eliminate the non-cash transactions from the net income figure to arrive at an accurate presentation of cash flow from operating activities.

**Table. Cash Flow from Operating Activities (two formats)**

| Direct | | Indirect | |
|---|---|---|---|
| Cash received from customers | $400,000 | Net Income | $30,000 |
| Cash paid to suppliers | -260,000 | Adjustments to reconcile net | |
| Cash paid to employees | -70,000 | income to net cash provided, | |
| Other cash operating expenditures | | by operating activities: | |
| Net cash provided by operating | Depreciation | | 25,000 |
| activities | $40,000 | Changes in other accounts | |
| affecting operations: | | | |
| (Increase) in receivables | | | -12,000 |
| Decrease in inventory | | | 5,000 |
| (Decrease) in payables | | | -8,000 |
| Net cash provided by operating activities | | | $40,000 |

## Method Used to Analyse the Cash Flow

- Scan the big picture
- Check the power of the cash flow engine
- Pinpoint the good news and the bad news
- Put the puzzle together

### *Step 1: Scanning The Big Picture*

- First, place your company in context in terms of its age, industry, and size. (Mature companies have different cash flows from start-up companies. And service industries look different from heavy manufacturing industries.)
- Flip through the annual report and other accounting records to determine how management believes the year progressed. Was it a good year? Perhaps a record-breaking year in terms of revenue or net income? Or is management explaining how the company has had some rough times?
- Look at net income. Does it show income or losses over the past few years? Is income (or loss) shrinking or growing?

### *Step 2: Checking The Power Of The Cash Flow Engine*

- The cash flow from operating activities part is the cash flow engine of the company. When this engine is working effectively, it provides the cash flows to cover the cash needs of operations.
- To check the cash flow check if the cash flow from operating activities is greater than zero. Also check whether it is growing or shrinking. Assuming it is positive, the next question is can it cover important, routine expenditures?
- An exception is start-up companies often have negative cash flow from operating activities because they had to spend a lot to get the company started and their cash flow engines are not yet up to speed.
- Examine the operating working capital accounts. Inventories, receivables, and accounts payable usually grow in expanding companies.

### *Step 3: Pinpointing The Good News And The Bad News*

- Begin with cash flow from investing activities. One systematic observation is to check whether the company is generating or using cash in its investing activities. A healthy company invests continually in more plant, equipment, land, and other fixed assets to replace the assets that have been used up or have become technologically obsolete.
- You must look at the entire package to evaluate whether your cash flows from financing are in the "good news" or "bad news" categories. One systematic way to begin is to compare borrowing and payments on debt with each other across the years and note the trends. Another way in uncovering the news in this part is to check the activities in the stock accounts.

### *Step 4: Putting The Puzzle Together*

- It would be rare to find a company in which all of the evidence is positive, or in which all of the evidence is negative.
- To make a balanced evaluation, you must use both the good news and the bad news identified in each part of the statement.
- Sometimes there are unusual or unknown items that may need further looked into (possibly by a professional).

## CASH FLOW FORECASTING

*Cash flow forecasting is*:

- In a corporate finance sense, the modeling of a company or asset's future financial liquidity over a specific timeframe. *Cash* usually refers to the company's total bank balances, but often what is forecast is treasury position which is cash plus short-term investments minus short-term debt. Cash flow is the change in cash or treasury position from one period to the next;

- In the context of the entrepreneur or manager, forecasting what cash will come into the business or business unit in order to ensure that outgoing can be managed to as to avoid them exceeding cashflow coming in. If there is one thing entrepreneurs learn fast, it is to become very good at cashflow forecasting.

## Importance of Cash Flow Forecast

Cash flow forecast shows the critical when of cash coming in and cash going out during a certain month. Preparing a monthly cash flow forecast provides you with the opportunity to show dollar figures, representing revenues and expenses, in the month the business expects to collect and spend the cash. A cash flow forecast does not show sales estimates or overhead expenses averaged across several months.

Used properly, this will provide you with the means to keep your business decision-making on track and your inventory purchasing in control. It will also serve as an early warning indicator when your expenditures are running out of line or your sales targets are not being met.

As the manager of your cash, you will have enough time to devise remedies for anticipated temporary cash shortfalls and ample opportunity to arrange short term investments for the business' temporary cash flow surpluses.

The completed cash flow forecast will clearly show a bank loans officer (or yourself) what additional working capital, if any, the business may need, and will offer proof that there will be sufficient cash on hand to make the interest payments to support a revolving line of credit (to cover the shortfalls). If the performance projections are realistic, they will also provide support for the feasibility of a term loan for an equipment purchase or for a master marketing campaign.

Computer spreadsheet programs such as Microsoft Excel, Lotus 123 or any of a variety of full-faceted business software can be very useful for cash flow worksheet development.

Reliable cash flow projections can bring a sense of order and well-being to your business and more calm to your life. The most important tool owners/managers have available to control the financial aspects of their business is the cash flow worksheet.

## Starting Steps

### *Step One: Consider Your Cash Flow Revenues*

For new operations, the basis can be the average monthly sales of a similar-sized competitor's operations who is operating in a similar market It is recommended that you make adjustments for this year's predicted trend for the industry. Be sure to reduce your figures by a start-up year factor of about 50% a month for the start-up months.

For existing operations, sales revenues from the same month in the previous year make a good base for forecasting sales for that month in the succeeding year. For example, if the trend readers in the economy and the industry predict a general growth of 4% for the next year, it will be entirely acceptable for you to show each month's projected sales at 4% higher than your actual sales the previous year. Include Notes to the Cash flow to explain any unusual variations from previous years' numbers.

If you sell products on credit terms or with instalment payments, you must be careful to enter only the part of each sale that is collectible in cash in the specific month you are considering (realized accounts receivable). Any amount collected after 30 days will be termed Collections on Accounts Receivable and will be shown in the month in which it will be collected.

It is critical to the credibility of your plan that any sales made should only be entered once the cash is received in payment. This is the critical test principle of the cash flow and should be applied whenever you are in doubt as to what amount to enter and when.

### *Step Two: Consider your Cash Flow Disbursements*

Project each of the various expense categories (that would normally be shown in your ledger) beginning with a summary for each month of the cash payments to trade suppliers (accounts payable). Again, follow the principle that there should not be any averaging or allocating of these inventory purchases (trade payables).

Each month must show only the cash you expect to pay out that month to your trade suppliers. For example, if you plan to pay your supplier invoices in 30 days, the cash payouts for January's purchases will be shown in February. If you can obtain trade credit for longer terms, then cash outlays will appear two or even three months after the stock purchase has been received and invoiced. An example of a different type of expense is your insurance expenditure. Your commercial insurance premium may be $2400 annually. Normally, this would be treated as a $200 monthly expense. But the cash flow will not see it this way. The cash flow wants to know exactly how it will be paid. If it is to be paid in two instalments, $1200 in January and $1200 in July, then that is how it must be entered on the cash flow worksheet. The exact same principle applies to all cash flow expense items.

Once total cash collections, total cash payments on goods purchased, and any other expected expenses have been estimated for each individual month of operation, it is necessary to link the cash flow status of each month to the cash flow status and activity of the preceding and succeeding months (i.e. the reconciliation).

### *Step Three: Reconciliation of the Cash Revenues to Cash Disbursements*

The reconciliation part of the cash flow worksheet begins by showing the balance carried over from the previous months' operations. To this it will add the total of the current month's revenues and subtract the total of the current month's expenditures. This adjusted balance will be carried forward to the first line of the reconciliation portion of the next month to become the base to which the next month's cash flow activity will be added and/or subtracted.

## Usage of Your Cash Flow

Cash flow plans are living entities and must constantly

be modified as you learn new things about your business and your paying customers. Since you will use this cash flow forecast to regularly compare each month's projected figures with each month's actual performance figures, it will be useful to have a second column for the actual performance figures right alongside each of the planned columns in the cash flow worksheet. As the true strengths and weaknesses of your business unfold before your eyes, actual patterns of cash movement emerge. Look for significant discrepancies between the planned and actual figures.

For example, if the business' actual figures are failing to meet your cash revenue projections for three months running, this is an unmistakable signal that it is time to revise the year's projections. It may be necessary to delay the stock replenishment plan, or apply to the bank to increase the upper limit of your revolving line of credit. Approaching the bank to increase an operating loan should be done well in advance of the date when the additional funds are required. Do not leave cash inflow to chance.

## Cash Flow Worksheet

There are a variety of ways a cash flow forecast can be structured. To gain the optimum benefit, it is recommended that it be structured to show only revenues from operations, and the proceeds from sales of company assets, if appropriate, in the revenues portion of the worksheet.

On occasion a prepared format will show a slot for proceeds of a term loan in this part; this may, however, take away from the value of the cash flow as an indicator of the business' operating performance and of the cash flow's ability to clearly show the real amount of working capital needs. If a fixed term loan amount is treated as revenue to the business, the balances carried forward each month cannot accurately reflect how the business is earning money (unless the reader takes the additional step of subtracting the loan proceeds from the equation).

Your general format should allow a double width column along the left side of the page for the account headings, then two side by side vertical columns for each month of the year, beginning from the month you plan to open (e.g. the first dual column might be labelled April Planned and April Actual etc.).

From there, the cash flow worksheet breaks into three distinctive parts. The first part (at the top left portion of the worksheet, starting below and to the left of the month names) is headed Cash Revenues (or Cash In). The second part is headed Cash Disbursements (or Cash Out). The final part is headed Reconciliation of Cash Flow.

*Example*:

| ITEM | April Planned | April Actual | May Planned | May Actual |
|---|---|---|---|---|
| Cash Revenues | | | | |
| Total Cash Revenues | $40 | $10 | $75 | $35 |
| Cash Disbursements | | | | |
| Total Cash Disbursements | $50 | $60 | $60 | $70 |
| Reconciliation of Cash Flow | | | | |
| Opening Cash Balance | $0 | $0 | ($10) | ($50) |
| Add: Total Cash Revenues | $40 | $10 | $75 | $35 |
| Deduct: Total Cash Disbursements | $50 | $60 | $60 | $70 |
| Closing Cash Balance (carry forward to next month) | ($10) | ($50) | $5 | ($85) |

## ASPECTS OF CASH FLOW

### Cash Flow Hedge

*A cash flow hedge is a hedge of the exposure to the variability of cash flow that*:

- Is attributable to a particular risk associated with a recognized asset or liability. Such as all or some future interest payments on variable rate debt or a highly probable forecast transaction and
- Could affect profit or loss

### Cash Flow Loan

Cash flow loan is a sort of debt financing, in which a bank lends funds against cash flows that a borrowing company generates. To secure repayment, the bank covenants a borrower on such levels and ratios as enterprise value, EBITDA, total interest coverage ratio, Total debt/EBITDA, and so on. In contrast, an asset-based loan is lent against company's assets. Senior stretch loan is the mix of the two.

Cash flow loans are usually senior term loans or subordinated debt, being used for funding growth or financing an acquisition.

## Discounted Cash Flow

In finance, discounted cash flow (DCF) analysis is a method of valuing a project, company, or asset using the concepts of the time value of money. All future cash flows are estimated and discounted to give their present values (PVs) – the sum of all future cash flows, both incoming and outgoing, is the net present value (NPV), which is taken as the value or price of the cash flows in question.

Using DCF analysis to compute the NPV takes as input cash flows and a discount rate and gives as output a price; the opposite process – taking cash flows and a price and inferring a discount rate, is called the yield.

Discounted cash flow analysis is widely used in investment finance, real estate development, and corporate financial management.

### *Discount Rate*

By far the most widely used method of discounting is exponential discounting, which values future cash flows as "how much money would have to be invested currently, at a given rate of return, to yield the cash flow in future". Other methods of discounting, such as hyperbolic discounting, are studied in academia and said to reflect intuitive decision-making, but are not generally used in industry.

The discount rate used is generally the appropriate Weighted average cost of capital (WACC), that reflects the risk of the cashflows.

*The discount rate reflects two things*:

1. *The time value of money (risk-free rate)*: The theory of time preference, investors would rather have cash

immediately than having to wait and must therefore be compensated by paying for the delay.

2. *A risk premium*: Reflects the extra return investors demand because they want to be compensated for the risk that the cash flow might not materialize after all.

An alternative to including the risk in the discount rate is to use the risk free rate, but multiply the future cash flows by the estimated probability that they will occur (the success rate). This method, widely used in drug development, is referred to as rNPV (risk-adjusted NPV), and similar methods are used to incorporate credit risk in the probability model of CDS valuation.

### *Methods of Appraisal of a Company or Project*

For these valuation purposes, a number of different DCF methods are distinguished today. The details are likely to vary depending on the capital structure of the company. However the assumptions used in the appraisal (especially the equity discount rate and the projection of the cash flows to be achieved) are likely to be at least as important as the precise model used.

Both the income stream selected and the associated cost of capital model determine the valuation result obtained with each method. This is one reason these valuation methods are formally referred to as the Discounted Future Economic Income methods.

- *Equity-Approach*:
  - Flows to equity approach (FTE)
    Discount the cash flows available to the holders of equity capital, after allowing for cost of servicing debt capital. *Advantages*: Makes explicit allowance for the cost of debt capital *Disadvantages*: Requires judgement on choice of discount rate
- *Entity-Approach*:
  - Adjusted present value approach (APV)
    Discount the cash flows before allowing for the

debt capital (but allowing for the tax relief obtained on the debt capital) *Advantages*: Simpler to apply if a specific project is being valued which does not have earmarked debt capital finance.*Disadvantages*: Requires judgement on choice of discount rate; no explicit allowance for cost of debt capital, which may be much higher than a "risk-free" rate

- Weighted average cost of capital approach (WACC)
  Derive a weighted cost of the capital obtained from the various sources and use that discount rate to discount the cash flows from the project. *Advantages*: Overcomes the requirement for debt capital finance to be earmarked to particular projects. *Disadvantages*: Care must be exercised in the selection of the appropriate income stream. The net cash flow to total invested capital is the generally accepted choice.
- Total cash flow approach (TCF)
  This distinction emphasises that the Discounted Cash Flow method can be used to determine the value of various business ownership interests. These can include equity or debt holders.

Alternatively, the method can be used to value the company based on the value of total invested capital. In each case, the differences lie in the choice of the income stream and discount rate.

For example, the net cash flow to total invested capital and WACC are appropriate when valuing a company based on the market value of all invested capital.

### *Shortcomings*

Commercial banks have widely used discounted cash flow as a method of valuing commercial real estate construction projects.

*This practice has two substantial shortcomings*:

1. The discount rate assumption relies on the market

for competing investments at the time of the analysis, which would likely change, perhaps dramatically, over time, and

2. Straight line assumptions about income increasing over ten years are generally based upon historic increases in market rent but never factors in the cyclical nature of many real estate markets. Most loans are made during boom real estate markets and these markets usually last less than ten years. Using DCF to Analyse commercial real estate during any but the early years of a boom market will lead to overvaluation of the asset.

Discounted cash flow models are powerful, but they do have shortcomings. DCF is merely a mechanical valuation tool, which makes it subject to the axiom "garbage in, garbage out". Small changes in inputs can result in large changes in the value of a company.

Instead of trying to project the cash flows to infinity, terminal value techniques are often used. A simple annuity is used to estimate the terminal value past 10 years, for example. This is done because it is harder to come to a realistic estimate of the cash flows as time goes on.

## Discounted Payback Period

The discounted payback period is the amount of time that it takes to cover the cost of a project, by adding positive discounted cash flow coming from the profits of the project.

## FCC LLC

FCC, LLC, also known as First Capital, is a commercial financial services firm providing working capital and outsourcing, primarily for middle-market companies and institutions.

The company reports over $1 billion in total committed lines. The firm focuses on asset-based lending, accounts receivable financing and management, factoring, credit protection, international supply chain financing and servicing for clients in North America and Asia.

The firm also manages asset portfolios and issues receivables-backed securities.

Based out of Boca Raton, Florida, the firm has offices in New York, Los Angeles, Oklahoma City and Atlanta as well as Asian subsidiaries in Hong Kong and Manila.

John Kiefer is Chief Executive Officer He previously held corporate management positions at Capital Factors, Inc., a subsidiary of Union Planters Corp and has held board positions at Capital Bank as well as Capital Factors.

## Forecast Period (Finance)

In finance, the forecast period is the time period in which the individual yearly cash flows are input to the discounted cash flow formula. Cash flows after the forecast period can only be represented by a fixed number such as the compound annual growth rate. There are no fixed rules for determining the duration of the forecast period.

### *No Set Maximum*

Determine a forecast period by choosing a number of years with excessive return. In the years chosen the company should plan to generate a return on new investments greater than its cost of capital. This can be based on factors such as comparing the company's competitiveness with it's competitors.

### *Predetermined Maximum, Based on Exit Strategy*

Determine a forecast period by choosing a number of years after which an exit is planned. A exit can either be positive (merger, acquisition, initial public offering) or negative (bankruptcy). This method is mostly used by investors, using venture capital for example, planning on a positive exit.

### *Predetermined Maximum, Based on Market*

Determine a forecast period by choosing a number of years based on characteristics of the market. Companies in established and well known market are better suited towards longer forecasting periods then companies opening up a new market.

## Free Cash Flow

In corporate finance, free cash flow (FCF) is cash flow available for distribution among all the securities holders of an organization. They include equity holders, debt holders, preferred stock holders, convertible security holders, and so on.

| Element | Data Source |
|---|---|
| Net Income | Current Income Statement |
| + Depreciation/Amortization | Current Income Statement |
| - Changes in Working Capital | Prior & Current Balance Sheets: Current Assets and Liability accounts |
| - Capital expenditure | Prior & Current Balance Sheets: Property, Plant and Equipment accounts |
| = Free Cash Flow | |

Note that the first three lines are calculated for you on the standard Statement of Cash Flows.

You can also calculate it by taking: (EBITDA-D&A)*(1–T)+D&A–CAPEX–Net Change in WC

| Element | Data Source |
|---|---|
| Net Income | Current Income Statement |
| + Depreciation/Amortization | Current Income Statement |
| - Changes in Working Capital | Prior & Current Balance Sheets: Current Assets and Liability accounts |
| = Cash Flows from Operations | same as Statement of Cash Flows: part 1, from Operations |

Therefore,

| Element | Data Source |
|---|---|
| Cash Flows from Operations | Statement of Cash Flows: part 1, from Operations |
| - Capital Expenditure | Statement of Cash Flows: part 2, from Investment |
| = Free Cash Flow | |

There are two differences between Net Income and Free Cash Flow that should be noted. The first is the accounting for the consumption of capital goods. The Net Income measure uses depreciation, while the Free Cash Flow measure uses last period's net capital purchases.

| Measurement Type | Component | Advantage | Disadvantage |
|---|---|---|---|
| Free Cash Flow | Prior period net investment spending | Spending is in current dollars | Capital investments are at the discretion of management, so spending may be sporadic. |
| Net Income | Depreciation charge | Charges are smoothed, related to cumulative prior purchases | Allowing for typical 2% inflation per year, equipment purchased 10 years ago for $100 would now cost about $122. With 10 year straight line depreciation the old machine would have an annual depreciation of $10, but the new, identical machine would have depreciation of $12.2, or 22% more. |

The second difference is that the Free Cash Flow measurement deducts increases in net working capital, where the net income approach does not. Typically, in a growing company with a 30 day collection period for receivables, a 30 day payment period for purchases, and a weekly payroll, it will require more and more working capital to finance the Labour and profit components embedded in the growing receivables balance. The net income measure essentially says, "You can take that cash home" because you would still have the same productive capacity as you started with. The Free Cash Flow measurement however would say, "You can't take that home" because you would cramp the enterprise from operating itself forward from there.

Likewise when a company has negative sales growth it's likely to diminish its capital spending dramatically. Receivables, provided they are being timely collected, will also ratchet down. All this "deceleration" will show up as additions to Free Cash Flow. However, over the longer term, decelerating sales trends will eventually catch up.

Net Free Cash Flow definition should also allow for cash available to pay off the company's short term debt. It should also take into account any dividends that the company means to pay.

*Net Free Cash Flow = Operation Cash flow – Capital Expenses to keep current level of operation – dividends – Current Portion of long term debt – Depreciation*

Here Capex Definition should not include additional investment on new equipment. However maintenance cost can be added.

Dividends - This will be base dividend that the company intends to distribute to its share holders.

Current portion of LTD - This will be minimum Debt that the company needs to pay in order to not create defaults. Depreciation - This should be taken out since this will account for future investment for replacing the current PPE. If the Net Income category includes the income from Discontinued operation and extraordinary income make sure it is not be part of Free Cash Flow.

## *Uses of the Metric*

Free cash flow measures the ease with which businesses can grow and pay dividends to shareholders. Even profitable businesses may have negative cash flows. Their requirement for increased financing will result in increased financing cost reducing future income. The discounted cash flow valuation model, the intrinsic value of a company is the present value of all future free cash flows, plus the cash proceeds from its eventual sale. The presumption is that the cash flows are used to pay dividends to the shareholders.

Some investors prefer using free cash flow instead of net income to measure a company's financial performance, because free cash flow is more difficult to manipulate than net income. The problems with this presumption are itemized at cash flow and return of capital.

The payout ratio is a metric used to evaluate the sustainability of distributions from REITs, Oil and Gas Royalty Trusts, and Income Trust. The distributions are divided by the free cash flow. Distributions may include any of income, flowed-through capital gains or return of capital.

## *Problems with Capital Expenditures*

The expenditures for maintenances of assets is only part of the capex reported on the Statement of Cash Flows. It must be separated from the expenditures for growth purposes.

This split is not a requirement under GAAP, and is not audited. Management is free to disclose maintenance capex or not. Therefore this input to the calculation of free cash flow may be subject to manipulation, or require estimation. Since it may be a large number, maintenance capex's uncertainty is the basis for some people's dismissal of 'free cash flow'.

A second problem with the maintenance capex measurement is its intrinsic 'lumpiness'. By their nature, expenditures for capital assets that will last decades may be infrequent, but costly when they occur.

'Free cash flow', in turn, will be very different from year to year. No particular year will be a 'norm' that can be expected to be repeated. For companies that have stable capital expenditures, free cash flow will (over the long term) be roughly equal to earnings

### *Agency Costs of Free Cash Flow*

In 1986, *American Economic Review,* Michael Jensen noted that free cash flows allowed firms' managers to finance projects earning low returns which therefore might not be funded by the equity or bond markets. Examining the US oil industry, which had earned substantial free cash flows in the 1970s and the early 1980s, he wrote that

[the] 1984 cash flows of the ten largest oil companies were $48.5 billion, 28 Per cent of the total cash flows of the top 200 firms in Dun's Business Month survey. Consistent with the agency costs of free cash flow, management did not pay out the excess resources to shareholders. Instead, the industry continued to spend heavily on [exploration and development] activity even though average returns were below the cost of capital.

Jensen also noted a negative correlation between exploration announcements and the market valuation of these firms - the opposite effect to research announcements in other industries.

## Operating Cash Flow

In financial accounting, operating cash flow (OCF), cash

flow provided by operations or cash flow from operating activities, refers to the amount of cash a company generates from the revenues it brings in, excluding costs associated with long-term investment on capital items or investment in securities.

Operating cash flow = Cash generated from operations less taxation and interest paid, investment income received and less dividends paid gives rise to operating cash flows per International Financial Reporting Standards.

To calculate cash generated from operations, one must calculate cash generated from customers and cash paid to suppliers. The difference between the two reflects cash generated from operations.

*Cash generated from customers*:

- Revenue as reported

  – increase (decrease) in trade receivables

  – investment income (disclosed separately)

  – other income that is non cash and non sales related

*Cash paid to suppliers*:

- Costs of sales
- \+ other expenses as reported less

  – increase (decrease) in trade payables

- – non cash items such as depreciation, provisioning, impairments, bad debts, etc.
- – financing expenses

## *Operating Cash Flow vs. Net Income, EBIT, and EBITDA*

Since it adjusts for liabilities, receivables, and depreciation, operating cash flow is a more accurate measure of how much cash a company has generated (or used) than traditional measures of profitability such as net income or EBIT.

For example, a company with numerous fixed assets on its books (e.g. factories, machinery, etc.) would likely have decreased net income due to depreciation; however, as depreciation is a non-cash expense the operating cash flow would provide a more accurate picture of the company's current cash holdings than the artificially low net income. Earnings before interest, taxes, depreciation and amortization (EBITDA) is a non-GAAP metric that can be used to evaluate a company's profitability based on net working capital.

The difference between EBITDA and OCF would then reflect how the entity finances its net working capital in the short term.

OCF is not a measure of free cash flow and the effect of investment activities would need to be considered to arrive at the free cash flow of the entity.

## Valuation Using Discounted Cash Flows

A method for determining the current value of a company using future cash flows adjusted for time value.

The future cash flow set is made up of the cash flows within the determined forecast period and a continuing value that represents the cash flow stream after the forecast period.

### *Basic Frmula for Firm valuation Using DCF Model*

$$\text{Value of firm} = \sum_{t=1}^{n} \frac{FCFF_t}{(1+WACC_{hg})^t} + \frac{\left[\frac{FCFF_n + 1}{(WACC_{st} - g_n)}\right]}{(1+WACC_{hg})^n}$$

*Where:*

- *FCFF* is the Free Cash Flow to the Firm (i.e. Operating cash flow minus capital expenditures)
- *WACC* is the Weighted Average Cost of Capital
- *t* is the time period
- *n* is the number of time periods
- *g* is the growth rate

### *Process Data Diagram*

The following diagram shows an overview of the process

of company valuation. All activities in this model are explained in more detail in part 3: Using the DCF method.

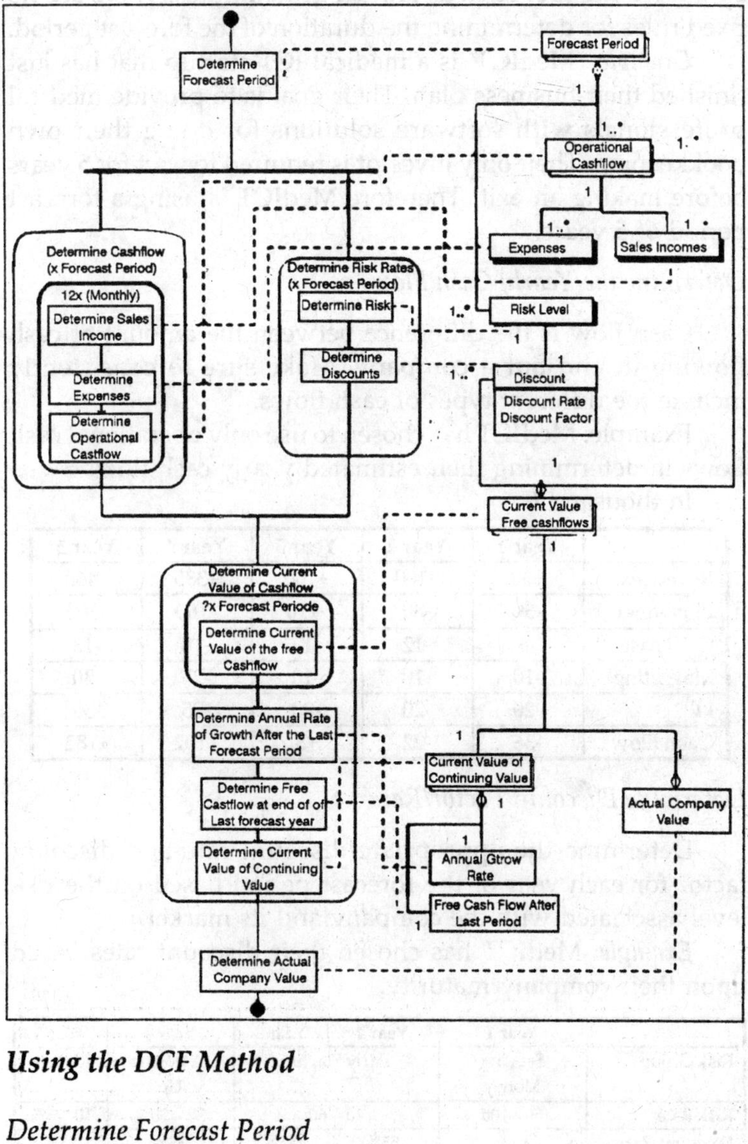


## *Using the DCF Method*

### *Determine Forecast Period*

The forecast period is the time period for which the

individual yearly cash flows are input to the DCF formula. Cash flows after the forecast period can only be represented by a fixed number such as annual growth rates. There are no fixed rules for determining the duration of the forecast period.

*Example*: 'MedICT' is a medical ICT startup that has just finished their business plan. Their goal is to provide medical professionals with software solutions for doing their own bookkeeping. Their only investor is required to wait for 5 years before making an exit. Therefore MedICT is using a forecast period of 5 years.

### *Determine the Yearly Cash Flow*

Cash flow is the difference between the amount of cash flowing in and out a company. Make sure to consistently include the different types of cash flows.

Example: MedICT has chosen to use only operational cash flows in determining their estimated yearly cash flow:

In thousand €

| | Year 1 | Year 2 | Year 3 | Year 4 | Year 5 |
|---|---|---|---|---|---|
| Revenues | +30 | +100 | +160 | +330 | +460 |
| Personnel | -30 | -80 | -110 | -160 | -200 |
| Car Lease | -6 | -12 | -12 | -18 | -18 |
| Marketing | -10 | -10 | -10 | -25 | -30 |
| IT | -20 | -20 | -20 | -25 | -30 |
| Cash Flow | -36 | -22 | +8 | +102 | +182 |

### *Determine Discount Factor/Rate*

Determine the appropriate discount rate and discount factor for each year of the forecast period based on the risk level associated with the company and its market.

*Example*: MedICT has chosen their discount rates based upon their company maturity.

| | Year 1 | Year 2 | Year 3 | Year 4 | Year 5 |
|---|---|---|---|---|---|
| Risk Group | Seeking Money | Early Startup | | Late Start Up | Mature |
| Risk Rate | 50 - 100 | 40 – 60 | | 30 – 50% | 10- 25% |
| Discount Rate | 65% | 55% | 45% | 35% | 25% |
| Discount Factor | 0.61 | 0.42 | 0.33 | 0.30 | 0.33 |

*Determine Current Value*

Calculate the current value of the future cash flows by multiplying each yearly cash flow by the discount factor for the year in question. This is known as the time value of money.

*Example:*

| | Year 1 | Year 2 | Year 3 | Year 4 | Year 5 |
|---|---|---|---|---|---|
| Cash Flow | -36 | -22 | +8 | +102 | +182 |
| Discount Factor | 0.61 | 0.42 | 0.33 | 0.30 | 0.33 |
| Current Value | € -21.96 | € -9.24 | € 2.64 | €30.6 | €60.1 |

*Determine the Continuing Value*

Calculating cash flows after the forecast period is much more difficult as uncertainty, and therefore the risk factor, rises with each additional year into the future. The continuing value, or terminal value, is a solution that represents the cash flows after the forecast period.

*Example*: MedICT has chosen the perpetuity growth model to calculate the value of cash flows after the forecast period. They estimate that they will grow at about 6% for the rest of these years. (182*1.06/ (0.25–0.06)) = 1015.34 This value however is a future value that still needs to be discounted to a current value: 1015.34 * 1/(1.25)^5 = 332.72

*Determining Equity Value*

The value of the equity can be calculated by subtracting any outstanding debts from the total of all discounted cash flows.

*Example*: MedICT doesn't have any debt so it only needs to add up the current value of the continuing value and the current value of all cash flows during the forecast period:

62.14 + 332.72= 394.86 The equity value of MedICT: € 394.86

# 4

# Capital Budgeting Techniques

## AN OVERVIEW

There are a number of techniques of capital budgeting. Some of the methods are based on the concept of incremental cash flows from the projects or potential investments.

There are some other techniques of capital budgeting that are based on the accounting rules and accounting earnings. However, the techniques based on the accounting rules are considered to be improper by the economists. The hybrid and simplified techniques of capital budgeting are also used in practice.

Capital budgeting is the process of managing the long-term capital of a firm in the most profitable way. The prime task of the capital budgeting is to estimate the requirements of capital investment of a business. The capital allocation to various projects depending on their needs and selection of proper project for the business also fall under the canopy of capital budgeting concept.

*Some of the major techniques of capital budgeting are*:

- Profitability index
- Net present value
- Modified Internal Rate of Return
- Equivalent annuity
- Internal rate of return

## PROFITABILITY INDEX

The profitability index is a technique of capital budgeting. This holds the relationship between the investment and a proposed project's payoff. Mathematically the profitability index is given by the following formula:

Profitability Index = (Present Value of future cash flows)/ (Present Value of Initial investment)

The profitability index is also sometimes called as value investment ratio or profit investment ratio. Profitability index is used to rank various projects.

## NET PRESENT VALUE

Net present value (NPV) is a widely used tool for capital budgeting. NPV mainly calculates whether the cash flow is in excess or deficit and also gives the amount of excess or shortfall in terms of the present value. The NPV can also be defined as the present value of the net cash flow.

Mathematically, NPV = ?(Ct/ (1+r)t) – C0, where the summation takes the value of t ranging from 1 to n Here, n stands for the total project time t stands for the cash flow time r stands for the rate of discount Ct stands for net cash flow at time t C0 stands for capital outlay when t = 0

## MODIFIED INTERNAL RATE OF RETURN

The Modified Internal Rate of Return (MIRR) gives the measure of an investment's attractiveness in a business. The prime use of the modified internal rate of return in the capital budgeting process is to rank various choices of projects.

## EQUIVALENT ANNUITY

Equivalent Annual Cost is widely used in capital budgeting as a decision making tool. This is mainly used to compare different projects having unequal project lifetime.

## INTERNAL RATE OF RETURN

The internal rate of return (IRR) is a metric used by the capital budgeting in order to determine whether the firm should make investments or not. The IRR indicates the efficiency of a particular investment.

## PAYBACK PERIOD METHOD

The payback is another method to evaluate an investment

project. The payback method focuses on the payback period. *The payback period is the length of time that it takes for a project to recoup its initial cost out of the cash receipts that it generates. This period is some times referred to as" the time that it takes for an investment to pay for itself."*

The basic premise of the payback method is that the more quickly the cost of an investment can be recovered, the more desirable is the investment. The payback period is expressed in years. When the net annual cash inflow is the same every year, the following formula can be used to calculate the payback period.

*The formula or equation for the calculation of payback period is as follows:*

Payback period = Investment required/ Net annual cash inflow*

*If new equipment is replacing old equipment, this becomes incremental net annual cash inflow.

To emphasise the payback method, consider the following example:

*Example*: York company needs a new milling machine. The company is considering two machines. Machine A and machine B. Machine A costs $15,000 and will reduce operating cost by $5,000 per year. Machine B costs only $12,000 but will also reduce operating costs by $5,000 per year.

*Required*:

- Calculate payback period.
- Which machine should be purchased just as to payback method?

*Calculation*:

Machine A payback period = $15,000/ $5,000 = 3.0 years

Machine B payback period = $12,000/ $5,000 = 2.4 years

Payback calculations, York company should purchase machine B, since it has a shorter payback period than machine A.

## EVALUATION OF THE PAYBACK PERIOD METHOD

The payback method is not a true measure of the

profitability of an investment. Rather, it simply tells the manager how many years will be required to recover the original investment. Unfortunately, a shorter payback period does not always mean that one investment is more desirable than another.

To emphasise since machine B has a shorter payback period than machine A, it appears that machine B is more desirable than machine A. But if we add one more piece of information, this illusion quickly disappears. Machine A has a project 10-years life, and machine B has a projected 5 years life. It would take two purchases of machine B to provide the same length of service as would be provided by a single purchase of machine A. Under these circumstances, machine A would be a much better investment than machine B, even though machine B has a shorter payback period. Unfortunately, the payback method has no inherent mechanism for highlighting differences in useful life between investments.

Such differences can be very important, and relying on payback alone may result in incorrect decisions.

Another *criticism of payback method* is that it does not consider the time value of money. A cash inflow to be received several years in the future is weighed equally with a cash inflow to be received right now.

*Assume that for an investment of $8,000 you can purchase either of the two following streams of cash inflows*:

| Years | 0 | 1 | 2 | 3 | 4 | 5 | 6 | 7 | 8 |
|---|---|---|---|---|---|---|---|---|---|
| Stream 1 | | | | | $8,000 | $2,000 | $2,000 | $2,000 | $2,000 |
| Stream 2 | | $2,000 | $2,000 | $2,000 | $2,000 | $8,000 | | | |

Which stream of cash inflows would you prefer to receive to receive in return for your $8,000 investment? Each stream has a payback period of four years. Therefore, if payback method alone were relied on in making the decision, you would be forced to say that the streams are equally desirable. However from the point of view of the time value of money, stream 2 is much more desirable than stream 1.

On the other hand, under certain conditions the payback method can be very useful. For one thing, it can help identify which investment proposals are in the "ballpark." That is, it can be used as a screening tool to help answer the question, "Should I consider this proposal further?" If a proposal does not provide a payback within some specified period, then there may be no need to consider it further.

In addition, the payback period is often of great importance to new firms that are "cash poor." When a firm is cash poor, a project with a short payback period but a low rate of return might be preferred over another project with a high rate of return but a long payback period.

The reason is that the company may simply need a faster return of its cash investment. And finally, the payback method is sometimes used in industries where products become obsolete very rapidly - such as consumer electronics. Since products may last only a year or two, the payback period on investments must be very short.

## EXTENSION OF PAYBACK METHOD

The payback period is calculated by dividing the investment in a project by the net annual cash inflows that the project will generate.

If equipment is replacing old equipment then any salvage to be received on disposal of the old equipment should be deducted from the cost of the new equipment, and only the incremental investment should be used in payback computation.

In addition, any depreciation deducted in arriving at the project's net operating income must be added back to obtain the project's expected net annual cash inflow.

*Example*: Goodtime Fun Centres, Inc., operates many outlets in the eastern states.

Some of the vending machines in one of its outlets provide very little revenue, so the company is considering removing the machines and installing equipment to dispense soft ice cream.

The equipment would cost $80,000 and have an eight-year useful life. Incremental annual revenues and costs associated with the sale of ice cream would be as follows:

| **Sales** | **$150,000** |
|---|---|
| Less cost of ingredients | 90,000 |
| Contribution margin | 60,000 |
| Less fixed expenses: | |
| Salaries | 27,000 |
| Maintenance | 3,000 |
| Depreciation | 10,000 |
| Total fixed expenses | 40,000 |
| Net operating income | $20,000 |

The vending machines can be sold for a $5,000 scrap value. The company will not purchase equipment unless it has a payback of three years or less. Should the equipment be purchased? An analysis of the payback period for the proposed equipment is given below:

- *Step: Compute the net annual cash inflow*: Since the net annual cash inflow is not given, it must be computed before the payback period can be determined:

| | |
|---|---|
| Net operating income | $20,000 |
| Add: Noncash deduction for depreciation | 10,000 |
| Net annual cash inflow | $30,000 |

- *Step: Compute the payback period*: Using the net annual cash inflow figure, the payback period can be determined as follows:

| | |
|---|---|
| Cost of the new equipment | $80,000 |
| Less salvage value of old equipment | 5,000 |
| Investment required | $75,000 |

Payback period = Investment required/ Net annual cash inflow
= $75,000/ $30,000
= 2.5 years

First, notice that depreciation is added back to net operating income to obtain the net annual cash inflow from the new equipment. Depreciation is not a cash outlay; thus, it must be added back to net operating income to adjust it to a cash basis. Second, notice in the payback computation that the salvage value from the old machines has been deducted from the cost of the new equipment, and that only the incremental investment has been used in computing the payback period. Since the proposed equipment has a payback period of less than three years, the company's payback requirement has been met.

## PAYBACK AND UNEVEN CASH FLOWS

When the cash flows associated with an investment project changes from year to year, the simple payback formula that we outlined earlier cannot be used.

*To understand this point consider the following data:*

*Example:*

| Year | Investment | Cash Inflow |
|---|---|---|
| 1 | $4,000 | $1,000 |
| 2 | | 0 |
| 3 | | 2,000 |
| 4 | 2,000 | 1,000 |
| 5 | | 500 |
| 6 | | 3,000 |
| 7 | | 2,000 |
| 8 | | 2,000 |

What is the payback period on this investment? The answer is 5.5 years, but to obtain this figure it is necessary to track the unrecovered investment year by year.

*The steps involved in this process are shown below:*

| Year | Beginning Unrecovered Investment | Investment | Cash Inflow | Ending Unrecovered Investment (1) + (2) - (3) |
|---|---|---|---|---|
| 1 | $ 0 | $4,000 | $1,000 | $3,000 |
| 2 | 3,000 | | 0 | 3,000 |
| 3 | 3,000 | | 2,000 | 1,000 |
| 4 | 1,000 | 2,000 | 1,000 | 2,000 |
| 5 | 2,000 | | 500 | 1,500 |
| 6 | 1,500 | | 3,000 | 0 |
| 7 | 0 | | 2,000 | 0 |
| 8 | 0 | | 2,000 | 0 |

By the middle of the sixth year, sufficient cash inflows will have been realized to recover the entire investment of $6,000 ($4,000 + $2,000)

## AVERAGE RATE OF RETURN

Arithmetic average of a portfolio's returns over a specific period of time or set of observations.

*In Russell Style Classification (RSC), average rate of return is calculated as follows:*

$$\bar{R} = \frac{\sum R_t}{T}$$

| Where | Equals |
|---|---|
| $\bar{R}$ | Average rate of return |
| *Rt* | Return at time t |
| *T* | Number of time points |

*In Russell Performance Universes (RPU), the formula for average rate of return is:*

$$u = \frac{\sum(R_i)}{n}$$

| Where | Equals |
|---|---|
| *u* | Average rate of return |
| *Ri* | *i*-th return |
| *n* | Number of observations |

## RATE OF RETURN

In finance, rate of return (ROR), also known as return on investment (ROI), rate of profit or sometimes just return, is the ratio of money gained or lost on an investment relative to the amount of money invested. The amount of money gained or lost may be referred to as interest, profit/loss, gain/loss, or net income/loss. The money invested may be referred to as the asset, capital, principal, or the cost basis of the investment. ROI is usually expressed as a percentage rather than a fraction.

## Calculation

The initial value of an investment, $V_i$, does not always have a clearly defined monetary value, but for purposes of measuring ROI, *the expected value must be clearly stated* along with the rationale for this initial value. The multiple value of an investment, $V_f$, also does not always have a clearly defined monetary value, but for purposes of measuring ROI, *the final value must be clearly stated* along with the rationale for this final value. The rate of return can be calculated over a single period, or expressed as an average over multiple periods.

## Single-Period

### *Arithmetic Return*

*The arithmetic return is:*

$$r_{arith} = \frac{V_f - V_i}{V_i}$$

$r_{arith}$ is sometimes referred to as the yield..

### *Logarithmic or Continuously Compounded Return*

*The logarithmic return or continuously compounded return, also known as force of interest, is cleared as:*

$$r_{log} = \ln\left(\frac{V_f}{V_i}\right)$$

It is the reciprocal of the e-folding time.

## Multiperiod Average Returns

### *Arithmetic Average Rate of Return*

*The arithmetic average rate of return over n periods is defined as:*

$$\bar{r}_{arithmetic} = \frac{1}{n}\sum_{i-1}^{n} r_{arith,i} = \frac{1}{n}(r_{aith,1} + \cdots + r_{arith,n})$$

### *Geometric Average Rate of Return*

*The geometric average rate of return, also known as the time-*

*weighted rate of return, over n periods is defined as:*

$$\bar{r}_{geometric} = -1 + \prod_{i=1}^{n} (1 + r_{arith,i})^{1/n}$$

The geometric average rate of return calculated over n years is also known as the annualized return.

### *Internal Rate of Return*

The internal rate of return (IRR), also known as the dollar-weighted rate of return, is defined as the value(s) of $\bar{r}$ that satisfies the following equation:

$$NPV = \sum_{t=o}^{n} \frac{C_t}{(1+\bar{r})^t} = 0$$

*where:*

- NPV = net present value of the investment
- $C_t$ = cashflow at time $t$

When the rate of return $r$ is smaller than the IRR rate $\bar{r}$, the investment is profitable, i.e., $NPV > 0$. Otherwise, the investment is not profitable.

## Comparisons Between Various Rates of Return

### *Arithmetic and Logarithmic Return*

The value of an investment is doubled over a year if the annual ROR $r_{arith}$ = +100%, that is, if $r_{log}$ = ln(200%/ 100%) = ln(2) = 69.3%. The value falls to zero when $r_{arith}$ = –100%, that is, if $r_{log} = -\infty$

Arithmetic and logarithmic returns are not equal, but are approximately equal for small returns. The difference between them is large only when Per cent changes are high. For example, an arithmetic return of +50% is equivalent to a logarithmic return of 40.55%, while an arithmetic return of -50% is equivalent to a logarithmic return of –69.31%.

Logarithmic returns are often used by academics in their research. The main advantage is that the continuously compounded return is symmetric, while the arithmetic return is not: positive and negative Per cent arithmetic returns are not equal. This means that an investment of $100 that yields an arithmetic return of 50% followed by an arithmetic return of -50% will result in $75, while an investment of $100 that yields a logarithmic return of 50% followed by an logarithmic return of -50% it will remain $100.

**Table. Comparison of Arithmetic and Logarithmic Returns for Initial Investment of $100**

| Initial investment, $V_i$ | $100 | $100 | $100 | $100 | $100 |
|---|---|---|---|---|---|
| Final investment, $V_f$ | $0 | $50 | $100 | $150 | $200 |
| Profit/loss, $V_f$ ? $V_i$ | -$100 | -$50 | $0 | $50 | $100 |
| Arithmetic return, $r_{arith}$ | -100% | -50% | 0% | 50% | 100% |
| Logarithmic return, $r_{log}$ | $-\infty$ | -69.31% | 0% | 40.55% | 69.31% |

## *Arithmetic Average and Geometric Average rates of Return*

Both arithmetic and geometric average rates of returns are averages of periodic percentage returns. Neither will accurately translate to the actual dollar amounts gained or lost if Per cent gains are averaged with Per cent losses. A 10% loss on a $100 investment is a $10 loss, and a 10% gain on a $100 investment is a $10 gain.

When percentage returns on investments are calculated, they are calculated for a period of time – not based on original investment dollars, but based on the dollars in the investment at the beginning and end of the period. So if an investment of $100 loses 10% in the first period, the investment amount is then $90.

If the investment then gains 10% in the next period, the investment amount is $99.

A 10% gain followed by a 10% loss is a 1% loss. The order in which the loss and gain occurs does not affect the result. A 50% gain and a 50% loss is a 25% loss. An 80% gain plus an 80% loss is a 64% loss. To recover from a 50% loss, a 100% gain is required.

The mathematics of this are beyond the scope of this substance, but since investment returns are often published as "average returns", it is important to note that average returns do not always translate into dollar returns.

*Example*: Level Rates of Return

| | Year 1 | Year 2 | Year 3 | Year 4 |
|---|---|---|---|---|
| Rate of Return | 5% | 5% | 5% | 5% |
| Geometric Average at End of Year | 5% | 5% | 5% | 5% |
| Capital at End of Year | $105.00 | $110.25 | $115.76 | $121.55 |
| Dollar Profit/(Loss) | $5.00 | $10.25 | $15.76 | $21.55 |
| Compound Yield | 5% | | | 5.4% |

*Example*: Volatile Rates of Return, including losses

| | Year 1 | Year 2 | Year 3 | Year 4 |
|---|---|---|---|---|
| Rate of Return | 50% | -20% | 30% | -40% |
| Geometric Average at End of Year | 50% | 9.5% | 16% | -1.6% |
| Capital at End of Year | $150.00 | $120.00 | $156.00 | $93.60 |
| Dollar Profit/(Loss) | | | | ($6.40) |
| Compound Yield | | | | -1.6% |

*Example*: Highly Volatile Rates of Return, including losses.

| | Year 1 | Year 2 | Year 3 | Year 4 |
|---|---|---|---|---|
| Rate of Return | -95% | 0% | 0% | 115% |
| Geometric Average at End of Year | -95% | -77.6% | -63.2% | -42.7% |
| Capital at End of Year | $5.00 | $5.00 | $5.00 | $10.75 |
| Dollar Profit/(Loss) | | | | ($89.25) |
| Compound Yield | | | | -22.3% |

### *Annual Returns and Annualized Returns*

Care must be taken not to confuse annual and annualized returns. An annual rate of return is a single-period return, while an annualized rate of return is a multi-period, geometric average return.

An annual rate of return is the return on an investment over a one-year period, such as January 1 through December 31, or June 3 2006 through June 2 2007. Each ROI in the cash flow example is an annual rate of return.

An annualized rate of return is the return on an investment over a period other than one year multiplied or divided to give a comparable one-year return. For instance, a one-month ROI of 1% could be stated as an annualized rate of return of 12%. Or a two-year ROI of 10% could be stated as an annualized rate of return of 5%. **For GIPS compliance: you do not annualize portfolios or composites for periods of less than one year. You start on the 13th month. The dollar returns for the four years add up to $265. The annualized rate of return for the four years is: $265 ÷ ($1,000 × 4 years) = 6.625%.

## Uses

- ROI is a measure of cash generated by or lost due to the investment. It measures the cash flow or income stream from the investment to the investor, relative to the amount invested. Cash flow to the investor can be in the form of profit, interest, dividends, or capital gain/loss. Capital gain/loss occurs when the market value or resale value of the investment increases or decreases. Cash flow here does not include the return of invested capital.

**Table. Cash Flow Example on $1,000 Investment**

| | Year 1 | Year 2 | Year 3 | Year 4 |
|---|---|---|---|---|
| Dollar Return | $100 | $55 | $60 | $50 |
| ROI | 10% | 5.5% | 6% | 5% |

- ROI values typically used for personal financial decisions include Annual Rate of Return and Annualized Rate of Return. For nominal risk investments such as savings accounts or Certificates of Deposit, the personal investor considers the effects of reinvesting/compounding on increasing savings balances over time. For investments in which capital is at risk, such as stock shares, mutual fund shares and home purchases, the personal investor considers the effects of price volatility and capital gain/loss on returns.
- Profitability ratios typically used by financial analysts to compare a company's profitability over time or compare profitability between companies include Gross Profit Margin, Operating Profit Margin, ROI ratio, Dividend yield, Net profit margin, Return on equity, and Return on assets.
- During capital budgeting, companies compare the

rates of return of different projects to select which projects to pursue in order to generate maximum return or wealth for the company's stockholders. Companies do so by considering the average rate of return, payback period, net present value, profitability index, and internal rate of return for various projects.

- A return may be adjusted for taxes to give the after-tax rate of return. This is done in geographical areas or historical times in which taxes consumed or consume a significant portion of profits or income. The after-tax rate of return is calculated by multiplying the rate of return by the tax rate, then subtracting that percentage from the rate of return.
- A return of 5% taxed at 15% gives an after-tax return of 4.25%
  0.05 × 0.15 = 0.0075
  0.05 – 0.0075 = 0.0425 = 4.25%
- A return of 10% taxed at 25% gives an after-tax return of 7.5%
  0.10 × 0.25 = 0.025
  0.10 – 0.025 = 0.075 = 7.5%
  Investors usually seek a higher rate of return on taxable investment returns than on non-taxable investment returns.
- A return may be adjusted for inflation to better indicate its true value in purchasing power. Any investment with a nominal rate of return less than the annual inflation rate represents a loss of value, even though the nominal rate of return might well be greater than 0%. When ROI is adjusted for inflation, the resulting return is considered an increase or decrease in purchasing power. If an ROI value is adjusted for inflation, it is stated explicitly, such as "The return, adjusted for inflation, was 2%."
- Many online poker tools include ROI in a player's tracked statistics, assisting users in evaluating an opponent's profitability.

## Cash or Potential Cash Returns

### *Time Value of Money*

Investments generate cash flow to the investor to compensate the investor for the time value of money.

Except for rare periods of significant deflation where the opposite may be true, a dollar in cash is worth less today than it was yesterday, and worth more today than it will be worth tomorrow.

*The main factors that are used by investors to determine the rate of return at which they are willing to invest money include*:

- Estimates of future inflation rates
- Estimates regarding the risk of the investment
- Whether or not the investors want the money available for other uses.

The time value of money is reflected in the interest rates that banks offer for deposits, and also in the interest rates that banks charge for loans such as home mortgages. The "risk-free" rate is the rate on U.S. Treasury Bills, because this is the highest rate available without risking capital.

The rate of return which an investor expects from an investment is called the Discount Rate. Each investment has a different discount rate, based on the cash flow expected in future from the investment.

The higher the risk, the higher the discount rate the investor will demand from the investment.

### *Compounding or Reinvesting*

Compound interest or other reinvestment of cash returns does not affect the discount rate of an investment, but it does affect the Annual Percentage Yield, because compounding/ reinvestment increases the capital invested.

For example, if an investor put $1,000 in a 1-year Certificate of Deposit (CD) that paid an annual interest rate of 4%, compounded quarterly, the CD would earn 1% interest per quarter on the account balance.

The account balance includes interest previously credited to the account.

**Table. Compound Interest Example**

| | 1st Quarter | 2nd Quarter | 3rd Quarter | 4th Quarter |
|---|---|---|---|---|
| Capital at the beginning of the period | $1,000 | $1,010 | $1,020.10 | $1,030.30 |
| Dollar return for the period | $10 | $10.10 | $10.20 | $10.30 |
| Account Balance at end of the period | $1,010.00 | $1,020.10 | $1,030.30 | $1,040.60 |
| Quarterly ROI | 1% | 1% | 1% | 1% |

The concept of 'income stream' may express this more clearly. At the beginning of the year, the investor took $1,000 out of his pocket to invest in a CD at the bank. The money was still his, but it was no longer available for buying groceries. The investment provided a cash flow of $10.00, $10.10, $10.20 and $10.30. At the end of the year, the investor got $1,040.60 back from the bank. $1,000 was return of capital.

Once interest is earned by an investor it becomes capital. Compound interest involves reinvestment of capital; the interest earned during each quarter is reinvested. At the end of the first quarter the investor had capital of $1,010.00, which then earned $10.10 during the second quarter. The extra dime was interest on his additional $10 investment. The Annual Percentage Yield or Future value for compound interest is higher than for simple interest because the interest is reinvested as capital and earns interest. The yield on the investment was 4.06%.

Bank accounts offer contractually guaranteed returns, so investors cannot lose their capital. Investors/Depositors lend money to the bank, and the bank is obligated to give investors back their capital plus all earned interest. Because investors are not risking losing their capital on a bad investment, they earn a quite low rate of return. But their capital steadily increases.

## Returns when Capital is at Risk

### *Capital Gains and Losses*

Many investments carry significant risk that the investor will lose some or all of the invested capital. For example, investments in company stock shares put capital at risk. The value of a stock share depends on what someone is willing to pay for it at a certain point in time. Unlike capital invested in a savings account, the capital value of a stock share constantly changes. If the price is relatively stable, the stock is said to have "low volatility." If the price often changes a great deal, the stock has "high volatility." All stock shares have some volatility, and the change in price directly affects ROI for stock investments. Stock returns are usually calculated for holding periods such as a month, a quarter or a year.

### *Reinvestment When Capital is at Risk: Rate of Return and Yield*

Yield is the compound rate of return that includes the effect of reinvesting interest or dividends.

*To the right is an example of a stock investment of one share purchased at the beginning of the year for $100*:

- The quarterly dividend is reinvested at the quarter-end stock price.
- The number of shares purchased each quarter = ($ Dividend)/($ Stock Price).
- The final investment value of $103.02 is a 3.02% Yield on the initial investment of $100. This is the compound yield, and this return can be considered to be the return on the investment of $100.

To calculate the rate of return, the investor includes the reinvested dividends in the total investment. The investor received a total of $4.06 in dividends over the year, all of which were reinvested, so the investment amount increased by $4.06.

- Total Investment = Cost Basis = $100 + $4.06 = $104.06.
- Capital gain/loss = $103.02 – $104.06 = –$1.04 (a capital loss)
- ($4.06 dividends – $1.04 capital loss )/ $104.06 total investment = 2.9% ROI

The disadvantage of this ROI calculation is that it does not take into account the fact that not all the money was invested during the entire year.

*The advantages are*:

- It uses the cost basis of the investment,
- It clearly shows which gains are due to dividends and which gains/losses are due to capital gains/losses,

- The actual dollar return of $3.02 is compared to the actual dollar investment of $104.06.

For U.S. income tax purposes, if the shares were sold at the end of the year, dividends would be $4.06, cost basis of the investment would be $104.06, sale price would be $103.02, and the capital loss would be $1.04.

Since all returns were reinvested, the ROI might also be calculated as a continuously compounded return or logarithmic return. The effective continuously compounded rate of return is the natural log of the final investment value divided by the initial investment value:

- $V_i$ is the initial investment ($100)
- $V_f$ is the final value ($103.02)

$$ROL_{Log} = \ln\left(\frac{V_f}{V_i}\right) = \ln\left(\frac{103.02}{100}\right) = 2.98\%$$

## *Mutual Fund and Investment Company Returns*

Mutual funds, exchange-traded funds (ETFs), and other equitized investments are essentially portfolios of various investment securities such as stocks, bonds and money market instruments which are equitized by selling shares or units to investors. Investors and other parties are interested to know how the investment has performed over various periods of time.

Performance is usually quantified by a fund's total return. In the 1990s, many different fund companies were advertising various total returns— some cumulative, some averaged, some with or without deduction of sales loads or commissions, etc. To level the playing field and help investors compare performance returns of one fund to another, the U.S. Securities and Exchange Commission (SEC) began requiring funds to compute and report total returns based upon a standardized formula— so called "SEC Standardized total return" which is the average annual total return assuming reinvestment of dividends and distributions and deduction of sales loads or charges. Funds may compute and advertise returns on other bases so long as they also publish no less prominently the "standardized" return data.

Subsequent to this, apparently investors who'd sold their fund shares after a large increase in the share price in the late 1990s and early 2000s were ignorant of how significant the impact of income/capital gain taxes was on their fund "gross" returns. That is, they had little idea how significant the difference could be between "gross" returns and "net" returns. In reaction to this apparent investor ignorance, and perhaps for other reasons, the SEC made further rule-making to require mutual funds to publish in their annual prospectus, among other things, total returns before and after the impact of U.S federal individual income taxes. And further, the after-tax returns would include 1) returns on a hypothetical taxable account after deducting taxes on dividends and capital gain distributions received during the emphasised periods and 2) the impacts of the items in #1) as well as assuming the entire investment shares were sold at the end of the period. These after-tax returns would apply of course only to taxable accounts and not to tax-deferred or retirement accounts such as IRAs.

Lastly, in more recent years, "personalized" investment returns have been demanded by investors. In other words, investors are saying more or less the fund returns may not be what their actual account returns are based upon the actual investment account transaction history. This is because investments may have been made on various dates and additional purchases and withdrawals may have occurred which vary in amount and date and thus are unique to the particular account. More and more fund and brokerage firms have begun providing personalized account returns on investor's account statements in response to this need.

With that out of the way, here's how basic earnings and gains/losses work on a mutual fund. The fund records income for dividends and interest earned which typically increases the value of the mutual fund shares, while expenses set aside have an offsetting impact to share value. When the fund's investments increase in market value, so too does the value of the fund shares owned by the investors. When investments increase in market value, so too the fund shares value increases. When the fund sells investments at a profit, it turns or reclassifies that paper profit or unrealized gain into an actual or realized gain.

The sale has no affect on the value of fund shares but it has reclassified a component of its value from one bucket to another on the fund books— which will have future impact to investors. At least annually, a fund usually pays dividends from its net income and net capital gains realized out to shareholders as an IRS requirement. This way, the fund pays no taxes but rather all the investors in taxable accounts do. Mutual fund share prices are typically valued each day the stock or bond markets are open and typically the value of a share is the net asset value of the fund shares investors own.

### *Total Returns*

This part addresses only total returns without the impact of U.S. federal individual income and capital gains taxes.

Mutual funds report total returns assuming reinvestment of dividend and capital gain distributions. That is, the dollar amounts distributed are used to purchase additional shares of the funds as of the reinvestment/ex-dividend date. Reinvestment rates or factors are based on total distributions (dividends plus capital gains) during each period.

$$\text{Year 1 Reinvestment Factor} = \frac{\text{Year 1 Total Distribution}}{\text{Year 1 Share Price}} + 1$$

$$\text{Year 2 Reinvestment Factor} = \frac{\text{Year 2 Total Distribution} \times \text{Year 1 Reinvestment Factor}}{\text{Year 2 Share Price}} + 1$$

$$\text{Year 3 Reinvestment Factor} = \frac{\text{Year 3 Total Distribution} \times \text{Year 2 Reinvestment Factor}}{\text{Year 3 Share Price}} + 1$$

$$\text{Year 4 Reinvestment Factor} = \frac{\text{Year 4 Total Distribution} \times \text{Year 3 Reinvestment Factor}}{\text{Year 4 Share Price}} + 1$$

$$\text{Year 5 Reinvestment Factor} = \frac{\text{Year 5 Total Distribution} \times \text{Year 4 Reinvestment Factor}}{\text{Year 5 Share Price}} + 1$$

Total Return = ((Final Price × Last Reinvestment Factor) – Beginning Price)/ Beginning Price

### *Average Annual Total Return (Geometric)*

Average Annual Return (geometric) US mutual funds are to compute total return as proscribed by the U.S. Securities and Exchange Commission in instructions to form N–1A as the average annual compounded rates of return for 1-year, 5-year and 10-year periods as the "average annual total return" for each fund.

*The following formula is used*:

P(1+T)n = ERV

*Where*:

P = a hypothetical initial investment of $1,000.

T = average annual total return.

n = number of years.

ERV = ending redeemable value of a hypothetical $1,000 payment made at the beginning of the 1–, 5–, or 10-year periods at the end of the 1–, 5–, or 10-year periods (or fractional portion).

$$= \left[ \left(1 + \frac{\text{Cumulative Return}}{100}\right)^{\text{Time in Years}-1} - 1 \right] \times 100$$

*Example*: Mutual Fund with low volatility and a regular annual dividend, reinvested at year-end share price, initial share value $100

| End of: | Year 1 | Year 2 | Year 3 | Year 4 | Year 5 |
|---|---|---|---|---|---|
| Dividend | $5 | $5 | $5 | $5 | $5 |
| Capital Gain Distribution | | | $2 | | |
| Total Distribution | $5 | $5 | $7 | $5 | $5 |
| Share Price | $98 | $101 | $102 | $99 | $101 |
| Shares Purchased | 0.05102 | 0.04950 | 0.06863 | 0.05051 | 0.04950 |
| Shares Owned | 1.05102 | 1.10053 | 1.16915 | 1.21966 | 1.26916 |
| Reinvestment Factor | 1.05102 | 1.05203 | 1.07220 | 1.05415 | 1.05219 |

- Total Return = (($101 × 1.05219) – $100)/ $100 = 6.27% (net of expenses)
- Average Annual Return (geometric) = (((28.19)/ 100)+1) ^ (1/5)) – 1) × 100 = 5.09%

Using a Holding Period Return calculation, after 5 years, an investor who reinvested owned 1.26916 share valued at $101 per share ($128.19 in value). ($128.19–$100)/$100/5 = 5.638% return. An investor who did not reinvest received total cash payments of $27 in dividends and $1 in capital gain. ($27+$1)/ $100/5 = 5.600% return.

Mutual funds include capital gains as well as dividends in their return calculations. Since the market price of a mutual fund share is based on net asset value, a capital gain distribution is offset by an equal decrease in mutual fund share value/price. From the shareholder's perspective, a capital gain distribution is not a net gain in assets, but it is a realized capital gain.

### Summary: Overall Rate of Return

Rate of Return and Return on Investment indicate cash flow from an investment to the investor over a specified period of time, usually a year.

ROI is a measure of investment profitability, not a measure of investment size. While compound interest and dividend reinvestment can increase the size of the investment, Return on Investment is a percentage return based on capital invested.

In general, the higher the investment risk, the greater the potential investment return, and the greater the potential investment loss.

## NET PRESENT VALUE METHOD

Widely used approach for evaluating an investment project. Under the net present value method, the present value*(PV)*of all cash inflows from the project is compared against the initial investment*(I)*. The Net Present Value (NPV) which is the difference between the present value and the initial investment (i.e., NPV =PV – I), determines whether the project is an acceptable investment. To compute the present value of cash inflows, a rate called the cost of capital is used for discounting. Under the method, if the net present value is positive(NPV > 0 or PV>I), the project should be accepted.

## NET PRESENT VALUE

In finance, the net present value (NPV) or net present worth (NPW) of a time series of cash flows, both incoming and outgoing, is defined as the sum of the present values (PVs) of the individual cash flows. In case when all future cash flows are incoming and the only outflow of cash is the purchase price, the NPV is simply the PV of future cash flows minus the purchase price.

NPV is a central tool in discounted cash flow (DCF) analysis, and is a standard method for using the time value of money to appraise long-term projects. Used for capital budgeting, and widely throughout economics, finance, and accounting, it measures the excess or shortfall of cash flows, in present value terms, once financing charges are met.

The NPV of a sequence of cash flows takes as input the cash flows and a discount rate or discount curve and outputting a price; the converse process in DCF analysis, taking as input a sequence of cash flows and a price and inferring as output a discount rate is called the yield, and is more widely used in bond trading.

### Formula

Each cash inflow/outflow is discounted back to its present value (PV). Then they are summed. Therefore NPV is the sum of all terms,

$$\frac{R_t}{(1+i)^t},$$

where

$t$ - the time of the cash flow

$i$ - the discount rate

$R_t$ - the net cash flow at time $t$ investment.

The result of this formula if multiplied with the Annual Net cash in-flows and reduced by Initial Cash outlay will be the present value but in case where the cash flows are not equal in amount then the previous formula will be used to determine the present value of each cash flow separately. Any cash flow within 12 months will not be discounted for NPV purpose.

**The Discount Rate**

The rate used to discount future cash flows to their present values is a key variable of this process.

A firm's weighted average cost of capital is often used, but many people believe that it is appropriate to use higher discount rates to adjust for risk for riskier projects or other factors. A variable discount rate with higher rates applied to cash flows occurring further along the time span might be used to reflect the yield curve premium for long-term debt.

Another approach to choosing the discount rate factor is to decide the rate which the capital needed for the project could return if invested in an alternative venture. If, for example, the capital required for Project A can earn five Per cent elsewhere, use this discount rate in the NPV calculation to allow a direct comparison to be made between Project A and the alternative.

Related to this concept is to use the firm's Reinvestment Rate. Reinvestment rate can be defined as the rate of return for the firm's investments on average. When analyzing projects in a capital constrained environment, it may be appropriate to use the reinvestment rate rather than the firm's weighted average cost of capital as the discount factor. It reflects opportunity cost of investment, rather than the possibly lower cost of capital.

A NPV amount obtained using variable discount rates better reflects the real situation than that calculated from a constant discount rate for the entire investment duration.

For some professional investors, their investment funds are committed to target a specified rate of return. In such cases, that rate of return should be selected as the discount rate for the NPV calculation. In this way, a direct comparison can be made between the profitability of the project and the desired rate of return.

To some extent, the selection of the discount rate is dependent on the use to which it will be put. If the intent is simply to determine whether a project will add value to the company, using the firm's weighted average cost of capital may be appropriate. If trying to decide between alternative investments in order to maximize the value of the firm, the corporate reinvestment rate would probably be a better choice.

Using variable rates over time, or discounting "guaranteed" cash flows differently from "at risk" cash flows may be a superior methodology, but is seldom used in practice. Using the discount rate to adjust for risk is often difficult to do in practice and is really difficult to do well. An alternative to using discount factor to adjust for risk is to explicitly correct the cash flows for the risk elements using rNPV or a similar method, then discount at the firm's rate.

## What NPV Means

NPV is an indicator of how much value an investment or project adds to the firm. With a particular project, if $R_t$ is a positive value, the project is in the status of discounted cash inflow in the time of $t$. If $R_t$ is a negative value, the project is in the status of discounted cash outflow in the time of $t$. Appropriately risked projects with a positive NPV could be accepted. This does not necessarily mean that they should be undertaken since NPV at the cost of capital may not account for opportunity cost, *i.e.* comparison with other available investments. In financial theory, if there is a choice between two mutually exclusive alternatives, the one yielding the higher NPV should be selected. The following sums up the NPVs in various situations.

| If... | It means... | Then... |
|---|---|---|
| NPV > 0 | the investment would add value to the firm | The project may be accepted |
| NPV < 0 | the investment would subtract value from the firm | The project should be rejected |
| NPV = 0 | the investment would neither gain nor lose value for the firm | We should be indifferent in the decision whether to accept or reject the project. This project adds no monetary value. Decision should be based on other criteria, e.g. strategic positioning or other factors not explicitly included in the calculation. |

**Example**

A corporation must decide whether to introduce a new product line. The new product will have startup costs, operational costs, and incoming cash flows over six years. This project will have an immediate (t=0) cash outflow of $100,000 (which might include machinery, and employee training costs). Other cash outflows for years 1–6 are expected to be $5,000 per year. Cash inflows are expected to be $30,000 each for years 1–6. All cash flows are after-tax, and there are no cash flows expected after year 6. The required rate of return is 10%. The present value (PV) can be calculated for each year:

| Year | Cashflow | Present Value |
|---|---|---|
| T=0 | $\frac{-100,000}{(1+0.10)^0}$ | -$100,000 |
| T=1 | $\frac{30,000-5,000}{(1+0.10)^1}$ | $22,727 |
| T=2 | $\frac{30,000-5,000}{(1+0.10)^2}$ | $20,661 |
| T=3 | $\frac{30,000-5,000}{(1+0.10)^3}$ | $18,783 |
| T=4 | $\frac{30,000-5,000}{(1+0.10)^4}$ | $17,075 |
| T=5 | $\frac{30,000-5,000}{(1+0.10)^5}$ | $15,523 |
| T=6 | $\frac{30,000-5,000}{(1+0.10)^6}$ | $14,112 |

The sum of all these present values is the net present value, which equals $8,881.52. Since the NPV is greater than zero, it would be better to invest in the project than to do nothing, and the corporation should invest in this project if there is no alternative with a higher NPV.

**Common Pitfalls**

- If for example the $R_t$ are generally negative late in

the project then at that stage the company owes money, so a high discount rate is not cautious but too optimistic. Some people see this as a problem with NPV. A way to avoid this problem is to include explicit provision for financing any losses after the initial investment, that is, explicitly calculate the cost of financing such losses.

- Another common pitfall is to adjust for risk by adding a premium to the discount rate. Whilst a bank might charge a higher rate of interest for a risky project, that does not mean that this is a valid approach to adjusting a net present value for risk, although it can be a reasonable approximation in some specific cases. One reason such an approach may not work well can be seen from the foregoing: if some risk is incurred resulting in some losses, then a discount rate in the NPV will reduce the impact of such losses below their true financial cost. A rigorous approach to risk requires identifying and valuing risks explicitly, *e.g.* by actuarial or Monte Carlo techniques, and explicitly calculating the cost of financing any losses incurred.
- Yet another issue can result from the compounding of the risk premium. R is a composite of the risk free rate and the risk premium. As a result, future cash flows are discounted by both the risk-free rate as well as the risk premium and this effect is compounded by each subsequent cash flow. This compounding results in a much lower NPV than might be otherwise calculated. The certainty equivalent model can be used to account for the risk premium without compounding its effect on present value.
- If NPV is less than 0, which is to say, negative, the project should not be immediately rejected. Sometimes companies have to execute an NPV-negative project if not executing it creates even more value destruction.
- Another issue with relying on NPV is that it does

not provide an overall picture of the gain or loss of executing a certain project. To see a percentage gain relative to the investments for the project, usually, Internal rate of return is used complimented to the NPV method.

## Alternative Capital Budgeting Methods

- *APV*: Adjusted present value, is the net present value of a project if financed solely by ownership equity plus the present value of all the benefits of financing.
- *Payback period*: Which measures the time required for the cash inflows to equal the original outlay. It measures risk, not return.
- *Cost-benefit analysis*: Which includes issues other than cash, such as time savings.
- *Real option method*: Which attempts to value managerial flexibility that is assumed away in NPV.
- *Internal rate of return*: Which calculates the rate of return of a project while disregarding the absolute amount of money to be gained.
- *Modified internal rate of return*: Similar to IRR, but it makes explicit assumptions about the reinvestment of the cash flows. Sometimes it is called Growth Rate of Return.
- *Accounting rate of return (ARR)*: A ratio similar to IRR and MIRR

### IRR

Internal rate of return (IRR) is a rate of return on an investment. The IRR of a project is the discount rate that will give it a net present value of zero. The IRR is calculated by a trial and error process.

*Starting with a guess at the IRR, r, the process is as follows*:

- The NPV is calculated using discount rate *r*.
- If the NPV is close to zero then *r* is the IRR.
- If the NPV is positive *r* is increased.
- If the NPV is negative *r* is decreased.

This is more tedious than calculating an NPV, but the extra

work can be automated. It avoids the need to estimate an appropriate discount rate which is a considerable simplification — this is a flaw because of the lack of risk adjustment. This can be done later by demanding risk premia for higher risk alternatives, but assessing this reintroduces the complexity. It is generally preferable to use NPV to IRR to make investment decisions. A smaller investment with a better rate of return will have a higher IRR, but investors' total wealth would be increased more by making a larger investment with a lower IRR but a higher total gain.

This is only a problem where investments are limited in size and mutually exclusive, so it is not a concern for securities valuation. However, the only common use of IRR for securities valuation is that of yield to maturity for bonds.

IRR has even worse failings. If the investment has negative cash flows following positive cash flows, then there may be more than one IRR, or even none at all. While it is possible to use more complex procedures to work around this, it is better to simply not use IRR. If used, it should not be used for any pattern of cash flows that ever changes from positive to negative.

## USES

Because the internal rate of return is a rate quantity, it is an indicator of the efficiency, quality, or yield of an investment. This is in contrast with the net present value, which is an indicator of the value or magnitude of an investment.

An investment is considered acceptable if its internal rate of return is greater than an established minimum acExample ceptable rate of return or cost of capital. In a scenario where an investment is considered by a firm that has equity holders, this minimum rate is the cost of capital of the investment. This ensures that the investment is supported by equity holders since, in general, an investment whose IRR exceeds its cost of capital adds value for the company.

## CALCULATION

Given a collection of pairs involved in a project, the

internal rate of return follows from the net present value as a function of the rate of return. A rate of return for which this function is zero is an internal rate of return.

Given the (period, cash flow) pairs ($n$, $C_n$) where $n$ is a positive integer, the total number of periods $N$, and the net present value NPV, the internal rate of return is given by $r$ in:

$$NPV = \sum_{n=o}^{N} \frac{C_n}{(1+r)^n} = 0$$

Note that the period is usually given in years, but the calculation may be made simpler if $r$ is calculated using the period in which the majority of the problem is defined and converted to a yearly period thereafter.

Note that any fixed time can be used in place of the present; the value obtained is zero if and only if the NPV is zero. In the case that the cash flows are random variables, such as in the case of a life annuity, the expected values are put into the formula.

Often, the value of $r$ cannot be found analytically. In this case, numerical methods or graphical methods must be used.

**Example**

If an investment may be given by the sequence of cash flows,

| Year ($n$) | Cash Flow ($C_n$) |
|---|---|
| 0 | –4000 |
| 1 | 1200 |
| 2 | 1410 |
| 3 | 1875 |
| 4 | 1050 |

then the IRR $r$ is given by

$$NPV = -400 + \frac{1200}{(1+r)^1} + \frac{1400}{(1+r)^2} + \frac{1875}{(1+r)^3} + \frac{1050}{(1+r)^4} = 0$$

In this case, the answer is 14.3%.

***Numerical Solution***

Since the manifestation of the general problem of finding

the roots of the equation NPV($r$), there are many numerical methods that can be used to estimate $r$. For example, using the secant method, $r$ is given by,

$$r_n + 1 = r_n - NPV_n \left( \frac{(r_n - r_n - 1)}{NPV_n - NPV_{n-1}} \right)$$

where $r_n$ is considered the $n^{th}$ approximation of the IRR.

This formula initially requires two unique pairs of estimations of the IRR and NPV ($r_0$,NPV$_0$) and ($r_1$,NPV$_1$), and produces a sequence of,

$$(r_0, NPV_0), (r_1, NPV_1), \cdots, (r_{n-1}, NPV_{n-1}),$$
$$(r_n, NPV_n), (r_{n+1}, NPV_{n+1})$$

that may converge to $(r, 0)$ as $n \to \infty$. If the sequence converges, then iterations of the formula can continue indefinitely so that $r$ can be found to an arbitrary degree of accuracy.

*The convergence behaviour of the sequence is governed by the following*:

- If the function NPV($i$) has a single real root $r$, then the sequence will converge reproducibly towards $r$.
- If the function NPV($i$) has $n$ real roots $r1, r2, \cdots, rn$, then the sequence will converge to one of the roots and changing the values of the initial pairs may change the root to which it converges.
- If function NPV($i$) has no real roots, then the sequence will tend towards $+\infty$.

Having $r1 > r0$ when NPV or $r1 < r0$ when NPV$_0 < 0$ may speed up convergence of $r_n$ to $r$.

## *Calculation of IRR With the Help of Trial and Error Method*

*IRR can also be calculated by Trial and error method if the data satisfy the following conditions:*

- Outflow take place one time
- Inflows are constant as per interval and amount
- Time period involve is significant so that the other methods become complicated

for example in a case there is a project with initial investment of $100 (year 0) and annual cash inflows of $20 at the end of each year till 10th year now here one want to calculate the IRR. IRR is the rate with which if all the cash inflows are discounted then the resultant figure will be equal to initial investment so here we use Trial and error method in this method one formula for aggression is used.

$$IRR = \text{Lower rate} + \frac{\text{NPV at lower rate}}{\text{NPV at lower rate} - \text{NPV at higher rate}} * (\text{Higher rate} - \text{Lower rate})$$

Here as suggested, calculate IRR at lower rate that will be in positive and NPV at Higher rate will negative and as suggested, put this value in NPV at lower rate – NPV at Higher rate the Minus sign will become positive as NPV at Higher rate also contain negative sign with it so the 2nd important thing is to guess higher rate and lower rate like in the case given suppose 10% as lower rate and 20% as higher rate NPV@10% will be 22.89 and NPV@20% will be -16.15 and at last if we apply the formula as suggested, get 15% that is IRR of the project

Now if all the inflows are discounted @15% the resultant figure will be 100 as the Present value factor @15% for 10years is 5.0 and 20*5 = $100 this method is also called Hit and Trail Method

## PROBLEMS WITH USING INTERNAL RATE OF RETURN

As an investment decision tool, the calculated IRR should *not* be used to rate mutually exclusive projects, but only to decide whether a single project is worth investing in.

In cases where one project has a higher initial investment than a second mutually exclusive project, the first project may have a lower IRR, but a higher NPV and should thus be accepted over the second project.

IRR assumes reinvestment of interim cash flows in projects with equal rates of return. Therefore, IRR overstates the annual equivalent rate of return for a project whose interim cash flows are reinvested at a rate lower than the calculated

IRR. This presents a problem, especially for high IRR projects, since there is frequently not another project available in the interim that can earn the same rate of return as the first project.

When the calculated IRR is higher than the **true** reinvestment rate for interim cash flows, the measure will overestimate — sometimes very significantly — the annual equivalent return from the project. The formula assumes that the company has additional projects, with equally attractive prospects, in which to invest the interim cash flows.

This makes IRR a suitable choice for analyzing venture capital and other private equity investments, as these strategies usually require several cash investments throughout the project, but only see one cash outflow at the end of the project.

Since IRR does not consider cost of capital, it should not be used to compare projects of different duration. Modified Internal Rate of Return does consider cost of capital and provides a better indication of a project's efficiency in contributing to the firm's discounted cash flow.

In the case of positive cash flows followed by negative ones the IRR may have multiple values. In this case a discount rate may be used for the borrowing cash flow and the IRR calculated for the investment cash flow. This applies for example when a customer makes a deposit before a specific machine is built.

In a series of cash flows like, one initially invests money, so a high rate of return is best, but then receives more than one possesses, so then one owes money, so now a low rate of return is best. In this case it is not even clear whether a high or a low IRR is better. There may even be multiple IRRs for a single project, like in the example 0% as well as 10%. Examples of this type of project are strip mines and nuclear power plants, where there is usually a large cash outflow at the end of the project.

In general, the IRR can be calculated by solving a polynomial equation. Sturm's theorem can be used to determine if that equation has a unique real solution. In general the IRR equation cannot be solved analytically but only iteratively.

When a project has multiple IRRs it may be more convenient to compute the IRR of the project with the benefits reinvestmented. MIRR is used, which has an assumed reinvestment rate, usually equal to the project's cost of capital.

Despite a strong academic preference for NPV, surveys indicate that executives prefer IRR over NPV. Apparently, managers find it easier to compare investments of different sizes in terms of percentage rates of return than by dollars of NPV. However, NPV remains the "more accurate" reflection of value to the business. IRR, as a measure of investment efficiency may give better insights in capital constrained situations. However, when comparing mutually exclusive projects, NPV is the appropriate measure.

## BENEFIT-COST RATIO

### GENERAL

The transferred Godavari waters will not only benefit the Krishna basin, but also accrue benefits to further south i.e., in Pennar, Cauvery, Vaigai basins. As such, it will be more appropriate to assess the overall benefits of the whole integrated net work, after the entire component of interlinking proposals under Peninsular rivers development of NPP i.e., Mahanadi - Godavari - Krishna - Pennar - Cauvery - Vaigai link is completed. The assessment of benefit - cost ratio for the singular link may not reflect the overall economics of the proposal. However, since the water diverted through Polavaram - Vijayawada link will not directly go beyond Krishna basin and as the basic criteria for the analysis of proposal is to be worked out to reflect a broad general idea of the economic viability of the plan, the B.C. ratio of this singular link has been estimated on the basis of benefits that accrue due to en route irrigation contemplated under the link.

### BENEFITS

#### Direct Benefits

The expected value of produce with and without

introduction of irrigation are worked out comprising the direct benefits from the project. The gross values of the benefits for the pre-project and post-project conditions are computed adopting the yields and prices of commodities collected from the Agricultural and Marketing Departments of the Government of Andhra Pradesh by the Polavaram project authorities and are incorporated in their project report. The net annual benefits by en route irrigation for the CCA of 139740 ha through Polavaram - Vijayawada link works out to Rs.20110 lakh. The net value of the benefits is computed after allowing for the loss in the area due to excavation of canal and distributaries, and land going out of cultivation in the project area etc.

## Indirect Benefits

*The Polavaram*: Vijayawada link canal project when implemented will have a positive impact on the socio-economic conditions of the en route area, which can be partly quantified and partly visualised in a broad perspective only.

- The assured irrigation in the command area will create direct additional employment opportunity in agriculture sector, besides job opportunities during construction of the project.
- Increased opportunities for agro based industries and other related cottage and small scale industries.
- General prosperity and upliftment of economic level of the people of the region.
- Augmented supply of drinking water due to ground water recharge from the regeneration of irrigated water.
- Communication system will improve because of canal roads and CD works raising marketing opportunities
- Industrial growth due to increase in infrastructural facilities.
- Afforestation programme could be implemented on canal banks resulting in environmental improvement.

- The formation of the reservoir will help tourism development, fish and aqua culture, bird sanctuaries etc.
- Increased civic amenities in the planned colonies for the resettled people.

## COST

While working out the cost of the plan, the cost of the link canal and the cost of command area development are considered as cost of this link. The total cost accordingly is estimated as Rs.148391 lakh based on 1994-95 schedule of rates. The annual cost is computed at 10% of interest and 1% depreciation on the total estimated cost.

## B. C. RATIO

| | Rs. in lakh |
|---|---|
| **I. Estimated cost of project** | |
| Cost of link canal, canal structures including command area development | 148391 |
| **II. Annual benefits** | |
| **a) Post-project** | |
| i) Gross value of produce | 57170 |
| ii) Cost of expenditure | 18782 |
| iii) Net value of produce | 38388 |
| **b) Pre-project** | |
| i) Gross value of produce | 28086 |
| ii) Cost of expenditure | 12617 |
| iii) Net value of produce | (–) 15469 |
| Loss in agricultural production in land going out of cultivation due to distributary system @10% of gross value of produce before irrigation (based on the figures adopted by the A.P. State in the Polavaram project report) | (-) 2809 |
| **Net Value** | **20110** |

| III. Annual cost | |
|---|---|
| a) Interest @ 10% of project cost | 14839 |
| b) Depreciation @ 1% of capital cost | 1484 |
| c) Annual O&M charges @ Rs.100 per ha for 139740 ha | 139.74 |
| **Total** | 16462.74 |
| **IV. Benefit-cost ratio** | 20110/16462.74 = 1.22* |

*The B.C. ratio is derived considering the annual benefits exclusively from the en route irrigation through the link canal.

The benefits to be accrued from the proposed diversion of 2265 Mm3 to the Krishna delta as proposed in the GWDTAward plus the additional diversion of 1236 Mm3 proposed by NWDA have not been considered.

But the cost of the canal for transportation of the entire waters (including 2265 + 1236) has been considered. The benefits from the diverted quantities to Krishna delta through the link canal could be estimated and included only after the finalisation of economic analysis of Peninsular links component which is being separately attempted by NWDA.

## INTERNAL RATE OF RETURN

The Internal Rate of Return for the whole project has been computed considering distributional and employment effect which works out to 8.63%. The details are given in Table.

*Details of Project*:

| | | |
|---|---|---|
| 1. Life of the project after completion | : | 100 years |
| 2. Construction period | : | 12 years |
| 3. Cost of project | : | Rs.1484 crore |
| 4. Annual benefits | : | Rs. 201 crore |
| 5. Maintenance cost @ 1% of the cost of I - works | : | Rs. 13 crore |

**Internal Rate of Return (IRR)**

**Cost/Benefit: Rs. in crore**

| Year(s) | Cost | Benefit | Net Benefit | Discounting factor | | Present worth of the net benefits | |
|---|---|---|---|---|---|---|---|
| | | | | (8%) | (10%) | (8%) | (10%) |
| 0 | 34 | – | – 34 | 1.000 | 1.000 | – 34 | –34 |
| 1 | 66 | – | – 66 | 0.926 | 0.909 | – 61 | – 60 |
| 2 | 125 | – | –125 | 0.857 | 0.826 | –107 | –103 |
| 3 | 182 | – | –182 | 0.794 | 0.751 | –145 | –137 |
| 4 | 173 | – | –173 | 0.735 | 0.683 | –127 | –118 |
| 5 | 165 | – | –165 | 0.681 | 0.621 | –112 | –102 |
| 6 | 147 | – | –147 | 0.630 | 0.564 | – 93 | –83 |
| 7 | 136 | – | –136 | 0.583 | 0.513 | –79 | – 70 |
| 8 | 130 | – | –130 | 0.540 | 0.467 | – 70 | – 61 |
| 9 | 156 | – | –156 | 0.500 | 0.424 | – 78 | – 66 |
| 10 | 113 | 39 | – 74 | 0.463 | 0.386 | – 34 | –29 |
| 11 | 57 | 101 | 44 | 0.429 | 0.350 | 19 | 15 |
| 12 | 13 | 201 | 188 | | | | |
| 13 | 13 | 201 | 188 | | | | |
| 14 | 13 | 201 | 188 | 5.355 | 3.505 | 1007 | 659 |
| – | ... | .... | .... | | | | |
| – | .... | .... | ..... | | | | |
| – | .... | ..... | ..... | | | | |
| (Continued up to 111th year) | | | | | | | |
| 111 | 13 | 201 | 188 | | | | |
| Total | | | | | | 86 | –189 |
| Internal Rate of Return | | | | 8 + {2 × (86/275)} = 8.63% | | | |

## CAPITAL RATIONING

Capital rationing has to do with the acquisition of new investments. More to the point, capital rationing is all about the acquisition of new investments based on such factors as the recent performance of other capital investments, the amount of disposable resources that are free to acquire a new asset, and the anticipated performance of the asset. In short, capital rationing is a strategy employed by companies to make investments based on the current relevant circumstances of the company.

Generally, capital rationing is utilized as a means of putting a limit or cap on the portion of the existing budget that may be used in acquiring a new asset. As part of this process, the investor will also want to consider the use of a high cost of capital when thinking in terms of the outcome of the act of acquiring a particular asset. Obviously, any responsible company will choose to employ strategies that support the productive use of disposable funds built within a capital budget. At the same time, it is important to understand what benefits can reasonably be expected from owing the asset in question. Since capital rationing is all about setting criteria that any investment opportunity must meet before the company will seriously entertain the purchase, many businesses choose this strategy as their guiding process for any acquisitions. Using the basic principles of the technique, a company can develop a list of standards that must be addressed before any capital purchase. If the standards are drafted in a manner that accurately reflects the current condition of the company, then there is a good chance the right types of investments will be considered.

Some of the more important factors to consider as part of a productive capital rationing approach are the financial condition of the company, the long and short term goals of the business, and proper attention to daily operations. One of the benefits of capital rationing is that the approach helps to ensure that funds for basic operations are not diverted in order to take advantage of a so-called "can't fail" opportunity, which helps to maintain the stability of the business.

# 5

# Capital Structure

## CONCEPT

The term capital structure refers to the percentage of capital at work in a business by type. Broadly speaking, there are two forms of capital: equity capital and debt capital. Each has its own benefits and drawbacks and a substantial part of wise corporate stewardship and management is attempting to find the perfect capital structure in terms of risk/ reward payoff for shareholders. This is true for Fortune 500 companies and for small business owners trying to determine how much of their startup money should come from a bank loan without endangering the business.

*Let's look at each in detail*:

*Equity Capital*: This refers to money put up and owned by the shareholders (owners).

*Typically, equity capital consists of two types*:

1. Contributed capital, which is the money that was originally invested in the business in exchange for shares of stock or ownership and
2. Retained earnings, which represents profits from past years that have been kept by the company and used to strengthen the balance sheet or fund growth, acquisitions, or expansion.

Many consider equity capital to be the most expensive type of capital a company can utilize because its "cost" is the return the firm must earn to attract investment. A speculative mining company that is looking for silver in a remote region of Africa may require a much higher return on equity to get investors to purchase the stock than a firm such as Procter & Gamble, which sells everything from toothpaste and shampoo to detergent and beauty products.

- *Debt Capital*: The debt capital in a company's capital structure refers to borrowed money that is at work in the business. The safest type is generally considered long-term bonds because the company has years, if not decades, to come up with the principal, while paying interest only in the meantime. Other types of debt capital can include short-term commercial paper utilized by giants such as Wal-Mart and General Electric that amount to billions of dollars in 24-hour loans from the capital markets to meet day-to-day working capital requirements such as payroll and utility bills. The cost of debt capital in the capital structure depends on the health of the company's balance sheet - a triple AAA rated firm is going to be able to borrow at extremely low rates versus a speculative company with tons of debt, which may have to pay 15% or more in exchange for debt capital.
- *Other Forms of Capital*: There are actually other forms of capital, such as vendor financing where a company can sell goods before they have to pay the bill to the vendor, that can drastically increase return on equity but don't cost the company anything. This was one of the secrets to Sam Walton's success at Wal-Mart. He was often able to sell Tide detergent before having to pay the bill to Procter & Gamble, in effect, using PG's money to grow his retailer. In the case of an insurance company, the policyholder "float" represents money that doesn't belong to the firm but that it gets to use and earn an investment on until it has to pay it out for accidents or medical bills, in the case of an auto insurer. The cost of other forms of capital in the capital structure varies greatly on a case-by-case basis and often comes down to the talent and discipline of managers.

## SEEKING THE OPTIMAL CAPITAL STRUCTURE

Many middle class individuals believe that the goal in life is to be debt-free. When you reach the upper echelons of finance, however, that idea is almost anathema. Many of the most successful companies in the world base their capital structure on one simple consideration: the cost of capital. If you can borrow money at 7% for 30 years in a world of 3% inflation and reinvest it in core operations at 15%, you would be wise to consider at least 40% to 50% in debt capital in your overall capital structure.

Of course, how much debt you take on comes down to how secure the revenues your business generates are - if you sell an indispensable product that people simply must have, the debt will be much lower risk than if you operate a theme park in a tourist town at the height of a boom market. Again, this is where managerial talent, experience, and wisdom comes into play. The great managers have a knack for consistently lowering their weighted average cost of capital by increasing productivity, seeking out higher return products, and more.

To truly understand the idea of capital structure, you need to take a few moments to read Return on Equity: The DuPont Model to understand how the capital structure represents one of the three components in determining the rate of return a company will earn on the money its owners have invested in it. Whether you own a doughnut shop or are considering investing in publicly traded stocks, it's knowledge you simply must have.

## CAPITAL STRUCTURE IN A PERFECT MARKET

Assume a perfect capital market; firms and individuals can borrow at the same interest rate; no taxes; and investment decisions aren't affected by financing decisions. Modigliani and Miller made two findings under these conditions. Their first 'proposition' was that the value of a company is independent of its capital structure. Their second 'proposition' stated that the cost of equity for a leveraged firm is equal to the cost of equity for an unleveraged firm, plus an added premium for financial risk. That is, as leverage increases, while the burden of individual risks is shifted between different investor classes, total risk is conserved and hence no extra value created.

Their analysis was extended to include the effect of taxes and risky debt. Under a classical tax system, the tax deductibility of interest makes debt financing valuable; that is, the cost of capital decreases as the proportion of debt in the capital structure increases. The optimal structure, then would be to have virtually no equity at all.

## DETERMINANTS OF CAPITAL STRUCTURE

### INTRODUCTION

The revolution and evolution of the new economy has created non-traditional channels for doing business. Newly formed high tech corporations attract many investors and are able to raise money easily to meet their capital needs in the 1990s. As a result, the capital structure or the determinants of the capital structure of the high tech industry seems to be significantly different from that of the traditional industry.

The determinants of corporate borrowing, literature on the determinants of capital structure has grown steadily. Titman and Wessels' article on the determinants of capital structure choice took such attributes of firms as asset structure, non-debt tax shields, growth, uniqueness, industries classification, size, earnings, volatility and profitability, but found only uniqueness was highly significant. But Harris and Raviv in their seminal article on the subject point out that the consensus among financial economists is that leverage increases with fixed costs, non-debt tax shields, investment opportunities and firm size. Leverage decreases with volatility, advertising expenditure, the probability of bankruptcy, profitability and uniqueness of the product. Moh'd, Perry, and Rimbey employ an extensive time-series and cross-sectional analysis to examine the influence of agency costs and ownership concentration on the capital structure of the firm. Results indicate that the distribution of equity ownership is important in explaining overall capital structure and that managers do reduce the level of debt as their own wealth is increasingly tied-to the firm.

It seems that financial decisions in developing countries are somehow different. Rajan and Zingales took asset structure, investment opportunities, firm size and profitability as the determinants of capital structure across the G–7 countries. They found that leverage increases with asset structure and size, but decreases with growth opportunities and profitability. Again firm leverage is fairly similar across the G–7 countries. Booth, Aivazian, Demirguc-Kunt, and Maksimovic took tax rate, business risk, asset tangibility, firm size, profitability, and market-to-book ratio as determinants of capital structure across ten developing countries. They found that long-term debt ratios decrease with higher tax rates, size, and profitability, but increase with tangibility of assets. Again the influence of the market-to-book ratio and the business-risk variables tends to be subsumed within the country dummies. Moreover, in time-series tests, Shyam-Sunder and Myers show that many of the current empirical tests lack sufficient statistical power to distinguish between the models. As a result, recent empirical research has focused on explaining capital structure choice by using cross-sectional tests.

*Our focus is on answering three quantitatively oriented questions and proposing a qualitative comment on the rise and fall of high tech dot com companies*:

- Do corporate financial leverage decisions differ significantly between high tech and traditional industries?
- Do the determinants of capital structure differ significantly between high tech and traditional industries?
- Is the time-series component important in resolving the conflicting results reported in prior research?

The rest of the paper is organized as follows. The data used in the investigation and four linear models for debt ratio. A comparative study of the determinants of capital structure choices and an attempt to rationalize the observed regularities.

## DATA SOURCE AND METHODOLOGY

### Data Description

*In this study, corporations are classified into two categories*: The high tech and the traditional corporations. High tech corporations include electronics, telecommunications, computer hardware, software, networking, information systems, and other related corporations. The rest are traditional corporations such as clothing, textile, trading, agriculture, manufacturing, etc. Corporations with sound financial statements are selected to create a database and it included a total of 168 observations of public trading corporations in Taiwan from 1996 to 1999.

There are 21 high tech corporations and 21 traditional corporations. All variables are compiled from the Taiwan Economic Journal. Basic statistics are estimated to describe each variable collected and T-tests are conducted to determine if variables of high tech corporations are different from that of traditional corporations. Correlation coefficients (CORR) are estimated to help identify potential problem of multicollinearity for regression models.

As for methodology, four models are used, with the total debt ratio (DEBT) as the dependent variables, and firm size (SIZE), growth opportunities (GRTH), profitability (ROA), tangibility of assets (TANG), non-debt tax shields (NDT), dividend payments (DIV), and business risk (RISK) as independent variables of corporation's feature. In each model, there are three external macro-economic control variables: capital market factor (MK), money market factor (M2), and inflation level (PPI).

### Multiple Linear Regression Models

In order to test the relationship between capital structure and its determinants, the following multiple regression equation is proposed for the panel data.

*Model 1*: [DEBT.sub.it]=[a.sub.0] [a.sub.1]L[SIZE.sub.it] [a.sub.2] [GRTH.sub.it] [a.sub.3] [ROA.sub.it] [a.sub.4] [TANG.sub.it] [a.sub.5]ND [T.sub.it] [a.sub.6][DIV.sub.it] [a.sub.7][RISK.sub.it] [a.sub.8] [MK.sub.it] [a.sub.9]M [2.sub.it] [a.sub.10]PP[I.sub.it] [u.sub.it], i=1..., N; t=1..., T

*The following notation is used to define the variables in the empirical model*:

- DEBT = the total book-debt/ total assets;
- LSIZE = In (Asset Size);
- GRTH = average sales growth rate over the previous two year;
- ROA = the earnings before interest and tax divided by total assets;
- TANG = fixed assets/ total assets;
- NDT = ratio of depreciation, investment tax credit, and tax loss carry forward to total assets;
- DIV = dividend payout ratio;
- RISK = variance of the return on assets;
- MK = rate of return of the overall stock market;
- M2 = annual growth rate;
- PPI = producers' price index

The estimation procedure involves two steps. In step one, each variable is normalized by subtracting its mean value and divided by its standard deviation to have zero mean value and unity variance for all variables. As a result, as suggested, not have an intercept in our results and we can determine the relative importance of each independent variable in explaining variations of the dependent variable based on its estimated coefficient. Variance inflation factor (VIF) is estimated for each independent variable to identify causes of multicollinearity. Pending on the results of step one, model one is re-estimated in step two by deleting variables with insignificant coefficient or significant VIF value one at a time (stepwise) (VIF>20 implies [R.sub.j.sup.2] >.95, i.e. independent variable j is highly correlated with other independent variables of the model).

## Variance Components Models

To determine if there is heteroscedasticity problem, model 1 is estimated based on a "variance-component" model in the later. The error term include three factors (firm, time, and random) and model 1 become:

*Model 2*: [DEBT.sub.it]=[a.sub.0] [a.sub.1]L[SIZE.sub.it] [a.sub.2] [GRTH.sub.it] [a.sub.3][ROA.sub.it] [a.sub.4] [TANG.sub.it] [a.sub.5]ND [T.sub.it] [a.sub.6][DIV.sub.it] [a.sub.7][RISK.sub.it] [a.sub.8] [MK.sub.it] [a.sub.9]M [2.sub.it] [a.sub.10]PP[I.sub.it] [u.sub.it], i=1..., N; t=1..., T
where, [u.sub.it] = [a.sub.i] [b.sub.t] [e.sub.it] (three error components: firm, time, and random).

The error structure is similar to the common two-way random effects model with covariates. The error components are estimated by the fitting-of-constants method, and the regression parameters are estimated with generalized least squares which resulted in unbiased and asymptotically normally distributed estimates. Independent variables with insignificant t-ratio are deleted from the model to finalize our estimates.

## First-order Autoregressive Models

To determine if there are autocorrelation problems, the Parks method is adopted to estimate model 1. The method assumes a first-order autoregressive error structure with contemporaneous correlation between cross sections. The covariance matrix is estimated by a two-stage procedure leading to the estimation of model regression parameters by GLS. The model and error term become:

*Model 3*: [DEBT.sub.it]=[a.sub.0] [a.sub.1]L[SIZE.sub.it] [a.sub.2] [GRTH.sub.it] [a.sub.3][ROA.sub.it] [a.sub.4] [TANG.sub.it] [a.sub.5]ND [T.sub.it] [a.sub.6][DIV.sub.it] [a.sub.7][RISK.sub.it] [a.sub.8] [MK.sub.it] [a.sub.9]M [2.sub.it] [a.sub.10]PP[I.sub.it] [u.sub.it], i=1..., N; t=1..., T where, [u.sub.it] = [[rho].sub.i] [u.sub.i,t-1] [[epsilon].sub.it]

For a stable Parks' estimate, the absolute value of [[rho].sub.ii] should be less than unity.

## Variance-component Moving Average Models (VCMA)

To determine if there are heteroscedasticity and autocorrelation problems, the Da Silva method is adopted to estimate the VCMA model. This method estimates the regression parameters using a two-step GLS-type estimator. The model and error term become:

*Model 4*: [DEBT.sub.it]=[a.sub.0] [a.sub.1]L[SIZE.sub.it] [a.sub.2] [GRTH.sub.it] [a.sub.3][ROA.sub.it] [a.sub.4] [TANG.sub.it] [a. sub.5]ND [T.sub.it] [a.sub.6] [DIV.sub.it] [a.sub.7][RISK.sub.it] [a.sub.8] [MK.sub.it] [a.sub.9]M [2.sub.it] [a.sub.10]PP[I.sub.it] [u.sub.it], i=1..., N; t=1..., T where [u.sub.it] = [a.sub.i] [b.sub.t] [e.sub.it], (three error components) and [e.sub.it] = [][[epsilon].sub.t] [[].sub.l] [[epsilon].sub.t-1] [[].sub.m][[epsilon].sub.t–m].

As the data set only includes a four year period, model four is estimated based on the first order of moving average error process, i.e. [e.sub.it] = [[alpha].sub.0] [[epsilon].sub.t] [[alpha].sub.l][[epsilon].sub.t–1]. We compare and interpret results of all estimates to determine if more advanced models will generate better results than that of the basic multiple regression. More advanced models assume their residual values behave differently and offer more options for better estimates. Policy implications are then drawn as valuable tools for managers in achieving optimal capital structure.

## CAPITAL STRUCTURE THEORY

Capital structure theory is one of the most puzzling issues in the corporate finance literature. Numerous empirical studies have shown that announcements of seasoned equity offerings (SEOs) cause negative price reactions, whereas the news of an additional debt issue is followed by an increase in stock prices. The majority of these studies use capital structure arguments emphasizing the importance of tax shield benefits from debt financing, as the explanation for this phenomenon. We investigate whether differences in tax regimes, in the relative size of the issues, the pre -offer debt-to-equity ratio, the underlying property type and operational performance can account for the price reactions to issue announcements that occurred in various European property share markets over the last decade.

The idea to test whether tax arguments can account for market reactions to the news of security issues by investigating tax-exempt companies is not novel. Howe and Shilling (1988) investigated the stock price reactions to the announcements of new security issues, both debt and equity, of tax-exempt Real Estate Investment Trusts (REITs). They found both the classical positive price reaction on debt issue announcements and the negative price reaction on equity issues. Documenting these typical price reactions in the absence of corporate taxation caused them to attribute these market reactions to the alternative negative signaling explanations. Ghosh, Nag and Sirmans repeated this effort by investigating a larger and more recent REIT -sample and reported results that corroborate with those of Howe and Shilling. But although the issue has been Analysed frequently over the years, some of the most fundamental questions on the cause of price reactions remain unanswered

One key attribution is that it investigates a unique data set consisting of European rights issues that occurred in countries with different tax regimes. We then continue by testing several explanations for these market reactions by investigating factors we derived from theory.

## REVIEW OF LITERATURE AND HYPOTHESES

Over the years numerous studies on capital structure theory have appeared1. Modigliani and Miller were the first who theorized the issue by posing their "M&M capital structure irrelevance proposition". By stating the circumstances under which capital structure does not influence firm value, the authors isolate factors that can explain why daily observations of reality prove the opposite. Modigliani and Miller showed how the relaxation of one of their crucial initial assumptions, the absence of corporate taxation, could attribute to the understanding of empirical findings, which typically exhibit negative price reactions on equity offering announcements. These two classical publications triggered a stream of studies and hypotheses over time, which contributed to the clarification of "the capital structure puzzle.

Howe and Shilling (1988) were the first to study the capital structure issue for listed property by analyzing price reactions to the news of security issues of REITs. They attributed the resulting negative price reactions to SEO-announcements to the negative signal content of equity offerings. Jaffe (1991) disputed this reasoning and argued that under a general model, based on Modigliani and Miller (1958), the value of a partnership, REIT, or related entity is invariant to leverage. The most recent contribution to this debate comes from Ghosh, Nag and Sirmans2 (1999, 2000), who re-examined the issue by investigating a sample of equity offerings in the U.S. REIT-market that occurred in the period 1991 -1996. In accordance with Howe and Shilling (1988) they document negative price reactions on equity offering announcements, and find evidence for the dominance of alternati ve hypotheses over the taxbased model. The focus is to contribute to this ongoing discussion by offering outcomes originating from a unique European data sample, that enables us to test both the tax-based model and the alternative hypotheses that will follow next

The most popular capital structure model is the *static trade-off theory3*, which claims that tax shield benefits of debt financing need to be adjusted for financial distress costs that rise with increasing debt levels, creating an optimal capital structure that balances both forces. Issuing equity means moving away from that optimum and should therefore be interpreted as bad news. The magnitude of this effect should be related to the size of the tax burden. Given the diversity of corporate tax rates in our sample we can test whether the size of the price reaction is related to the corporate tax regime.

One of the alternative hypotheses that as suggested, test is the so-called *implied cash flow change hypothesis4*, which claims that by raising additional resources a company signals that the net operating cash flows of current operations are disappointing. In the opinion of investors changing the financing policy may indicate that the future looks less bright then expected. Since relatively large issues imply more severe cash flow changes we expect equity offerings of relatively large size to be associated with more severe price reactions than issues of more modest magnitudes.

A second signaling hypothesis is the *informational asymmetry hypothesis*. Here Myers and Majluf (1984) assumed that firm managers have superior information about the true value of the company. Managers will therefore time a new equity issue if the market price exceeds their own assessment of the stock value – if the stocks are overvalued by the market. Since investors are aware of the existence of the information asymmetry they will interpret the announcement of an equity issue as a signal that the listed stocks are overvalued, which subsequently will cause a negative price reaction.

Although information asymmetry is difficult to measure we follow the example of Ling and Ryngaert (1992), who showed that the transparency of property companies varies among the different property types.

These variations are partly due to differences in lease contract structures. Offices, for instance, are typically managed using long-term lease contracts, in which the future rent is known in advance. Retail properties, however, are often managed using percentage rent contracts in which future rents are linked to the sales of the store, which make future rental inflows harder to predict, thus increasing information asymmetry.

An alternative hypothesis we derived from Bayless and Chaplinsky (1991) is the *debt market accessibility hypothesis*. The rationale of this theory is based upon the consideration of investors for the decision of managers to issue equity. If a company is already highly levered it will be regarded as being relatively risky by capital suppliers. Hence accessing the debt market will be less attractive and issuing additional equity instead becomes a sound decision. Assuming investors reason in this manner we expect highly levered equity issuers to be associated with better post-issue stock performance than issuers with relatively low debt-to-equity ratios.

A more recent stream of literature focuses on the slump in operational profitability that tends to occur in the year following a security issue. This phenomenon has been documented by studies like McLaughlin, Safieddine and Vasudevan (1996, 1998) and Loughran, Ritter (1997). A general explanation for this post-issue slump in earnings originates from Jensen's (1986) free cash flow theory, which claims that managers have incentives to invest issue proceeds in unprofitable projects due to *agency problems* causing earnings to decrease.

A second explanation for the post-issue operational slump is the slow start of new projects that are initiated with the proceeds of the issues. In the case of property companies these projects are real estate assets that will need to be leased, managed and maybe renovated, which will take time and delay optimal payoffs.

Both these explanations indicate that equity offerings are likely to be followed by a year in which earnings slow down, which can drive the negative price reaction. In line with Friday, Howton and Howton (2000) as suggested, investigate whether this operational slump is also present in the European listed property market.

## DATA

By combining the Global Property Research database with Datastream and the Bloomberg News Retrieval Services we retrieved the necessary data on a sample of seasoned equity offerings for the period 1990 to 2000. Our efforts resulted in a unique data set covering 113 SEOs in 13 different countries and 26 debt offerings in 6 different countries. Table provides a distribution of the sample by country and by year. Besides the announcement dates and the corresponding stock return series we also obtained the offering size, the pre - offer debt-ratio, the underlying property types and the corporate tax rate for each offering in our sample.

**Table. Distribution of Announcement Dates by country and by Year**

| A: Sample distribution by country | | | | | |
|---|---|---|---|---|---|
| **Country Issue** | **Rights Offering** | **Debt** | **Country Issue** | **Rights Offering** | **Debt** |
| Austria | 7 | 0 | Norway | 3 | 3 |
| Belgium | 3 | 0 | Portugal | 2 | 1 |

| | | | | | |
|---|---|---|---|---|---|
| Denmark | 4 | 0 | Spain | 11 | 2 |
| Finland | 1 | 0 | Sweden | 7 | 0 |
| France | 1 | 6 | Switzerl- | 15 | 0 |
| | | and | | | |
| Germany | 15 | 0 | United | 35 | 13 |
| | | Kingdom | | | |
| The Netherlands | 9 | 1 | | | |
| Total | | | | 113 | 26 |

**B: Sample distribution by year**

| Year | Rights Issue | Debt Offering | Country | Rights Issue | Debt Offering |
|---|---|---|---|---|---|
| 1990 | 3 | 0 | 1996 | 13 | 0 |
| 1991 | 4 | 1 | 1997 | 18 | 5 |
| 1992 | 3 | 0 | 1998 | 13 | 6 |
| 1993 | 21 | 0 | 1999 | 15 | 12 |
| 1994 | 10 | 0 | 2000 | 8 | 1 |
| 1995 | 5 | 1 | | | |
| Total | | | | 113 | 26 |

**C: Tax regimes for property companies**

| Country rate | Corporate tax | Country rate | Corporate tax |
|---|---|---|---|
| Austria | 34% | Norway | 28% |
| Belgium* | 0%* | Portugal | 37.4% |
| Denmark | 34% | Spain | 35% |
| Finland | 28% | Sweden | 28% |
| France | 33% | Switzerland | 22% |
| Germany | 39% | United | 29% |
| | Kingdom | | |
| The Netherlands 0%** | | | |

*The corporate tax rate in Belgium is 0% for companies with the so-called SICAFIstructure.To qualify as such, a company has to comply with certain regulations. Investing solely in real estate, a maximum of 20% of investments in one single asset and not more than 33% of assets as borrowing capacity are the most prominent ones. Furthermore, at least 80% of profits have to be distributed to investors.

** Dutch property companies are structured as so-called "erkende beleggingsinstellingen", which means that they have to distribute at least 95% of their profits in dividends. Being an "erkende beleggingsinstelling" the property companies do not have to pay any corporate taxes.

## COST OF CAPITAL

The important concept that the expected return on an investment should be a function of the "market risk" embedded in that investment – the risk–return tradeoff.

The firm must earn a minimum of rate of return to cover the cost of generating funds to finance investments; otherwise, no one will be willing to buy the firm's bonds, preferred stock, and common stock.

This point of reference, the firm's required rate of return, is called the COST OF CAPITAL.

The cost of capital is the required rate of return that a firm must achieve in order to cover the cost of generating funds in the marketplace. Based on their evaluations of the riskiness of each firm, investors will supply new funds to a firm only if it pays them the required rate of return to compensate them for taking the risk of investing in the firm's bonds and stocks. If, indeed, the cost of capital is the required rate of return that the firm must pay to generate funds, it becomes a guideline for measuring the profitabilities of different investments. When there are differences in the degree of risk between the firm and its divisions, a risk-adjusted discount-rate approach should be used to determine their profitability.

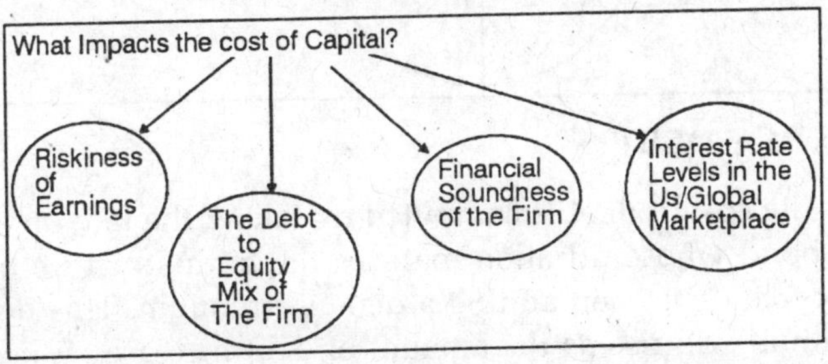

The Cost of Capital becomes a guideline for measuring the profitabilities of different investments. Another way to think of the cost of capital is as the opportunity cost of funds, since this represents the opportunity cost for investing in assets with the same risk as the firm. When investors are shopping for places in which to invest their funds, they have an opportunity cost. The firm, given its riskiness, must strive to earn the investor's opportunity cost. If the firm does not achieve the return investors expect, investors will not invest in the firm's debt and equity. As a result, the firm's value will decline.

## WEIGHTED AVERAGE COST OF CAPITAL (WACC)

The firm's WACC is the cost of Capital for the firm's mixture of debt and stock in their capital structure.

$WACC = W_d$ (Cost of Debt) + $W_s$ (Cost of Stock/RE) + $W_p$(Cost of PF. Stock)

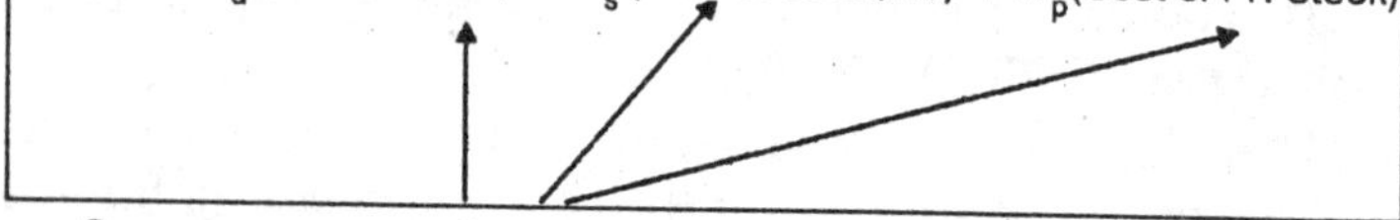

So now we need to calculate these to find the WACC!

- $w_d$ = weight of debt (i.e. fraction of debt in the firm's capital structure)
- $w_s$ = weight of stock
- $w_p$ = weight of prefered stock

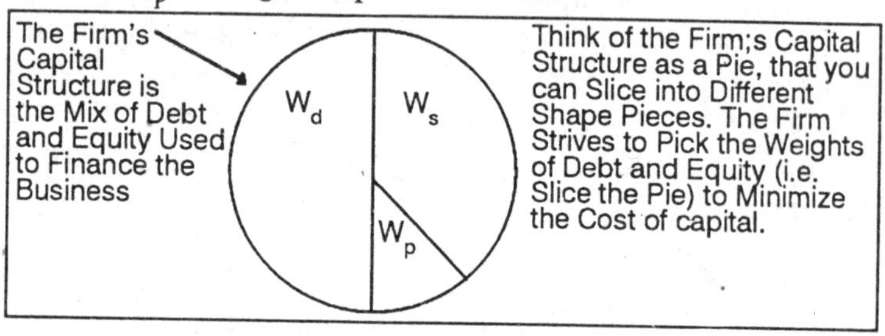


## COST OF DEBT

The cost of debt is computed by taking the rate on a risk free bond whose duration matches the term structure of the corporate debt, then adding a default premium. This default premium will rise as the amount of debt increases (since the risk rises as the amount of debt rises). Since in most cases debt expense is a deductible expense, the cost of debt is computed as an after tax cost to make it comparable with the cost of equity.

Thus, for profitable firms, debt is discounted by the tax rate. The formula can be written as (Rf + credit risk rate)(1–T), where T is the corporate tax rate and Rf is the risk free rate.

## COST OF EQUITY

Cost of equity = Risk free rate of return + Premium expected for risk.

### Expected Return

The expected return (or required rate of return for investors) can be calculated with the "dividend capitalization model", which is,

$$K_{cs} = \frac{\text{Dividend}_{\text{Payment/Share}}}{\text{Price}_{\text{Market}}} + \text{Growth}_{\text{rate}}.$$

*That equation is also seen as*: Expected Return = dividend yield + growth rate of dividends.

### Capital Asset Pricing Model

The capital asset pricing model (CAPM) is used in finance to determine a theoretically appropriate price of an asset such as a security. The expected return on equity according to the capital asset pricing model. The market risk is normally characterized by the β parameter.

*Thus, the investors would expect (or demand) to receive*:

$$E_s = R_f + \beta_s(R_m - R_f).$$

*Where*:

$E_s$: The expected return for a security

$R_f$: The expected risk-free return in that market (government bond yield)

$\beta_s$: The sensitivity to market risk for the security

$R_M$: The historical return of the stock market/ equity market

$(R_M - R_f)$: *The risk premium of market assets over risk free assets.*

*In writing*:

- The expected return (%) = risk-free return (%) + sensitivity to market risk * (historical return (%) – risk-free return (%))
- Put another way the expected rate of return (%) = the yield on the treasury note closest to the term of your project + the beta of your project or security * (the market risk premium)
- The market risk premium has historically been between 3-5%

### Comments

The models states that investors will expect a return that is the risk-free return plus the security's sensitivity to market risk times the market risk premium.

The risk free rate is taken from the lowest yielding bonds in the particular market, such as government bonds.

The risk premium varies over time and place, but in some developed countries during the twentieth century it has averaged around 5%. The equity market real capital gain return has been about the same as annual real GDP growth. The capital gains on the Dow Jones Industrial Average have been 1.6% per year over the period 1910-2005. The dividends have increased the total "real" return on average equity to the double, about 3.2%.

The sensitivity to market risk (β) is unique for each firm and depends on everything from management to its business and capital structure. This value cannot be known "ex ante" (beforehand), but can be estimated from *ex post* (past) returns and past experience with similar firms.

### Cost of Retained Earnings/Cost of Internal Equity

Note that retained earnings are a component of equity, and therefore the cost of retained earnings (internal equity) is equal to the cost of equity. Dividends (earnings that are paid to investors and not retained) are a component of the return on capital to equity holders, and influence the cost of capital through that mechanism.

## WEIGHTED AVERAGE COST OF CAPITAL

Corporations create value for shareholders by earning a return on the invested capital that is the cost of that capital. WACC (Weighted Average Cost of Capital) is an expression of this cost and is used to see if certain intended investments or strategies or projects or purchases are worthwhile to undertake.

WACC is expressed as a percentage, like interest. So for example if a company works with a WACC of 12%, than this means that only (and all) investments should be made that give a return higher than the WACC of 12%.

The cost of capital for any investment, whether for an entire company or for a project, is the rate of return capital providers would expect to receive if they would invest their capital elsewhere. In other words, the cost of capital is an *opportunity cost*.

How can the Weighted Average Cost of Capital (WACC) be calculated?

The easy part of WACC is the debt part of it. In most cases it is clear how much a company has to pay their bankers or bondholders for *debt finance*. More elusive however, is the cost of *equity finance*. Normally, the cost of equity finance is higher than the cost debt finance, because the cost of equity involves a *risk premium*. Calculating this risk premium is one thing that makes calculating WACC complicated.

Another important complication is which *mix* of debt and equity should be used to maximize shareholder value (This is what "*Weighted*" means in WACC).

Finally, also the *corporate tax rate* is important, because normally interest payments are tax-deductible.

## CAPITAL STRUCTURE

Because of tax advantages on debt issuance, it will be cheaper to issue debt rather than new equity (this is only true for profitable firms, tax breaks are available only to profitable firms). At some point, however, the cost of issuing new debt will be greater than the cost of issuing new equity. This is because adding debt increases the default risk - and thus the interest rate that the company must pay in order to borrow money. By utilizing too much debt in its capital structure, this increased default risk can also drive up the costs for other sources (such as retained earnings and preferred stock) as well. Management must identify the "optimal mix" of financing – the capital structure where the cost of capital is minimized so that the firm's value can be maximized.

The Thomson Financial league tables show that global debt issuance exceeds equity issuance with a 90 to 10 margin.

## MODIGLIANI-MILLER THEOREM

The Modigliani-Miller Theorem holds that a firm's market value is calculated by the risk associated with the underlying assets of the firm and also on the earning capacity of the firm. The theorem further states that the market value of the firm is not affected by the choice of financing the investments or on the decisions of distributing the dividends. The three ways that a firm can select to finance the investments are - borrowing outside capital, issuing the shares and reinvesting the profits. The theory, under some market assumptions whether or not the firm investments are financed with equity or debt makes no difference. The Modigliani-Miller theorem is very often called as the capital structure irrelevance principle. Economist Modigliani was awarded Nobel Prize in Economics in the year of 1985 for introducing this theory and his other contributions to economic studies.

Merton Miller explains the theorem with an example. Let us compare the firm with a huge tub of whole milk. The farmer, who owns it, can sell the whole milk entirely or can separate the cream from the milk and then sell the cream with a higher price. The skim milk that is left can be sold by the farmer at a relatively lower price than the whole milk. This practice relates to levered equity concept of the firms. Now, Modigliani-Miller Theorem, if the separation of milk does not contain any cost then selling the cream milk and the skim milk will bring the same price, as the whole milk would do. The Modigliani-Miller theorem is considered to construct the modern thinking base for the capital structure of a firm. The theorem, the firm's market value is independent of the decisions regarding how the firm is financed under certain assumptions, which are -no bankruptcy cost, no corporate tax, no asymmetric information and efficient market.

## OPERATING AND FINANCIAL LEVERAGE

Should a business increase or reduce the number of units it is producing? Should it rely more or less heavily on borrowed money? The answer depends upon how a change would affect risk and return. Operating leverage is the name given to the impact on operating income of a change in the level of output.

Financial leverage is the name given to the impact on returns of a change in the extent to which the firm's assets are financed with borrowed money. Despite the fact that both operating leverage and financial leverage are concepts that have been discussed and Analysed for decades, there is substantial disparity in how they are defined and measured by academics and practitioners.

Weston and Brigham told some of today's businessmen and women that, "High fixed costs and low variable costs provide the greater percentage change in profits both upward and downward."

Brigham, "If a high percentage of a firm's costs are fixed, and hence do not decline when demand decreases, this increases he company's business risk. This factor is called operating leverage." "If a high percentage of a firm's total costs are fixed, the firm is said to have a high degree of operating leverage." "The degree of operating leverage (DOL) is defined as the percentage change in operating income (or EBIT) that results from a given percentage change in sales....In effect, the DOL is an index number which measures the effect of a change in sales on operating income, or EBIT."

Grunewald and Nemmers, "When fixed costs are very large and variable costs consume only a small percentage of each dollar of revenue, even a slight change in revenue will have a large effect on reported profits."

Cherry, "Operating leverage, then, refers to the magnified effect on operating earnings (EBIT) of any given change in sales...And the more important, proportionally, are fixed costs in the total cost structure, the more marked is the effect on EBIT."

Van Horne, "one of the most dramatic examples of operating leverage is in the airline industry, where a large portion of total costs are fixed." Archer and D'Ambrosio, "The higher the proportion of fixed costs to total costs the higher the operating leverage of the firm..."

Schultz and Shultz, "Since a fixed expense is being compared to an amount which is a function of a fluctuating base (sales), profit-and-loss results will not bear a proportionate relationship to that base. These results in fact will be subject to magnification, the degree of which depends on the relative size of fixed costs vis-a-vis the potential range of sales volume. This entire subject is referred to as operating leverage."

*where*:

- q = quantity
- p = price per unit
- v = variable cost per unit
- f = total fixed costs

Block and Hirt, operating leverage measures the effect of fixed costs on the firm, and that the degree of operating leverage (DOL) equals:

DOL = q(p – v) divided by q(p – v) – f

*that is*:

Degree of operating leverage =

Sales revenue less total variable cost divided by sales revenue less total cost

In 1997, Buccino and McKinley define operating leverage as the impact of a change in revenue on profit or cash flow. It arises whenever a firm can increase its revenues without a proportionate increase in operating expenses. Cash allocated to increasing revenue, such as marketing and business development expenditures, are quickly."consumed by high fixed expenses." (This is certainly a different definition!)

In 1997 Rushmore, that positive operating leverage occurs at the point at which revenue exceeds the total amount of fixed costs.

There seems to be more uniformity in the definition of financial leverage."Financial leverage," Block and Hirt, reflects the amount of debt used in the capital structure of the firm. Because debt carries a fixed obligation of interest payments, we have the opportunity to greatly magnify our results at various levels of operations.

Weston and Brigham back in 1969, the degree of financial leverage is computed as the percentage change in earnings available to common stockholders associated with a given percentage change in earnings before interest and taxes.

Brigham in 1995,"The degree of financial leverage (DFL) is defined as the percentage change in earnings per share [EPS] that results from a given percentage change in earnings before interest and taxes (EBIT), and it is calculated as follows:"

DFL = Percentage change in EPS divided by Percentage change in EBIT

This calculation produces an index number which if, for example, it is 1.43, this means that a 100 Per cent increase in EBIT would result in a 143 Per cent increase in earnings per share. (It makes no difference mathematically if return is calculated on a per share basis or on total equity, as in the solution of the equation EPS cancels out.)

Clarity in regard to operating and financial leverage is important because these concepts are important to businesses. Small and medium-sized business often have difficulty using the highly sophisticated quantitative methods large companies use. Fortunately, he observes, the simple break-even graph is simple and easy to interpret; yet it can provide a significant amount of information. The algebra necessary to compute operating and financial leverage, too, is not very complex. Unfortunately, it comes in a several guises; not all equally easy to understand or equally useful.

## FINANCIAL LEVERAGE

Operating leverage refers to the fact that a lower ratio of

variable cost per unit to price per unit causes profit to vary more with a change in the level of output than it would if this ratio was higher. Financial leverage refers to the fact that a higher ratio of debt to equity causes profitability to vary more when earnings on assets changes than it would if this ratio was lower. Obviously, the profits of a business with a high degree of both kinds of leverage vary more, everything else remaining the same, than do those of businesses with less operating and financial leverage. Greater variability of profits, of course, means risk is higher. Therefore, in deciding what is the optimum level of leverage, what is an acceptable risk/ return tradeoff must be determined.

*The degree of financial leverage (DFL) is sometimes measured in the following manner*:

DFL = [q(p – v) – f – i]/ e divided by [q(p –v) – f]/ [e + d]

*where*: d is the value of a firm's liabilities and equity plus liabilities = assets = e + d that is:

DFL = rate of return on equity when borrowed money is used divided by rate of return on assets

By assuming various levels of debt financing at various interest rates, equation 13 can be used to judge the impact at various levels of output of using more or less debt financing or paying different interest rates for a given amount of debt financing.

## Suggested New Way to Measure Financial Leverage

It is quite simple to compute what the impact on owners' rate of return will be as a result of borrowing a given Per cent of the money used to finance a firm's assets:

$$r_e = (d/e)(r_a - r_d) + r_a$$

*where*:

- d = debt (either as $ or%)
- e = equity (either as $ or%)
- $r_d$ = interest rate on debt (%)
- $r_a$ = return on assets (%)

*Example*: Assuming 70 Per cent of a firm's assets are financed with debt costing 8 Per cent and return on assets is

12 Per cent, this equation indicates owners will earn 21.33 Per cent:

$$2.33\ (.12 - .08) + .12 = 2.33(.04) + .12 = .093 + .12 = .213$$

Owners' return rises by 9.33 Per cent as a result of the financial leverage obtained by 70 Per cent debt financing at a cost of 8 Per cent. If borrowing rose above 70 Per cent that is, financial leverage would be greater. If financial leverage is measured, instead, as an index number, an additional calculation is necessary to determine what return on equity it produces.

To confirm that this equation is a valid way to measure the impact on the bottom line of financial leverage, assume that assets = \$100,000. This means that EBIT = \$12,000. Interest cost is \$5,600 (.08 x \$70,000). So EBT is \$6,400 (\$12,000 - \$5,600). \$6,400 is a 21.3 Per cent return on equity of \$30,000.

The return on assets would, of course, vary with the assumed level of output.

The return on assets and the return on equity =

$r_a = (qp - qv - f)/a$ and

$r_e = (d/e)[(qp - qv - f)/a) - r_d] + (qp - qv - f)/a$

*that is:*

The return on equity = (the ratio of debt to equity) times (the return on assets minus the cost of debt plus the return on assets)

## Measuring Combined Leverage

The combined impact of operating and financial leverage can be measured by an index number in the following manner:

$$\text{OFL} = [q2(p - v) - f - i]/\,e \text{ divided by } [q1(p - v) - f]/(e + d)$$

*Solving this equation where:*

$p = \$\,2$ $v = \$\,1$ $f = \$\,50$ $i = \$\,50$

$e = \$1{,}000$ $d = \$1{,}000$ $q_1 = 200$ $q_2 = 400$

*means*: DFL =.30/.075 = 4.0

Adding 200 additional units of output and obtaining half the firm's financing from lenders will increase owners' rate of return from 7.5 Per cent to 30 Per cent (4.0 times 7.5 Per cent = 30 Per cent.).

# RETAINED EARNINGS AND DIVIDEND POLICY

## RETAINED EARNINGS

In accounting, retained earnings refers to the portion of net income which is retained by the corporation rather than distributed to its owners as dividends. Similarly, if the corporation takes a loss, then that loss is retained and called variously retained losses, accumulated losses or accumulated deficit. Retained earnings and losses are cumulative from year to year with losses offsetting earnings.

Retained earnings are reported in the shareholders' equity part of the balance sheet. Companies with net accumulated losses may refer to negative shareholders' equity as a shareholders' deficit. A complete report of the retained earnings or retained losses is presented in the Statement of retained earnings or Statement of retained losses.

### Stockholders' Equity

When total assets are greater than total liabilities, stockholders have a positive equity. Conversely, when total liabilities are greater than total assets, stockholders have a negative stockholders' equity— also sometimes called stockholders' deficit.

A stockholders' deficit does not mean that stockholders owe money to the corporation as they own only its net assets and are not accountable for its liabilities. It means that the value of the assets of the company must rise its liabilities before the stockholders hold positive equity value in the company. Liabilities that exceed assets is the classic definition of bankruptcy.

### Dividends

*The decision of whether a firm should retain net income or have it paid out as dividends depends on several factors including, but not limited to the*:

- Tax treatment of dividends; and
- Funds required for reinvestment in the corporation.

## DIVIDEND POLICY

Dividend policies are the regulations and guidelines that companies develop and implement as the means of arranging to make dividend payments to shareholders. Establishing a specific dividend policy is to the advantage of both the company and the shareholder. In order to make sure the policy is workable, a company should develop a viable policy and then run this policy through a number of test scenarios in order to determine what impact the dividend policy would have on the operation of the business.

In many cases, companies choose to explicitly state the provisions within the dividend policy. This is definitely to the advantage of the shareholder, as a well defined policy makes it much easier to project the amount of payout profits generated for the period under consideration and thus be able to determine the size of the dividends that will be issued. When the dividend policy is well defined and documented, it is easy for the shareholder to obtain a written copy and thus be fully informed as to how the policy works.

However, there are cases where the dividend policy is not so well documented. When this is the case, investors sometimes base their assumptions on upcoming dividend payments on what has occurred in the past. While less systematic, it is still possible to project a more or less accurate estimate of what the dividend payout will actually be.

In cases where the dividend policy is not specifically defined, investors often look at the history to spot any trends that emerged in the past. If the dividend payments have been more or less constant for the last several years, and there has been no loss in business volume, it is reasonable to assume the payments will still be in the same general range as before. However, if the dividend history is more volatile, the shareholder may attempt to identify what factors led to the up and down movement of the dividends and determine if any of those factors are relevant to the current dividend period.

In both expressed and implied dividend policy procedures, it is less common for the dividends to be increased. Part of the reason for that is companies tend to look closely at retained earnings and want to make sure the increased level of earnings will be sustained over the long term. Once this upward trend is deemed to be more or less permanent, the company may choose to increase dividends.

Far more common is the practice of reducing dividends. This usually takes place because there is a decrease in the company's business volume that is not anticipated to be recaptured in the foreseeable future. At other times, the decrease may be due to the need to retain more cash on hand for capital expenses. In both these scenarios, companies tend to notify the shareholders in advance that these factors exist and a chance in dividends will take place in order to meet the challenge to remain profitable.

## LEGAL CONSIDERATIONS IN DIVIDEND POLICY

While designing a dividend policy for a firm the legal and statutory framework should also be considered as the dividend policy is often constrained by legal and contractual factors. For public and private companies, the companies Act 1985 defines distributable profit as "Accumulated retained profits, so far as not previously utilized by distribution or capitalization, less accumulated realized losses, so far as not previously written off in a reduction or reorganization of capital duly made".

In India, several restrictions have been imposed on companies in respect of dividend payment. These provisions regarding quantum and procedure for payment of dividend are contained in section 205,205A, 206,206A and 207 of the Companies Act, 1956.

*These provisions may be summarized as follows*:

- A Company can pay dividends to shareholders only if sufficient provision has been made for the redemption of preference shares, if any and also that sufficient depreciation has been provided as per Schedule XIII annexed to the Companies Act, 1956.
- All dividends must be paid in cash the cash dividend may be paid either as
  - Final dividend which is payable after

recommendation of the board of directors and approved by the shareholders at the annual general meeting of the company. There are certain procedural constraints and formalities in respect of payment of final dividend given in the bye-laws of the stock exchange where the shares are listed.

- Interim dividend which is payable after passing a resolution by the Board of Directors and even before the finalization of accounts for that year. So, the interim dividend is paid in between two annual general meetings. The board may pay such dividend only if it expects sufficient profits for the period. The Companies Act, 1956 does not provide for payment of interim dividend and therefore, a company can pay interim dividend only if authorized by the Articles of Association of the Company.

Dividend is payable only out of current year revenue profits of the company. However, in certain cases, dividend can also be paid out of accumulated profits in case of inadequate or no current year profit. In this context, the following rules are worth noting:

The prescribed rules framed by the Central Government in this respect known as the Companies Rules, 1975 Rule 2 provides that in the event of inadequacy or in the absence of profits in any year, dividend may be declared by it in the previous years and transferred by it to the reserves, subject to the conditions that:

- The rate of dividend shall not exceed the average of the rate at which dividend was declared by it in the five years immediately preceding that year or 10 per cent of its paid up capital, whichever is less.
- The total amount to be drawn from the accumulated profits earned in previous years and transferred to the reserve shall not exceed an amount equal to one-tenth of the sum of its paid up capital and free reserves and the amount so drawn shall first be

utilized to set off the losses in the financial year before any dividend in respect of preference or equity shares is declared; and

- The balance of reserves after such draw shall not fall below 15 per cent of its paid up capital

For the purposes of the rules, profit earned by a company in previous years and transferred by its to the'reserves' shall mean the total amount of net profits after tax, transferred to reserves as at the beginning of the year for which the dividend is to be declared; and in computing the said amount, the appropriation out of the amount transferred from the Development Rebate Reserve shall be included and all items of capital reserves including reserves created by revaluation of assets shall be excluded.

Further that dividend is payable out of revenue profits only, however, in certain cases dividends can be paid out of capital profits also, subject to fulfillment of the following conditions:

- Such capital profits are realized in cash.
- The Articles of Association of the Company permits such payment.
- Such capital profits exist after revaluation of other assets.

The payment of dividend out of capital profits is not very common in India. Glaxo ltd, sold a part of its undertaking and out of the realized capital profit from such sale, it paid a special dividend @175% during 1994. Laking ltd. Also declared a special dividend of 600% in 1998 out of the profits resulting from the sale of undertaking to the Hindustan Lever Ltd.

Further, at the time of payment of dividend out of current year revenue profits, the company has to take care of the relevant rules as given in the Companies Act, 1956 as follows:

Sections 205 (2A) of the Companies Act, 1956 provides that before declaration and payment of dividend out of current year's profit, a company is required to transfer such percentage of its profits for the current year to reserves, not exceeding 10 Per cent, as may be prescribed. The Central Government has prescribed such percentage by framing the Companies Rules

1975. Rule 2 provides that no dividend shall be declared or paid by a company for any financial year out of its profits for that year arrived at after providing for depreciation in accordance with the provisions of sub section (2) of Section 205 of the Act except after the transfer to reserves of the company of a percentage of its profits for that year as specified below:

*When the dividend proposed Amount to be transferred to the reserves not less than:*

- Exceed 10% but not 12.5% of the 2.5% of the current year profits
  Paid up Capital
- Exceed 12.5% but not 15% of the 5% of the current year profits
  Paid up Capital
- Exceed 15% but not 20% of the 7.5% of the current year profits
  Paid up Capital
- Exceeds 20% of the paid up 10% of the current year profits.
  Capital

It is evident that percentage of profit required to be transferred to reserves are linked to the rates of dividends. Thus, where the proposed dividend is exactly 10% or less of the paid up capital of the company, it is not obligatory to transfer any portion of the profits to the reserves. The dividends, once declared at the annual general meeting of the company must be paid within 42 days of the declaration. If not, then within 7 days from the date of expiry of the said period of 42 days, the company must deposit the unpaid dividends to a separate bank account to be opened by the company in a Scheduled Bank, to be called "Unpaid Dividend Account". If the money remains unpaid/ unclaimed in this account for a period of three years from the date of transfer, then the company shall transfer such money to the General Revenue Account of the Central Government.

The most widely used method of distribution of earnings among the shareholders is to distribute by way of cash dividends. However, there is a number of other also of dividend payments. More common of these methods are the issue of bonus shares.

## DIVIDEND THEORIES

### DIVIDEND IRRELEVANCE THEORY

Much like their work on the capital-structure irrelevance proposition, Modigliani and Miller also theorized that, with no taxes or bankruptcy costs, dividend policy is also irrelevant. This is known as the "dividend-irrelevance theory", indicating that there is no effect from dividends on a company's capital structure or stock price.

MM's dividend-irrelevance theory, that investors can affect their return on a stock regardless of the stock's dividend. For example, suppose, from an investor's perspective, that a company's dividend is too big. That investor could then buy more stock with the dividend that is over the investor's expectations. Likewise, if, from an investor's perspective, a company's dividend is too small, an investor could sell some of the company's stock to replicate the cash flow he or she expected. As such, the dividend is irrelevant to investors, meaning investors care little about a company's dividend policy since they can simulate their own.

### BIRD-IN-THE-HAND THEORY

The bird-in-the-hand theory, however, states that dividends are relevant. Remember that total return (k) is equal to dividend yield plus capital gains. Myron Gordon and John Lintner took this equation and assumed that k would decrease as a company's payout increased. As such, as a company increases its payout ratio, investors become concerned that the company's future capital gains will dissipate since the retained earnings that the company reinvests into the business will be less. Gordon and Lintner argued that investors value dividends more than capital gains when making decisions related to stocks. The bird-in-the-hand may sound familiar as it is taken from an old saying: "a bird in the hand is worth two in the bush." In this theory "the bird in the hand' is referring to dividends and "the bush" is referring to capital gains.

## TAX-PREFERENCE THEORY

Taxes are important considerations for investors. Remember capital gains are taxed at a lower rate than dividends. As such, investors may prefer capital gains to dividends. This is known as thè "tax Preference theory". Additionally, capital gains are not paid until an investment is actually sold. Investors can control when capital gains are realized, but, they can't control dividend payments, over which the related company has control. Capital gains are also not realized in an estate situation. For example, suppose an investor purchased a stock in a company 50 years ago. The investor held the stock until his or her death, when it is passed on to an heir. That heir does not have to pay taxes on that stock's appreciation.

## DIVIDEND-IRRELEVANCE THEORY AND COMPANY VALUATION

In the determination of the value of a company, dividends are often used. However, MM's dividend-irrelevance theory indicates that there is no effect from dividends on a company's capital structure or stock price. MM's dividend-irrelevance theory, that investors can affect their return on a stock regardless of the stock's dividend. For example, suppose, from an investor's perspective, that a company's dividend is too big. That investor could then buy more stock with the dividend that is over his or her expectations. Likewise, if, from an investor's perspective, a company's dividend is too small, an investor could sell some of the company's stock to replicate the cash flow he or she expected. As such, the dividend is irrelevant to investors, meaning investors care little about a company's dividend policy since they can simulate their own.

## PRINCIPAL CONCLUSION FOR DIVIDEND POLICY

The dividend-irrelevance theory with no taxes or

bankruptcy costs, assumes that a company's dividend policy is irrelevant. The dividend-irrelevance theory indicates that there is no effect from dividends on a company's capital structure or stock price. MM's dividend-irrelevance theory assumes that investors can affect their return on a stock regardless of the stock's dividend. As such, the dividend is irrelevant to an investor, meaning investors care little about a company's dividend policy when making their purchasing decision since they can simulate their own dividend policy.

## HOW ANY SHAREHOLDER CAN CONSTRUCT HIS OR HER OWN DIVIDEND POLICY

The MM's dividend-irrelevance theory says that investors can affect their return on a stock regardless of the stock's dividend.

*As a result, a stockholder can construct his or her own dividend policy*:

- Suppose, from an investor's perspective, that a company's dividend is too big. That investor could then buy more stock with the dividend that is over the investor's expectations.
- Likewise, if, from an investor's perspective, a company's dividend is too small, an investor can sell some of the company's stock to replicate the cash flow the investor expected.

As such, the dividend is irrelevant to an investor, meaning investors care little about a company's dividend policy since they can simulate their own.

## BONUS SHARE

The term bonus means an extra dividend paid to shareholders in a joint stock company from surplus profits. When a company has accumulated a large fund out of profits - much beyond its needs, the directors may decide to distribute a part of it amongst the shareholders in the form of bonus Bonus can be paid either in cash or in the form of shares. Cash bonus is paid by the company when it has large accumulated profits as well as cash to pay dividend. Many a time, a company is not in a position to pay bonus in cash in spite of sufficient profits because of unsatisfactory cash position or because of its adverse effects on the working capital of the company. In such a position, the company pays a bonus to its shareholders in the form of shares; a free share thus issued is known as a bonus share.

## EXPLANATION

A bonus share is a free share of stock given to current/ existing shareholders in a company, based upon the number of shares that the shareholder already owns at the time of announcement of the bonus. While the issue of bonus shares increases the total number of shares issued and owned, it does not increase the value of the company. Although the total number of issued shares increases, the ratio of number of shares held by each shareholder remains constant. Whenever a company announces a bonus issue, it also announces a"Book Closure Date" which is a date on which the company will ideally temporarily close its books for fresh transfers of stock. Read"Book Closure" for a better understanding. An issue of bonus shares is referred to as a bonus issue. Depending upon the constitutional documents of the company, only certain classes of shares may be entitled to bonus issues, or may be entitled to bonus issues in preference to other classes. Bonus share is free share in fixed ratio to the shareholders. Sometimes a company will change the number of shares in issue by capitalising its reserve.In other words,it can convert the right of the sahreholders because each individual will hold the same proportion of the outstanding shares as before. Main reason for issuance is the price of the existing share has become unwieldy.

# 6

# Lease Financing

In order to start and sustain a business one needs finance. In the unit one on feasibility study, you have already seen the process of estimating financial requirements.

*The process involved*:

- Making a list of all the assets
- Identifying the sources of supply
- Estimating the cost of acquisition when the assets are to be acquired on outright basis.

Then investment requirements as well as entrepreneur's fear will increase. To scare away the entrepreneur's fear, the emphasis should be given to resources and not to the ownership. In this unit we intend to familiarize you with some important financial innovations i.e., leasing, hire purchase and ctoring.

## OBJECTIVES

*After going through this unit you should be able to*:

- Describe the meaning of leasing
- Explain the role and importance of lease financing in economic development of a country
- Distinguish between the various types of leases
- Describe the meaning of hire purchase
- Distinguish between leasing and hire purchase
- Describe the meaning of factoring

## CONCEPT 0F LEASE FINANCING

Lease financing denotes procurement of assets through lease. The subject of leasing falls in the category of finance.

Leasing has grown as a big industry in the USA and UK and spread to other countries during the present century. In India, the concept was pioneered in 1973 when the First Leasing Company was set up in Madras and the eighties have seen a rapid growth of this business. Lease as a concept involves a contract whereby the ownership, financing and risk taking of any equipment or asset are separated and shared by two or more parties. Thus, the lessor may finance and lessee may accept the risk through the use of it while a third party may own it. Alternatively the lessor may finance and own it while the lessee enjoys the use of it and bears the risk. There are various combinations in which the characteristics are shared by the lessor and lessee.

## MEANING OF LEASE FINANCING

A lease transaction is a commercial arrangement whereby an equipment owner or Manufacturer conveys to the equipment user the right to use the equipment in return for a rental. In other words, lease is a contract between the owner of an asset and its user for the right to use the asset during a specified period in return for a mutually agreed periodic payment. The important feature of a lease contract is separation of the ownership of the asset from its usage. Lease financing is based on the observation made by Donald B. Grant: "Why own a cow when the milk is so cheap? All you really need is milk and not the cow."

## IMPORTANCE OF LEASE FINANCING

Leasing industry plays an important role in the economic development of a country by providing money incentives to lessee. The lessee does not have to pay the cost of asset at the time of signing the contract of leases. Leasing contracts are more flexible so lessees can structure the leasing contracts according to their needs for finance. The lessee can also pass on the risk of obsolescence to the lessor by acquiring those appliances, which have high technological obsolescence. To day, most of us are familiar with leases of houses, apartments, offices, etc.

## TYPES OF LEASE AGREEMENTS

Lease agreements are basically of two types.

*They are*:

1. Financial lease and
2. Operating lease.

*The other variations in lease agreements are*:

- Sale and lease back
- Leveraged leasing and
- Direct leasing.

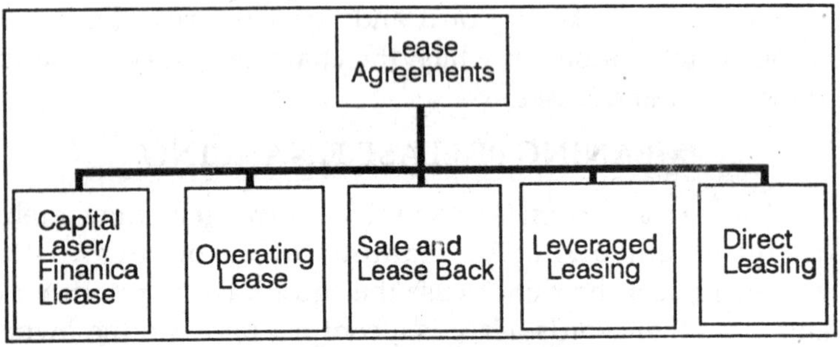


**Fig.** Types of Leases

## FINANCIAL LEASE

Long-term, non-cancellable lease contracts are known as financial leases. The essential point of financial lease agreement is that it contains a condition whereby the lessor agrees to transfer the title for the asset at the end of the lease period at a nominal cost.

At lease it must give an option to the lessee to purchase the asset he has used at the expiry of the lease. Under this lease the lessor recovers 90% of the fair value of the asset as lease rentals and the lease period is 75% of the economic life of the asset. The lease agreement is irrevocable. All the risks incidental to the asset ownership and all the benefits arising there from are transferred to the lessee who bears the cost of maintenance, insurance and repairs. Only title deeds remain with the lessor. Financial lease is also known as 'capital lease'. In India, financial leases are very popular with high-cost and high technology equipment.

## OPERATING LEASE

An operating lease stands in contrast to the financial lease in almost all aspects. This lease agreement gives to the lessee only a limited right to use the asset. The lessor is responsible for the upkeep and maintenance of the asset. The lessee is not given any uplift to purchase the asset at the end of the lease period.

Normally the lease is for a short period and even otherwise is revocable at a short notice. Mines, Computers hardware, trucks and automobiles are found suitable for operating lease because the rate of obsolescence is very high in this kind of assets.

## SALE AND LEASE BACK

It is a sub-part of finance lease. Under this, the owner of an asset sells the asset to a party, who in turn leases back the same asset to the owner in consideration of lease rentals. However, under this arrangement, the assets are not physically exchanged but it all happens in records only. This is nothing but a paper transaction. Sale and lease back transaction is suitable for those assets, which are not subjected depreciation but appreciation, say land. The advantage of this method is that the lessee can satisfy himself completely regarding the quality of the asset and after possession of the asset convert the sale into a lease arrangement. The sale and lease back transaction can be expressed with the help of the following figure.

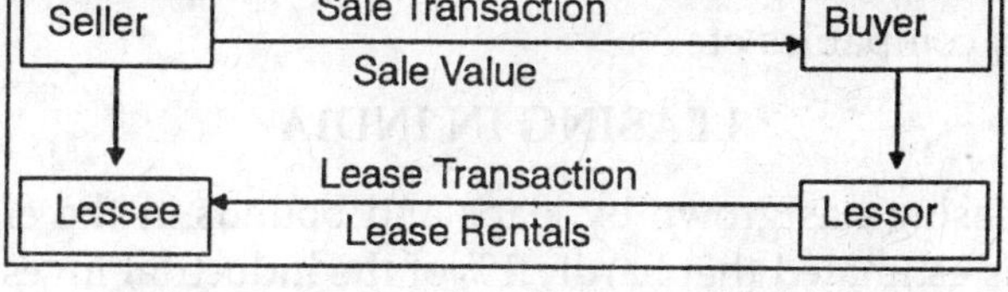


**Fig.** Structure of a sale and Leaseback Deal

Under this transaction, the seller assumes the role of a lessee and the buyer assumes the role of a lessor. The seller gets the agreed selling price and the buyer gets the lease rentals. It is possible to structure the sale at agreed value and to adjust difference in the lease rentals. Thus the effect of profit/ loss on sale of assets can be deferred.

## LEVERAGED LEASING

Under leveraged leasing arrangement, a third party is involved beside lessor and lessee. The lessor borrows a part of the purchase cost of the asset from the third party i.e., lender and the asset so purchased is held as security against the loan. The lender is paid off from the lease rentals directly by the lessee and the surplus after meeting the claims of the lender goes to the lessor. The lessor, the owner of the asset is entitled to depreciation allowance associated with the asset.

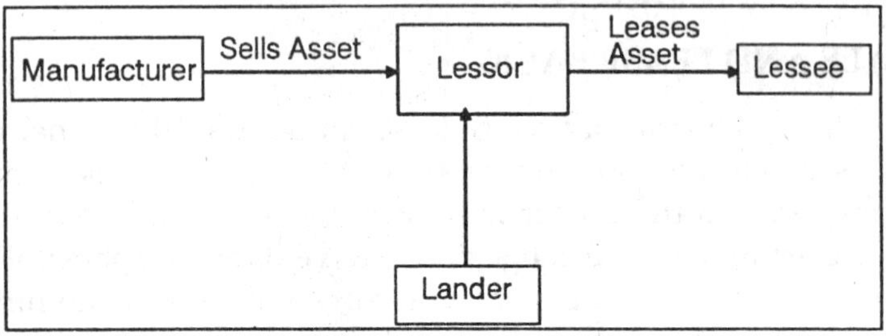


**Fig.** Leveraged Lease

## DIRECT LEASING

Under direct leasing, a firm acquires the right to use an asset from the manufacturer directly. The ownership of the asset leased out remains with the manufacturer itself. The major types of direct lessor include manufacturers, finance companies, independent lease companies, special purpose leasing companies etc

## LEASING IN INDIA

Leasing has grown by leaps and bounds in the eighties but it is estimated that hardly 1% of the industrial investment in India is covered by the lease finance, as against 40% in USA and 30% in UK and 10% in Japan.

The prospects of leasing in India are good due to growing investment needs and scarcity of funds with public financial institutions. This type of lease finances is particularly suitable in India where a large number of small companies have emerged more recently. Leasing in the sphere of land and building has been in existence in India for a long time, while equipment leasing has become very common in the recent times.

## CONCEPT AND MEANING OF HIRE PURCHASE

Hire purchase is a type of instalment credit under which the hire purchaser, called the hirer, agrees to take the goods on hire at a stated rental, which is inclusive of the repayment of principal as well as interest, with an option to purchase. Under this transaction, the hire purchaser acquires the property immediately on signing the hire purchase agreement but the ownership or title of the same is transferred only when the last instalment is paid. The hire purchase system is regulated by the Hire Purchase Act 1972.

This Act defines a hire purchase as"an agreement under which goods are let on hire and under which the hirer has an option to purchase them in accordance with the terms of the agreement and includes an agreement under which:

- The owner delivers possession of goods thereof to a person on condition that such person pays the agreed amount in periodic instalments.
- The property in the goods is to pass to such person on the payment of the last of such instalments, and
- Such person has a right to terminate the agreement at any time before the property so passes".

Hire purchase should be distinguished from instalment sale wherein property passes to the purchaser with the payment of the first instalment. But in case of HP buyer gets ownership after paying the last instalment. HP also differs form leasing.

**Table. Defference between Lease Financing and Hire Purchase**

| Basis | Lease Financing | Hire Purchase |
|---|---|---|
| Meaning | A lease transaction is a | Hire purchase is a |

| | | |
|---|---|---|
| | commercial arrangement whereby an equipment owner or manufacturer conveys to the equipment user the right to use the equipment in return for a rental. | type of instalment credit under which the hire purchaser agrees to take the goods on hire at a stated rental, which is inclusive of the repayment of principal as well as interest, with an option to purchase. |
| Option to user | No option is provided to the lessee (user) to purchase the goods. | Option is provided to the hirer (user). |
| Nature of expenditure | Lease rentals paid by the lessee are entirely revenue ependiture of the lesses. | Only Interest element included in the HP instalments is revenue expenditure by nature. |
| Components | Lease rentals comprise of 2 elements 1. finance charge and 2. Capital recovery. | HP instalments compriseof 3 elements 1. Normal trading profit 2. Finance charge and 3. Recovery of cost of goods/assest. |

## NSIC AND HIRE PURCHASE

Small scale firms can acquire industrial machinery, office equipment, vehicles, etc., without making full payment through hire purchase.

With the help of assets acquired through hire purchase they can produce and sell. From the earning payments can easily be made in instalments. Ultimately the ownership of assets can be acquired. Now several agencies like National Small Industries Corporation provide machinery and equipment to small scale units on hire purchase basis and on lease basis.

NSIC follows the following Hire Purchase procedure and Hire Purchase Plan for financing plant and machinery to small scale units.

## FACTORING

Factoring is another type of financial service provided by the specialist organizations. When small scale firms sell on credit basis, collection of receivable poses a problem. In that case factoring organizations play an important role in collection of debtors. Factoring involves sale of receivables to specialized firm, called factors. Factors collect receivables and also advance cash against receivables to solve the client firm's liquidity problem. For providing their services, they charge interest on advance and commission for other services. In other words, factoring is an arrangement under which a financial institution undertakes the task of collecting the book debts of its client in return for a service charge in the form of discount or rebate. The factoring institution eliminates the client's risk of bad debts by taking over the responsibility of book debts due to the client. The factoring institution advances a proportion of the value of book debts of the client immediately and the balance on maturity of book debts.

### FACTORING PROCEDURE

The agreement between the supplier and the factor specifies the factoring procedure. Usually the firm sends the customer's order to the factor for evaluating the customer's creditworthiness and approval. Once the factor is satisfied about the customer's credit worthiness and agrees to buy receivables, the firm dispatches goods to the customer.

The customer will be informed that his account has been sold to the factor, and he is instructed to make payment directly to the factor. To perform his functions of credit evaluation and collection for a large number of clients, a factor may maintain a credit department with specialized staff. Once the factor has purchased a firm's receivables and if he agrees to own them, he will have to provide protection against any bad-debt losses to the firm.

### MERITS

- As a result of factoring services, the enterprise can concentrate on manufacturing and selling.

- The risk of bad debts is eliminated.
- The factoring institution also provides advice on business trends and other related matters. In India, subsidiaries of four Indian banks-State Bank of India, Canara Bank, Punjab National Bank and Allahabad Bank are providing factoring services.

## ADVANTAGES OF LEASING

*Equipment leasing offers a number of important advantages:*

### LEASING PROVIDES 100 PER CENT FINANCING

Most leases simply require first and last payments paid in advance and a small documentation fee. No security deposits or up-front money is required. Enterprise Financial Solutions, Inc. pays your vendor in full including installation, delivery and taxes unless state law prohibits.

### LEASING PRESERVES CREDIT LINES

Credit lines with banks and other depository institutions are precious and hard to establish. Conserve those lines for inventory, A/R or other uses and emergencies. EFSI will take care of the financing for your capital equipment so that your lines of credit remain free.

### LEASING INCREASES PURCHASING POWER

Your needs may be for a $50,000 machine but your available cash/credit only allows for $30,000, hence you settle for a smaller piece of machinery that only meets your needs half-way. EFSI can increase your purchasing power by allowing you to finance the needed equipment for the job. That way you get the equipment you need to meet demand and promote growth.

### LEASING BALANCES USAGE AND COST

Leasing makes sense when the equipment you use creates a return that exceeds its cost. In other words, leasing allows you to set a fixed monthly payment for the use of equipment that creates an anticipated return exceeding that payment. That way you are certain that your operation is profitable and the equipment serves its purpose.

## LEASING PROVIDES FIXED RATE FINANCING

Leasing is not subject to market fluctuations and interest rate increases. You can negotiate the monthly payments up front and secure a fixed rate for the life of the lease. This makes it much easier to project cash flow and budgets for planning purposes.

## LEASING CONSERVES WORKING CAPITAL

Keep your hard-earned cash on hand or invested. Enterprise Financial Solutions, Inc. enables you to enjoy the working capital your company receives since it covers all costs associated with capital equipment purchases. This ability to grow and keep your cash ultimately puts you ahead of your competition and ensures long-term profitability.

## LEASING IS CONVENIENT

Unlike dealing with bank loans and other alternative types of financing, leasing is an easy and convenient process. Typically, all we require is a one-page application for any request up to $50,000.

## LEASING IS TAX-ADVANTAGED

When structured properly, a lease agreement may allow you to receive tax benefits. These benefits and their availability are subject to an array of factors and we suggest you talk with your accountant about these benefits. Similarly, any tax benefit received from the ownership of the equipment by EFSI is passed on to the lessee through competitive rates and lower fees.

## LEASING IS A HEDGE AGAINST INFLATION

Since your payments apply to the use of the equipment

you do not pay for ownership on equipment that consistently depreciates.

Furthermore, your cash savings can yield a return that fights inflationary pressures.

### LEASING PROVIDES FLEXIBLE PAYMENTS

Lease payments can be structured to meet your needs. This adjustment is possible by correcting the residual value of the equipment due at lease end. By changing your end of lease balloon payment from $10,000 to $25,000 for example, you can lower your monthly payment significantly.

### LEASING PROVIDES OPTIONS

Leasing provides flexible end of lease options. Equipment at the end of the lease term can returned, extended or purchased.

## DISADVANTAGES OF LEASING

Leasing is a preferred means of financing for certain businesses. However it is not for everyone. The type of industry and type of equipment required also need to be considered.

*Tax implications also need to be compared between leasing and purchasing equipment*:

- You have an obligation to continue making payments. Typically, leases may not be terminated before the original term is completed. Therefore, the renter is responsible for paying off the lease. This can pose a major financial problem for the owners of a business experiences a downturn.
- You have no equity until you decide to purchase the equipment at the end of the lease term, at which point the equipment has depreciated significantly.
- Although you are not the owner, you are still responsible for maintaining the equipment as specified by the terms of the lease. Failure to do so can prove costly.

## EVALUATION OF LEASE AGREEMENT

A Lease Agreement is a written document that sets down terms, rules and obligations that exist between the owner of the property and the person or entity that desires to lease the space. Rent or lease payments are the consideration paid by the renter to the owner in exchange for the renter's exclusive use of the property. Each and every term of a commercial lease agreement is negotiable - that is, the terms of the lease are contractually agreed-upon by the renter and the owner. Residential leases have certain statutory protections in so much as the State may require the owner to cap security deposits or follow rules protecting a tenant's privacy.

# 7

# Working Capital

## CONCEPT OF WORKING CAPITAL

Working capital is a measurement of an entity's current assets, after subtracting its liabilities. Sometimes referred to as operating capital, it is a valuation of the amount of liquidity a business or organization has for the running and building of the business. Generally speaking, companies with higher amounts of working capital are better positioned for success. They have the liquid assets needed to expand their business operations as desired.

Sometimes, a company will have a large amount of assets, but have very little with which to build the business and improve processes. Even a profitable company may have this problem. This can occur when a company has assets that are not easy to convert into cash.

Working capital can be expressed as a positive or negative number. When a company has more debts than current assets, it has negative working capital. When current assets outweigh debts, a company has positive working capital.

Changes in working capital will impact a business' cash flow. When working capital increases, the effect on cash flow is negative. This is often caused by the liquidation of inventory or the drawing of money from accounts that are due to be paid by the business. On the other hand, a decrease in working capital translates into less money to settle short-term debts.

Working capital is among the many important things that contribute to the success of a business. Without it, a business may cease to function properly or at all. Not only does a lack of working capital render a company unable to build and grow, but it may also leave a company with too little cash to pay its short-term obligations. Simply put, a company with a very low amount of working capital may be at risk of running out of money.

When a company has too little working capital, it can face financial difficulties and may even be forced toward bankruptcy. This is true of both very small companies and billion-dollar organizations. A company with this problem may pay creditors late or even skip payments. It may borrow money in an attempt to remain afloat. If late payments have affected the company's credit rating, it may have difficulty obtaining a loan at an affordable interest rate.

In some types of businesses, it isn't as much of a problem to have a lower amount of working capital. Companies that are operated on as cash basis, have fast inventory turnovers, and can generate cash quickly don't necessarily need as much working capital. For example, a grocery store might meet these requirements and do well with less working capital.

## CALCULATION

Current assets and current liabilities include three accounts which are of special importance.

*These accounts represent the areas of the business where managers have the most direct impact*:

- Accounts receivable
- Inventory, and
- Accounts payable.

The current portion of debt is critical, because it represents a short-term claim to current assets and is often secured by long term assets. Common types of short-term debt are bank loans and lines of credit.

An increase in working capital indicates that the business has either increased current assets or has decreased current liabilities, for example has paid off some short-term creditors.

*Implications on M&A*: The common commercial definition of working capital for the purpose of a working capital adjustment in an M&A transaction is equal to:

*Current Assets:* Current Liabilities excluding deferred tax assets/liabilities, excess cash, surplus assets and/or deposit balances.

Cash balance items often attract a one-for-one purchase price adjustment.

## WORKING CAPITAL MANAGEMENT

Decisions relating to working capital and short term financing are referred to as *working capital management*. These involve managing the relationship between a firm's short-term assets and its short-term liabilities. The goal of working capital management is to ensure that the firm is able to continue its operations and that it has sufficient cash flow to satisfy both maturing short-term debt and upcoming operational expenses.

### Decision Criteria

By definition, working capital management entails short term decisions - generally, relating to the next one year period - which are "reversible". These decisions are therefore not taken on the same basis as Capital Investment Decisions rather they will be based on cash flows and/ or profitability.

- One measure of cash flow is provided by the cash conversion cycle - the net number of days from the outlay of cash for raw material to receiving payment from the customer. As a management tool, this metric makes explicit the inter-relatedness of decisions relating to inventories, accounts receivable and payable, and cash. Because this number effectively corresponds to the time that the firm's cash is tied up in operations and unavailable for other activities, management generally aims at a low net count.
- In this context, the most useful measure of profitability is Return on capital. The result is shown as a percentage, determined by dividing relevant income for the 12 months by capital employed; Return on equity shows this result for the firm's shareholders. Firm value is enhanced when, and if, the return on capital, which results from working

capital management, exceeds the cost of capital. ROC measures are therefore useful as a management tool, in that they link short-term policy with long-term decision making.

## Management of Working Capital

Management will use a combination of policies and techniques for the management of working capital. These policies aim at managing the current assets and the short term financing, such that cash flows and returns are acceptable.

- *Cash management*: Identify the cash balance which allows for the business to meet day to day expenses, but reduces cash holding costs.
- *Inventory management*: Identify the level of inventory which allows for uninterrupted production but reduces the investment in raw materials - and minimizes reordering costs - and hence increases cash flow.
- *Debtors management*: Identify the appropriate credit policy, i.e. credit terms which will attract customers, such that any impact on cash flows and the cash conversion cycle will be offset by increased revenue and hence Return on Capital.
- *Short term financing*: Identify the appropriate source of financing, given the cash conversion cycle: the inventory is ideally financed by credit granted by the supplier; however, it may be necessary to utilize a bank loan or to"convert debtors to cash" through"factoring".

## FACTORS THAT AFFECT WORKING CAPITAL

How is it possible to calculate in advance how much working capital will be required, and thus keep on the safe side in providing capital funds? It is not possible to give an exact formula for answering this question, but an approximate answer in any given case may be reached. First of all, it is clear that the proportion of working capital in some lines of business is far greater than in other lines. This may be emphasised by two extreme cases. Telephone companies necessarily have large sums invested in wiring, poles, central offices, and other equipment, but after a complete telephone plant has been installed in a community the running expenses consist simply in maintenance and in the salaries of officers and employees and are comparatively light. It is the custom for telephone companies to render bills for their services once a month in advance; consequently, all the money which is required for running expenses from month to month is provided before the expenses are really incurred. Evidently there is no necessity in this instance for working capital, because the current receipts may safely be depended upon to take care of the current outgo.

On the other hand, let us take a retail store which occupies rented quarters. The only fixed assets required will consist of store furniture and equipment; all the other assets, including the stocks of merchandise, the accounts receivable, and the cash, are"current" or"working." The greater portion of the capital that must be invested in such an enterprise, will consist of working capital. This is true, all trading enterprises, and is particularly true of financial enterprises. Banks must keep all, or nearly all, of their assets in such a form as to be converted into cash almost at a moment's notice.

We may consider, therefore, as the first factor which determines the requirements of working capital, the general nature of the business. If the business consists merely of leasing real estate, providing facilities for transportation, and the like, all or nearly all of the investment will be in fixed forms. If the business is manufacturing, then a relatively small proportion will consist of working capital. If it is trading or financing, the chief requirement will be for working capital.

A second factor obviously is the volume of business. Generally speaking, the necessity for working capital will vary in proportion to the volume of sales. Making the assumption that methods, expenses, and terms of buying and selling goods and of producing the goods are standardized, then we may safely say that a 50% increase in output and sales will necessitate a proportionate increase in working capital. But these general remarks as to the nature and volume of business are serviceable chiefly in forestalling any misunderstanding of what follows.

*The practical considerations that require thought and are helpful in making estimates of working capital are:*

- Length of period of manufacture.
- Turnover.
- Terms of sale.
- Terms of purchase.
- Facilities for converting working assets into cash.
- Seasonal variations in business.

## DETERMINING WORKING CAPITAL REQUIREMENTS

- *Availability of Credit*: The amount of credit that a firm can obtain, as also the length of the credit period significantly affects the working capital requirement. The greater the prospects of getting credit, the smaller will be its requirement of working capital because it can easily purchase raw materials and other requirements on credit.

  Creditworthiness can also the interpreted to mean that the firm can function smoothly even with a smaller amount of working capital if it is assured that it can obtain loans from the bank immediately and easily. The firm does not need then to keep a wide margin of safety.
- *Growth and Expansion*: The working capital requirements increase with growth and expansion of business. Hence planning of the working capital requirements and its procurement must go hand in hand with the planning of the growth and expansion of the firm. The implementation of the production plan that aims at the growth or expansion of the unit necessitates more of fixed capital and working capital both.

  Even the expansion of the volume of sales increases the requirements of working capital. Of course, it is difficult to establish a quantitative relationship between them. An important point to be noted is that the requirements of working capital emerge before the growth or expansion actually takes place.

- *Profit and its Distribution*: The net profit of a firm is a good index of the resources available to it to meet its capital requirements. But, from the viewpoint of working capital requirement, it is the profit in the form of cash which is important, and not the net profit. The profit available in the form of cash is called cash profit and it can be assessed by adding or deducting non-cash items from the net profit of the firm. The larger the amount of cash profit, the greater will be the possibility of acquiring working capital.

  But, in fact the entire amount of cash profit may not be available to meet working capital needs. The portion of cash profit which is available for this purpose depends on the profit distribution policy. The policies with regard to distribution of dividends, ploughing back of profit and tax payments will determine the portion of cash profit which the firm can use to meet its working capital needs. Even depreciation policy can influence the amount of cash available, as depreciation of capital assets is deductible item of expenditure and it reduces tax liability.

- *Price Level Fluctuations*: A general statement may be made that with price rise, a firm will require more funds to purchase its current assets. In other words, the requirements of working capital will increase with the rise in prices. But all firms may not be affected equally. The prices of all current assets never go up to the same extent. Price of some current assets rise less rapidly than those of the others. Hence for the firms which use such current assets, the working capital need will increase by a smaller amount. Besides, if it is possible to pass on the burden of high prices of raw materials to the customers by raising the prices of final product, then also there will be no increase in working capital requirements.

- Operating Efficiency: If a firm is efficient, it can use its resources economically, and thereby it can reduce cost and earn more profit. Thus, the working capital requirement can be reduced by more efficient use of the current assets.

## RECEIVABLES MANAGEMENT

Managing and collecting commercial receivables is linked to the credit insurance business and the information business.

Coface has succeeded in considerably reducing its claims expenses by setting up efficient receivables management processes, developing excellent knowledge of local payment and collection regulations and practices, accurately predicting the commercial and financial behaviour of buyers throughout the world and closely monitoring changes in their behaviour.

Coface RBI provides a tailor-made service for the recovery of large trade debts in all countries. In the field of debt collection, Coface RBI responds to the needs of credit managers and financial groups with regard to atypical or complex transactions.

Collecting debts is a full time job that requires experienced, fully trained and efficient resources. Coface allows you to take advantage of its negotiating skills and legal expertise to collect cash on your behalf, either in our name or yours, on a confidential basis.

## INVENTORY MANAGEMENT

### INVENTORY

Inventory is a list for goods and materials, or those goods and materials themselves, held available in stock by a business. It is also used for a list of the contents of a household and for a list for testamentary purposes of the possessions of someone who has died. In accounting inventory is considered an asset.

In business management, inventory consists of a list of

goods and materials held available in stock. Labels: Inventory Management, Procurement, Supply Chain, Supply Chain Management

## INVENTORY MANAGEMENT

Inventory management is primarily about specifying the size and placement of stocked goods. Inventory management is required at different locations within a facility or within multiple locations of a supply network to protect the regular and planned course of production against the random disturbance of running out of materials or goods.

The scope of inventory management also concerns the fine lines between replenishment lead time, carrying costs of inventory, asset management, inventory forecasting, inventory valuation, inventory visibility, future inventory price forecasting, physical inventory, available physical space for inventory, quality management, replenishment, returns and defective goods and demand forecasting. Balancing these competing requirements leads to optimal inventory levels, which is an on-going process as the business needs shift and react to the wider environment.

*Other definitions of inventory management from across the web*: Involves a retailer seeking to acquire and maintain a proper merchandise assortment while ordering, shipping, handling, and related costs are kept in check. Systems and processes that identify inventory requirements, set targets, provide replenishment techniques and report actual and projected inventory status.

Handles all functions related to the tracking and management of material. This would include the monitoring of material moved into and out of stockroom locations and the reconciling of the inventory balances. Also may include ABC analysis, lot tracking, cycle counting support etc. Management of the inventories, with the primary objective of determining/controlling stock levels within the physical distribution function to balance the need for product availability against the need for minimizing stock holding and handling costs.

## BUSINESS INVENTORY

### Reasons for Keeping Stock

*There are three basic reasons for keeping an inventory:*

1. *Time*: The time lags present in the supply chain, from supplier to user at every stage, requires that you maintain certain amount of inventory to use in this"lead time".
2. *Uncertainty*: Inventories are maintained as buffers to meet uncertainties in demand, supply and movements of goods.
3. *Economies of scale*: Ideal condition of"one unit at a time at a place where user needs it, when he needs it" principle tends to incur lots of costs in terms of logistics. So bulk buying, movement and storing brings in economies of scale, thus inventory.

*All these stock reasons can apply to any owner or product stage*:

- Buffer stock is held in individual workstations against the possibility that the upstream workstation may be a little delayed in long setup or change-over time. This stock is then used while that change-over is happening. This stock can be eliminated by tools like SMED.

These classifications apply along the whole Supply chain not just within a facility or plant. Where these stocks contain the same or similar items it is often the work practice to hold all these stocks mixed together before or after the sub-process to which they relate. This'reduces' costs. Because they are mixed-up together there is no visual reminder to operators of the adjacent sub-processes or line management of the stock which is due to a particular cause and should be a particular individual's responsibility with inevitable consequences. Some plants have centralized stock holding across sub-processes which makes the situation even more acute.

### Special Terms Used in Dealing With Inventory

- *Stock Keeping Unit* is a unique combination of all the components that are assembled into the purchasable item. Therefore any change in the packaging or product is a new SKU. This level of detailed specification assists in managing inventory.

- *Stockout* means running out of the inventory of an SKU.
- "New old stock" is a term used in business to refer to merchandise being offered for sale which was manufactured long ago but that has never been used. Such merchandise may not be produced any more, and the new old stock may represent the only market source of a particular item at the present time.

## PRINCIPLE OF INVENTORY PROPORTIONALITY

### Purpose

Inventory proportionality is the goal of demand driven inventory management. The primary optimal outcome is to have the same number of days worth of inventory on hand across all products so that the time of runout of all products would be simultaneous. In such a case, there is no "excess inventory", that is, inventory that would be left over of another product when the first product runs out. Excess inventory is sub-optimal because the money spent to obtain it could have been deployed better elsewhere, i.e. to the product that just ran out.

The secondary goal of inventory proportionality is inventory minimization. By integrating accurate demand forecasting with inventory management, replenishment inventories can be scheduled to arrive just in time to replenish the product destined to run out first, while at the same time balancing out the inventory supply of all products to make their inventories more proportional, and thereby closer to achieving the primary goal. Accurate demand forecasting also allows the desired inventory proportions to be dynamic by determining expected sales out into the future; this allows for inventory to be in proportion to expected short term sales or consumption rather than to past averages, a much more accurate and optimal outcome.

Integrating demand forecasting with inventory management in this way also allows for the prediction of the "can fit" point when inventory storage is limited on a per product basis.

## Applications

The technique of inventory proportionality is most appropriate for inventories that remain unseen by the consumer. As opposed to "keep full" systems where a retail consumer would like to see full shelves of the product they are buying so as not to think they are buying something old, unwanted, or stale; and differentiated from the "trigger point" systems where product is reordered when it hits a certain level; inventory proportionality is used effectively by just-in-time manufacturing processes and retail applications where the product is hidden from view.

One early example of inventory proportionality used in a retail application in the United States is for motor fuel. Motor fuel is generally stored in underground storage tanks. The motorists do not know whether they are buying gasoline off the top or bottom of the tank, nor need they care. Additionally, these storage tanks have a maximum capacity and cannot be overfilled.

Finally, the product is expensive. Inventory proportionality is used to balance the inventories of the different grades of motor fuel, each stored in dedicated tanks, in proportion to the sales of each grade. Excess inventory is not seen or valued by the consumer, so it is simply cash sunk into the ground. Inventory proportionality minimizes the amount of excess inventory carried in underground storage tanks. This application for motor fuel was first developed and implemented by Petrolsoft Corporation in 1990 for Chevron Products Company. Most major oil companies use such systems today.

## Roots

The use of Inventory Proportionality in the United States is thought to have been inspired by Japanese just-in-time parts inventory management made famous by Toyota Motors in the 1980s.

## HIGH LEVEL INVENTORY MANAGEMENT

It seems that around about 1880 there was a change in manufacturing practice from companies with relatively homogeneous lines of products to vertically integrated companies with unprecedented diversity in processes and products.

Those companies attempted to achieve success through economies of scope - the gains of jointly producing two or more products in one facility.

The managers now needed information on the effect of product mix decisions on overall profits and therefore needed accurate product cost information. A variety of attempts to achieve this were unsuccessful due to the huge overhead of the information processing of the time.

However, the burgeoning need for financial reporting after 1900 created unavoidable pressure for financial accounting of stock and the management need to cost manage products became overshadowed. In particular it was the need for audited accounts that sealed the fate of managerial cost accounting.

The dominance of financial reporting accounting over management accounting remains to this day with few exceptions and the financial reporting definitions of 'cost' have distorted effective management 'cost' accounting since that time. This is particularly true of inventory.

*Hence high level financial inventory has these two basic formulas which relate to the accounting period:*

- Cost of Beginning Inventory at the start of the period + inventory purchases within the period + cost of production within the period = cost of goods
- Cost of goods " cost of ending inventory at the end of the period = cost of goods sold

The benefit of these formulae is that the first absorbs all overheads of production and raw material costs in to a value of inventory for reporting.

Manufacturing management is more interested in *inventory turnover ratio* or *average days to sell inventory* since it tells them something about relative inventory levels.

Inventory turn over ratio = cost of goods sold/ Average Inventory = Cost of Goods Sold/ ((Beginning Inventory + Ending Inventory)/ 2) and its inverse

Average Days to Sell Inventory = Number of Days a Year/ Inventory Turn Over Ratio = 365 days a year/ Inventory Turn Over Ratio. This ratio estimates how many times the inventory turns over a year. This number tells us how much cash/goods are tied up waiting for the process and is a critical measure of process reliability and effectiveness. So a factory with two inventory turns has six months stock on hand which generally not a good figure whereas a factory that moves from six turns to twelve turns has probably improved effectiveness by 100%. This improvement will have some negative results in the financial reporting since the 'value' now stored in the factory as inventory is reduced.

Whilst the simplicity of these accounting measures of inventory are very useful they are in the end fraught with the danger of their own assumptions. There are in fact so many things which can vary hidden under this appearance of simplicity that a variety of 'adjusting' assumptions may be used.

*These include*:

- Specific Identification
- Weighted Average Cost
- Moving-Average Cost
- FIFO and LIFO.

Inventory Turn is a financial accounting tool for evaluating inventory and it is not necessarily a management tool. Inventory management should be forward looking. The methodology applied is based on historical cost of goods sold. The ratio may not be able to reflect the usability of future production demand as well as customer demand.

Business models including Just in Time Inventory, Vendor Managed Inventory and Customer Managed Inventory attempt to minimize on-hand inventory and increase inventory turns. VMI and CMI have gained considerable attention due to the success of third party vendors who offer added expertise and knowledge that organizations may not possess.

## Specific Identification

Specific Identification is a method of finding out ending inventory cost. It requires a very detailed physical count, so that the company knows exactly how many of each goods brought on specific dates remained at year end inventory. When this information is found, the amount of goods are multiplied by their purchase cost at their purchase date, to get a number for the ending inventory cost.

On theory, this method is the best method, since it relates the ending inventory goods directly to the specific price they were bought for. However, this method allows management to easily manipulate ending inventory cost, since they can choose to report that the cheaper goods were sold first, hence increasing ending inventory cost and lowering Cost of Goods Sold. This will increase the income. Alternatively, management can choose to report lower income, to reduce the taxes they needed to pay. This method is also very hard to use on interchangeable goods. For example, it is hard to relate shipping and storage costs to a specific inventory item. These number will need to be estimated, and hence reducing the specific identification 's benefit of being extremely specific.

## Weighted Average Cost

Weighted Average Cost is a method of calculating Ending Inventory cost. It takes Cost of Goods Available for Sale and divides it by the total amount of goods from Beginning Inventory and Purchases. This gives a Weighted Average Cost per Unit. A physical count is then performed on the ending inventory to determine the amount of goods left. Finally, this amount is multiplied by Weighted Average Cost per Unit to give an estimate of ending inventory cost.

## Moving-Average Cost

Moving-Average Unit Cost is a method of calculating

Ending Inventory cost. Assume that both Beginning Inventory and beginning inventory cost are known. From them the *Cost per Unit of Beginning Inventory* can be calculated. During the year, multiple purchases were made. Each time, purchase costs are added to beginning inventory cost to get *Cost of Current Inventory*.

Similarly, the number of units bought is added to beginning inventory to get *Current Goods Available for Sale*. After each purchase, Cost of Current Inventory is divided by Current Goods Available for Sale to get *Current Cost per Unit on Goods*. Also during the year, multiple sales happened. The Current Goods Available for Sale is deducted by the amount of goods sold, and the Cost of Current Inventory is deducted by the amount of goods sold times the latest. Current Cost per Unit on Goods. This deducted amount is added to Cost of Goods Sold. At the end of the year, the last Cost per Unit on Goods, along with a physical count, is used to determine ending inventory cost.

## FIFO and LIFO Accounting

FIFO and LIFO accounting Methods are means of managing inventory and financial matters involving the money a company tied up within inventory of produced goods, raw materials, parts, components, or feed stocks. FIFO stands for first-in, first-out, meaning that the oldest inventory items are recorded as sold first. LIFO stands for last-in, first-out, meaning that the most recently purchased items are recorded as sold first. Since the 1970s, U.S. companies have tended to use LIFO, which reduces their income taxes in times of inflation.

### *LIFO Liquidation*

Notwithstanding its deferred tax advantage, a LIFO inventory system can lead to LIFO liquidation, a situation where in the absence of new replacement inventory or a search for increased profits, older inventory is increasingly liquidated. If prices have been rising, for example through inflation, this older inventory will have a lower cost, and its liquidation leads to the recognition of higher net income and the payment of higher taxes, thus reversing the deferred tax advantage that initially encouraged the adoption of a LIFO system. Some companies who use LIFO have decades-old inventory recorded on their books at a very low cost. For these companies a LIFO liquidation results in an inflated net income. Companies can use liquidations to manage their earnings.

Also mobile telecom operators either use FIFO or LIFO to allocate remaining call credit a customer did not fully use in a billing period. In telecom terms FIFO is good for the customers while LIFO is good for the telecom operator. With small amount of carry over duration, call credit is to be lost sooner with LIFO then with FIFO as a customer first uses his old call credit rather than first needing to use all the new credit before using the old call credit.

## ACCOUNTING FOR INVENTORY

Each country has its own rules about accounting for inventory that fit with their financial reporting rules.

So for example, organizations in the U.S. define inventory to suit their needs within US Generally Accepted Accounting Practices (GAAP), the rules defined by the Financial Accounting Standards Board (FASB) and enforced by the U.S. Securities and Exchange Commission (SEC) and other federal and state agencies. Other countries often have similar arrangements but with their own GAAP and national agencies instead.

It is intentional that financial accounting uses standards that allow the public to compare firms' performance, cost accounting functions internally to an organization and potentially with much greater flexibility. A discussion of inventory from standard and Theory of Constraints-based cost accounting perspective follows some examples and a discussion of inventory from a financial accounting perspective.

The internal costing/valuation of inventory can be complex. Whereas in the past most enterprises ran simple one process factories, this is quite probably in the minority in the

21st century. Where 'one process' factories exist then there is a market for the goods created which establishes an independent market value for the good. Today with multi-stage process companies there is much inventory that would once have been finished goods which is now held as 'work-in-process'. This needs to be valued in the accounts but the valuation is a management decision since there is no market for the partially finished product. This somewhat arbitrary 'valuation' of WIP combined with the allocation of overheads to it has led to some unintended and undesirable results.

## Financial Accounting

An organization's inventory can appear a mixed blessing, since it counts as an asset on the balance sheet, but it also ties up money that could serve for other purposes and requires additional expense for its protection. Inventory may also cause significant tax expenses, depending on particular countries' laws regarding depreciation of inventory, as in Thor Power Tool Company v. Commissioner.

Inventory appears as a current asset on an organization's balance sheet because the organization can, in principle, turn it into cash by selling it. Some organizations hold larger inventories than their operations require in order to inflate their apparent asset value and their perceived profitability.

In addition to the money tied up by acquiring inventory, inventory also brings associated costs for warehouse space, for utilities, and for insurance to cover staff to handle and protect it, fire and other disasters, obsolescence, shrinkage and others. Such holding costs can mount up: between a third and a half of its acquisition value per year.

Businesses that stock too little inventory cannot take advantage of large orders from customers if they cannot deliver. The conflicting objectives of cost control and customer service often pit an organization's financial and operating managers against its sales and marketing departments. Sales people, in particular, often receive sales commission payments, so unavailable goods may reduce their potential personal income. This conflict can be minimised by reducing production time to being near or less than customer expected delivery time. This effort, known as "Lean production" will significantly reduce working capital tied up in inventory and reduce manufacturing costs.

## Role of Inventory Accounting

By helping the organization to make better decisions, the accountants can help the public sector to change in a very positive way that delivers increased value for the taxpayer's investment. It can also help to incentivise progress and to ensure that reforms are sustainable and effective in the long term, by ensuring that success is appropriately recognized in both the formal and informal reward systems of the organization.

To say that they have a key role to play is an understatement. Finance is connected to most, if not all, of the key business processes within the organization. It should be steering the stewardship and accountability systems that ensure that the organization is conducting its business in an appropriate, ethical manner. It is critical that these foundations are firmly laid. So often they are the litmus test by which public confidence in the institution is either won or lost.

Finance should also be providing the information, analysis and advice to enable the organizations' service managers to operate effectively. This goes beyond the traditional preoccupation with budgets – how much have we spent so far, how much have we left to spend? It is about helping the organization to better understand its own performance. That means making the connections and understanding the relationships between given inputs – the resources brought to bear – and the outputs and outcomes that they achieve. It is also about understanding and actively managing risks within the organization and its activities.

## FIFO vs. LIFO Accounting

When a merchant buys goods from inventory, the value of the inventory account is reduced by the cost of goods sold. This is simple where the CoG has not varied across those held in stock; but where it has, then an agreed method must be derived to evaluate it. For commodity items that one cannot track individually, accountants must choose a method that fits the nature of the sale. Two popular methods which normally exist are: FIFO and LIFO accounting. FIFO regards the first unit that arrived in inventory as the first one sold. LIFO considers the last unit arriving in inventory as the first one sold. Which method an accountant selects can have a significant effect on net income and book value and, in turn, on taxation. Using LIFO accounting for inventory, a company generally reports lower net income and lower book value, due to the effects of inflation. This generally results in lower taxation. Due to LIFO's potential to skew inventory value, UK GAAP and IAS have effectively banned LIFO inventory accounting.

**Standard Cost Accounting**

Standard cost accounting uses ratios called efficiencies that compare the labour and materials actually used to produce a good with those that the same goods would have required under "standard" conditions. As long as similar actual and standard conditions obtain, few problems arise. Unfortunately, standard cost accounting methods developed about 100 years ago, when Labour comprised the most important cost in manufactured goods. Standard methods continue to emphasize Labour efficiency even though that resource now constitutes a small part of cost in most cases.

Standard cost accounting can hurt managers, workers, and firms in several ways. For example, a policy decision to increase inventory can harm a manufacturing managers' performance evaluation. Increasing inventory requires increased production, which means that processes must operate at higher rates. When something goes wrong, the process takes longer and uses more than the standard Labour time. The manager appears responsible for the excess, even though s/he has no control over the production requirement or the problem.

In adverse economic times, firms use the same efficiencies

to downsize, rightsize, or otherwise reduce their Labour force. Workers laid off under those circumstances have even less control over excess inventory and cost efficiencies than their managers. Many financial and cost accountants have agreed for many years on the desirability of replacing standard cost accounting. They have not, however, found a successor.

### Theory of Constraints Cost Accounting

Eliyahu M. Goldratt developed the Theory of Constraints in part to address the cost-accounting problems in what he calls the"cost world". He offers a substitute, called throughput accounting, that uses throughput in place of output and considers Labour as a fixed rather than as a variable cost. He defines inventory simply as everything the organization owns that it plans to sell, including buildings, machinery, and many other things in addition to the categories listed here. Throughput accounting recognizes only one class of variable costs: the trully variable costs like materials and components that vary directly with the quantity produced.

Finished goods inventories remain balance-sheet assets, but Labour efficiency ratios no longer evaluate managers and workers. Instead of an incentive to reduce Labour cost, throughput accounting focuses attention on the relationships between throughput on one hand and controllable operating expenses and changes in inventory on the other. Those relationships direct attention to the constraints or bottlenecks that prevent the system from producing more throughput, rather than to people - who have little or no control over their situations.

## NATIONAL ACCOUNTS

Inventories also play an important role in national accounts and the analysis of the business cycle. Some short-term macroeconomic fluctuations are attributed to the inventory cycle.

## DISTRESSED INVENTORY

Also known as distressed or expired stock, distressed

inventory is inventory whose potential to be sold at a normal cost has or will soon pass. In certain industries it could also mean that the stock is or will soon be impossible to sell. Examples of distressed inventory include products that have reached their expiry date, or have reached a date in advance of expiry at which the planned market will no longer purchase them, clothing that is defective or out of fashion, and old newspapers or magazines. It also includes computer or consumer-electronic equipment that is obsolescent or discontinued and whose manufacturer is unable to support it. One current example of distressed inventory is the VHS format.

## INVENTORY CREDIT

Inventory credit refers to the use of stock, or inventory, as collateral to raise finance. Where banks may be reluctant to accept traditional collateral, for example in developing countries where land title may be lacking, inventory credit is a potentially important way of overcoming financing constraints. This is not a new concept; archaeological evidence suggests that it was practiced in Ancient Rome. Obtaining finance against stocks of a wide range of products held in a bonded warehouse is common in much of the world. It is, for example, used with Parmesan cheese in Italy. Inventory credit on the basis of stored agricultural produce is widely used in Latin American countries and in some Asian countries. A precondition for such credit is that banks must be confident that the stored product will be available if they need to call on the collateral; this implies the existence of a reliable network of certified warehouses. Banks also face problems in valuing the inventory. The possibility of sudden falls in commodity prices means that they are usually reluctant to lend more than about 60% of the value of the inventory at the time of the loan.

## INVENTORY CONTROL

Inventory control means keeping the overall costs associated with having inventory as low as possible without creating problems. This is also sometimes called stock control.

It is an important part of any business that must have a stock of products or items on hand.

Correctly managing inventory control is a delicate balance at all times between having too much and too little in order to maximize profits. The costs associated with holding stock, running out of stock, and placing orders must all be looked at and compared in order to find the right formula for a particular business.

It is impossible to have an unlimited supply on hand, for a number of different reasons. Many businesses simply don't have enough money to keep excessively large inventories. There are costs associated with purchasing the items as well as storing them, and having too many products leads to further losses when they don't move off of the shelves.

At the same time, there are issues with inventory control when there isn't enough stock on hand. One common problem is running out of inventory, which is caused by trying to reduce inventory costs too much. This is something that no business wants to have happen, but it happens to virtually all of them at some point. Even the largest stores run out of certain products from time to time when they sell or use more than they expected.

This can cause financial losses when inventory is not available for customers to purchase. Part of inventory control is trying to minimize shortages so these are rare occurrences. Most businesses expect they will have shortages on occasion and they have calculated that the small loss is worth the money saved by not having an overstock.

Another important element of inventory control is called reorder point. Businesses need to think ahead and calculate the best time for reordering products.

Doing so too soon may cause financial difficulties or running out of space. On the other hand, waiting to long to reorder will result in a shortage and running out of inventory before the next shipment arrives. When figuring out a reorder point, it's necessary to calculate how long it will take the shipment to arrive and the amount of demand for a particular item. The overhead costs, fees, and shipping expenses of ordering large versus small quantities should also be looked at. Inventory control is an ongoing process that is rarely, if ever, executed perfectly. Experience, expertise, and practice help people to make the best decisions regarding stock, but there are always unknown circumstances and variables. Stores can make good estimates about how many of a specific product they will sell, but they get things wrong from time to time. This is unavoidable. Inventory control can break a business if it is executed poorly, because either expenses will be too high or customers will get tired of dealing with shortages and find another place to spend their money.

## ORDER PICKING

Order picking is the process by which products are retrieved from specified storage locations on the basis of customer orders. In general, the order picking process is the most laborious of alle warehouse processes. It may consume as much as 60% of all labour activities in the warehouse.

*Improving order picking efficiency generally means minimizing the total expected order picking time, which includes four components*:

- Travel time incurred in picking an order which corresponds to the length of a picking tour starting and ending at a depot. Travel time can be seen as the sum of the 'within aisle' travel time, i.e. time spent travelling within stocking aisles, and the 'across aisles' travel time, i.e. time spent moving along cross-aisles from one stocking aisle to another.
- Processing time at the location points, i.e. the time required to execute tasks such as searching for pick locations, extracting items, documenting picking activity.
- Administrative time incurred at the start and finish of a picking tour, i.e. the time spent on administrative and start-up tasks, e.g. collecting or depositing a pick device, obtaining a pick list, etc.
- A fourth component of the total order picking time is the waiting time for the next job. If one job is

finished and the next can not be executed yet, then the picker has to wait.

## AVERAGE COST

The term average cost has slightly different meanings in economics and accounting. In economics it is simply the total cost of products manufactured over a period divided by the number of units produced.

It accounting it is a method of allocating costs to units of stock: i.e.: an alternative to FIFO, LIFO and replacement cost. An average cost is a weighted average of the cost of all units available over a period, both those remaining from previous periods, and those purchased during a period. More recent purchases are more heavily weighted.

## CUMULATIVE/PERPETUAL AVERAGE COSTING

When using this method a new cost per unit is calculated whenever new stocks are received:

*unit cost = (total value of old stock + total cost of receipts) ÷ (units of old stocks + units of received)*

*total cost of old stock = old unit cost × units of old stock, bar rounding errors.*

When stocks are issued they are costed at the unit cost recalculated after the last receipt and *unit cost × quantity issued* is deducted from the total cost of stocks.

## PERIODIC WEIGHTED AVERAGE COST

This calculation is broadly similar, except that the unit cost is calculated only at the end of a period. Issues during that period are issued at that unit cost. This calculation is simpler, both to calculate and because record keeping is simpler. The disadvantage is obvious: the numbers are not available until the period end.

## CAPITAL SPARE

Capital Spare are those specific spare parts although acknowledged to have a long life or a small chance of failure would cause shutdown of equipment for a prolonged period because of the long delivery of their replacement.

## CARRYING COST

Carrying cost is the cost of maintaining, and holding inventory. Warehouse, insurance costs, financing costs, pilferage, obsolescence, and spoilage are the major components of this cost.

In business case analysis, carrying costs could be entered as non-capital expenses on scenario cash flow statements. On the other hand, carrying cost savings or costs avoided could be entered directly on an incremental cash flow statement as benefits/gains. For more on the treatment of costs, cost savings, avoided costs, and cash flow in the business case.

## COST OF GOODS SOLD

Cost of goods sold is the expense a company incurred in order to manufacture, create, or sell a product. It includes the purchase price of the raw material as well as the expenses of turning it into a product. Cost of goods sold is also known as cost of revenue or cost of sales.

Going back to our pizza parlor example, your cost of goods sold include the amount of money you spent purchasing items such as flour and tomato sauce.

The cost of goods sold per dollar of sales is going to be different depending upon the type of business you own or in which you buy shares of stock. A licensing company or law firm will have virtually no cost of goods sold because they are selling a service and not a tangible product.

Before you invest in a business, you'll want to research the industry you are examining and find out what is considered "good". For corporations that drill for oil, for instance, one of the most important figures you need to consider is the cost per barrel to get the oil out of the ground. This is, in effect, the cost of goods sold for the oil company. If one firm can get crude at far lower costs than its competitors, it has a distinct advantage and will result in more profit flowing to the owners or shareholders.

Another thing you want to try and figure out is how exposed a company is to a particular input cost. For Southwest Airlines, the cost of jet fuel is the most important cost the company has. For Starbucks or Folgers, now a division of J.M. Smucker's, it's coffee. For Coca-Cola, sugar prices are extremely important. One of the reasons some investors are extremely successful is because they know the exact relationship between profits and cost of goods sold. It's been noted that Warren Buffett knows the per 12 ounce can profitability figures for a serving of Coca-Cola and watches sugar prices regularly. If you were a small candy company, or even a giant like Coke, periods of time such as April to July of 2009 would have been hard for your business as sugar prices nearly doubled without warning. As an investor, you need to be aware of the risk a business faces due to unexpected higher cost of goods sold regardless of if you are buying shares of stock, purchasing a local business, or launching your own start-up.

## COST OF GOODS AVAILABLE FOR SALE

Cost of Goods Available for Sale is the maximum amount of goods, or inventory, that a company can possibly sell during this fiscal year. It has the formula: Beginning Inventory + Purchases + Production = Cost of Goods Available for Sale Notice that purchases and production might not be the same throughout the year, since purchase cost and production cost might vary during the year. But at the end, the total cost of purchases and production are added to beginning inventory cost to give Cost of Goods Available for Sale.

## DECOMPOSITION

Decomposition or rotting is the process by which tissues of a dead organism break down into simpler forms of matter. The process is essential for new growth and development of living organisms because it recycles the finite matter that occupies physical space in the biome. Bodies of living organisms begin to decompose recently after death. It is a cascade of processes that go through distinct phases. It may be categorized in two stages by the types of end products. The first stage is characterized by the formation of liquid materials; flesh or plant matter begin to decompose. The second stage is limited to the production of vapors. The science which studies such decomposition generally is called *taphonomy* from the Greek word *taphos*, which means grave.

*Historically, the progression of decomposition of the flesh of dead organisms has been viewed also as four phases*:

1. Fresh,
2. Bloat,
3. Decay,
4. Dry.

## AMBIENT CONDITIONS

### Exposed to the Elements

A dead body that is exposed to the open elements, such as water and air, will decompose more quickly and attract much more insect activity than a body that is buried or confined in special protective gear or artifacts. This is due, in part, to the limited number of insects that can penetrate a coffin and the lower temperatures under soil.

### Media for Bacterial Growth

Similarly, a submerged body is shielded from air-living organisms; however, it is exposed to a new set of waterborne breakdown agents such as the bountiful water life and marine bacteria.

### Ambient Temperature

Ultimately, the rate of bacterial decomposition acting on the tissue will depend upon the temperature of the surroundings. Colder temperatures decrease the rate of decomposition while warmer temperatures increase it.

## PLANT DECOMPOSITION

Decomposition of plant matter occurs in many stages. It begins with leaching by water; the most easily lost and soluble carbon compounds are liberated in this process. Another early process is physical breakup or fragmentation of the plant material into smaller bits which have greater surface area for microbial colonization and attack. In smaller dead plants, this process is largely carried out by the soil invertebrate fauna, whereas in the larger plants, primarily parasitic life-forms such as insects and fungi play a major breakdown role and are not assisted by numerous detritivore species.

Following this, the plant detritus undergoes chemical alteration by microbes. Different types of compounds decompose at different rates.

This is dependent on their chemical structure. For instance, lignin is a component of wood, which is relatively resistant to decomposition and can in fact only be decomposed by certain fungi, such as the black-rot fungi. Said fungi are thought to be seeking the nitrogen content of lignin rather than its carbon content.

Lignin is one such remaining product of decomposing plants with a very complex chemical structure causing the rate of microbial breakdown to slow. Warmth determines the speed of plant decay, with the rate of decay increasing as heat increases, e.g. a plant in a warm environment will decay over a shorter period of time.

In most grassland ecosystems, natural damage from fire, insects that feed on decaying matter, termites, grazing mammals, and the physical movement of animals through the grass are the primary agents of breakdown and nutrient cycling, while bacteria and fungi play the main roles in further decomposition. The chemical aspects of plant decomposition always involve the release of carbon dioxide.

## ENDING INVENTORY

Ending inventory is the amount of inventory a company have in stock at the end of this fiscal year. It is closely related with Ending Inventory Cost, which is the amount of money spent to get these goods in stock. It should be calculated at the Lower of Cost or Market.

## FINISHED GOOD

Finished goods are goods that have completed the manufacturing process but have not yet been sold or distributed to the end user.

### Manufacturing

*Manufacturing has three classes of inventory:*

1. Raw material
2. Work in process
3. Finished goods

A good purchased as a "raw material" goes into the manufacture of a product. A good only partially completed during the manufacturing process is called "work in process". When the good is completed as to manufacturing but not yet sold or distributed to the end-user, it is called a "finished good". Finished goods is a relative term. In a Supply chain management flow, the finished goods of a supplier can constitute the raw material of a buyer.

## STOCK-TAKING

A Stocktake involves the physical verification of the quantities and condition of items held in an inventory, warehouse etc, in order to provide an accurate audit of existing inventory and stock valuation. It is also the source of stock discrepancy information.

## STOCK OBSOLESCENCE

Obsolete stock or stock obsolescence calculations are done by companies to determine how much of their stock on hand is unlikely to be used in the future.

The financial value of stock obsolescence that is calculated can be entered into a general ledger system to create a "stock obsolescence provision" which can reduce the tax liability of a company. For this reason, a systematic and auditable approach to designing a stock obsolescence report should be used. Estimation of stock obsolescence without any traceable calculations will probably not be acceptable to an auditor.

Typically, a stock obsolescence report uses the value of "stock on hand" as a starting point, and then reduces this value based on the potential that stock will be used up in the future. The higher the probability that stock will be used in the future, the more the on-hand stock value can be reduced. Sometimes a historical usage of the item can also reduce the value, in this case, the more recently the item was used, the more the on-hand value can be reduced.

The formulae that calculate how much the on-hand value can be reduced by may vary from company to company and are normally described in a general way in the GAAP for that company or country. For example one formula may be: "If there is any future usage of the item in the next 3 months then reduce the value by 100%, if there is usage in the next 6 months then reduce by 50%, and if it is only going to be used in a year's time then reduce by 10%, if it has been used in the past 6 months then reduce by 70%, if there has been usage in the past year then reduce by 30%".

*Some formulae may also take into account the volume used e.g.:* reduce the on-hand value by the percentage of product used in the past 6 months.

## STOCK AND FLOW

Economics, business, accounting, and related fields often distinguish between quantities that are stocks and those that are flows. These differ in their units of measurement. A *stock* variable is measured at one specific time, and represents a quantity existing at that point in time, which may have accumulated in the past.

A *flow* variable is measured over an interval of time. Therefore a flow would be measured *per unit of time*. Flow is roughly analogous to rate or speed in this sense.

For example, U.S. nominal gross domestic product refers to a total number of dollars spent during a specific time period, such as a year. Therefore it is a flow variable, and has units of dollars/year. In contrast, the U.S. nominal capital stock is the total value, in dollars, of equipment, buildings, inventories, and other real assets in the U.S. economy, and has units of dollars. An intuitive illustration of how the *stock* of capital currently available is increased by the *flow* of new investment and depleted by the *flow* of depreciation.

### Stocks and Flows in Accounting

Thus, a stock refers to the value of an asset at a balance

date, while a flow refers to the total value of transactions during an accounting period. If the flow value of an economic activity is divided by the average stock value during an accounting period, we obtain a measure of the number of turnovers of a stock in that accounting period. Some accounting entries are normally always represented as a flow, while others may be represented both as a stock or as a flow.

A person or country might have stocks of money, financial assets, liabilities, wealth, real means of production, capital, and human capital. Income, spending, saving, debt repayment, Labour, or stocks averaged over a unit of time, such as the money in circulation per year.

## Comparing Stocks and Flows

Stocks and flows have different units and are thus not *commensurable* – they cannot be meaningfully *compared, equated, added, or subtracted*. However, one may meaningfully take *ratios* of stocks and flows, or multiply or divide them. This is a point of some confusion in economics, as some confuse taking ratios with comparing. The ratio of a stock over a flow has units of (units)/(units/time) = time. For example, the debt to GDP ratio has units of years (as GDP is generally GDP per year), which yields the interpretation of the debt to GDP ratio as "number of years to pay off all debt, assuming all GDP devoted to debt repayment".

A confusing point is that fixing a standard increment of time allows one to convert a flow to a stock by multiplying by time—in calculus terms, integrating over time. For example, the total US GDP in 2000 has units of dollars. Thus in ratios of stocks to flows, the time dimension is often eliminated and the ratio expressed as a percentage.

## More General Uses

Stocks and flows also have natural meanings in many contexts outside of business and its related fields. Thus stocks and flows are the basic building blocks of system dynamics models. Jay Forrester originally referred to them as"levels" and"rates".

A stock in this broader sense is some entity that is accumulated over time by inflows and/or depleted by outflows. Stocks can only be changed via flows. Mathematically a stock can be seen as an accumulation or integration of flows over time - with outflows subtracting from the stock. Stocks typically have a certain value at each moment of time - e.g. the number of population at a certain moment.

A flow changes a stock over time. Usually we can clearly distinguish inflows and outflows. Flows typically are measured over a certain interval of time - eg. the number of births over a day or month.

## SOFT RECONCILIATION

A soft reconciliation is a bias selection that one ties to the corresponding selection from the authoritative source. A soft reconciliation differs from a full reconciliation because it does not review every line item nor is it a statistical representation of the authoritative source.

*Example*: If your significant other went grocery shopping and you asked for 25 items but you didn't want to take the time to look for every item already put away, you can select any number of items until you are comfortable that they are all there. Since you are only worried about a few items simply look for those. If they are there, you can infer the carrots and green beans were also purchased. If not, you have reconciling items and need to determine the root cause.

## SAFETY STOCK

Safety stock is normally required by companies to ensure that they have sufficient quantities of material in stock. The safety stock is there to provide coverage for unexpected customer demand, damage in the warehouse or required due to quality issues found in production. However, there are situations where companies do not require inventory to be in stock. These"out of stock" situations should not be confused with the highly undesirable"stock-out" predicament where customer's orders cannot be shipped or production is halted due to lack of lack of components. The"out of stock" situation is beneficial to companies when the company has no demand for certain items and zero inventory means a no warehouse costs.

When supply chain professionals determine the optimum level of safety stock there are a number of scenarios that they will consider. Many companies look at the costs involved in having a certain level of safety stock. The costs include the initial purchase of the stock from the vendor, the cost of storing the material in the warehouse and the potential depreciation of the material over time, especially when considering material that has a finite shelf life.

However there is a cost associated with having a situation where the material is not in stock. Stock-outs can cause non-monetary results such as loss of customer satisfaction when items cannot be shipped on time. Whereas the cost of a production stoppage can be calculated when a production line stops and has to be retooled for a new order when the stock-out of a component occurs.

There are three techniques that are used to calculate safety stocks; statistical based, fixed quantity and time period based.

## Statistical Based Safety Stock

The statistical method to calculate safety stock is based on the premise that is possible to mathematically calculate the level of safety stock to prevent a stock-out situation. The traditional method used to statistically calculate safety stock is the used of the normal distribution or bell-shaped curve. In a normal distribution curve, the mid-point of the curve is the forecast, which represents the average value. As the curve moves away from the centre there is a deviation from the average and the probability of a high deviation from the forecast is represented by a smaller and smaller percentage. For example a 48% deviation from the forecast may represent a 2% possibility.

There are pros and cons of selecting a statistical based safety stock. Although the statistical method is based in accurate mathematics, predicting business is not always as accurate. There are always situations that occur that cannot be forecasted. For example, a statistical method may calculate an item to have a safety stock even when the item is no longer required in manufacturing. In addition some business methods employed by companies to improve efficiencies in the supply chain may work against the mathematical equations used in calculating safety stock. Just-In-Time techniques can adversely affect the requirements of safety stock and render the calculation inaccurate.

## Fixed Safety Stock

Companies can decide to have a fixed value for the level of safety stock for some materials. This will require a production planner to determine a value for the safety stock rather than rely on a quantity determined by a statistical calculation. The value that is determined by planner will remain the same until manually changed. When the actual inventory level reaches or falls below the safety stock level, this will trigger a replenishment order for a quantity of material. The quantity of material on the replenishment order is determined by demand. The fixed safety stock level can also be set to zero when a company wants to phase out an item, if it is being superceded or the finished good is no longer being manufactured.

## Time Period Based Safety Stock

The time period based safety stock level is used to calculate the stock required over a fixed period. For example, if manufacturing demand requires 100 cases of part A to be consumed each day, the safety stock for a week would be 700 cases. The time period based safety stock is therefore determined by the forecast for the material in future periods. The forecast will include usually include a combination of actual demand from sales orders placed by customers and a forecast based on a statistical calculation.

Whatever method is used to calculate safety stock, it should be monitored periodically to ensure that it is accurate and satisfies the need it is intended for. Having safety stock in a warehouse has a cost associated with it and unnecessary safety stock is a scenario that should be avoided.

## PHANTOM INVENTORY

Phantom inventory is a common expression for goods that an inventory accounting system considers to be on-hand at a storage location, but are not actually available. This could be due to the items being moved without recording the change in the inventory accounting system, breakage, theft, data entry errors or deliberate fraud.

The resulting discrepancy between the online inventory balance and physical availability can delay automated reordering and lead to out-of-stock incidents. If not addressed, phantom inventory can also result in broader accounting issues and restatements. A number of techniques have been used to correct phantom inventory problems, including physical cycle counts, RFID tagging of items and statistical modeling of phantom inventory conditions.

## GMROII

Gross Margin Return on Inventory Investment is a ratio in microeconomics that describes a seller's income on every dollar spent on inventory. It is one way to determine how valuable the seller's inventory is, and describes the relationship between total sales, total profit from total sales, and the amount of resources invested in the inventory sold. A seller will aim for a high GMROII. Since the inventory is a very widely-ranging factor in a seller's investment, it is important for the seller to know how much she might expect to gain from it. The GMROII answers the question "for each dollar at cost, how many dollars of gross profit will I generate in one year?" GMROII is traditionally calculated by using one year's gross profit against the average of 12 or 13 units of inventory at cost. A rule of thumb is that a GMROII of at least 3.2 is the breakeven for a business.

### GMROII in the Retail Industry

GMROII is particularly important in the retail industry where stock turn and Gross Margin Per cent can vary heavily by item, location, and week. GMROII can act as the main driver for retailers to Analyse their product and store offering. This metric does not suffer from the major disadvantages some of the other main performance metrics do.

*For example*:

- Products or stores with high sales often have lower margin or excessive inventory
- Products with a high stock turn often have a low margin
- High margin items are often slow sellers and thus produce low profits
- High profit products often have low margin, high volume sales but also high inventory levels that prevent other products from being displayed and sold

Retailers usually drive their business based on sales or margin. In a retailer where budgets and bonuses are based on sales, employees often achieve that by lowering the margin or putting too much stock in their stores. A high GMROII indicates a good balance of sales, margin, and inventory cost.

## Average GMROII

When tactical decisions are required for variable time periods, it is helpful for systems to be set up so that GMROII can be Analysed at either the yearly, monthly, or weekly level.

Therefore it is advantageous to use Average Weekly GMROII which takes time out of the picture. That way, the retailer looks at similar types of numbers regardless of how many weeks are being looked at. The formula is: Average Weekly GMROII = (Profits for the total time period)/ (Sum of each week ending inventory cost value)

## Short-coming of GMROII

A short-coming of GMROII driven analysis is that items with high sell-offs appear better than items with constant inventory supplies. Fashionable items that totally sold off will appear better than basic items such as black socks that are replenished by reorders. This is particularly evident when analyzing shorter time periods or item level information rather than higher level information.

## INVENTORY BOUNCE

Inventory bounce is a term used in economics to describe an economy's bounce back to normal GDP levels after a recession. Firms usually keep a certain amount of inventory. When an economy faces a recession, sales might be unexpectedly low, which results in unexpectedly high inventory. In the next period, firms cut production so that inventory will drop to their desired levels, which results in even lower GDP. Subsequently, firms might increase the production back up to maintain the usual level of inventory, which causes the GDP to bounce back. This bounce back is called an inventory bounce. We care about it because if GDP recovers is only an inventory bounce, the recovery of GDP might not be sustained, which means that economy might not have truly recovered from the recession.

## INVENTORY CONTROL PROBLEMS

In actual practice the vast majority of manufacturing and distribution companies suffer from lower customer service, higher costs and excessive inventories than are necessary. Inventory control problems are usually the result of using poor processes, practices and antiquated support systems. The inventory management process is much more complex than the uninitiated understand. In fact, in many companies the inventory control department is perceived as little more than a clerical function. When this is the case, the fact is the function is probably not very effective.

The likely result of this approach to inventory control is lots of material shortages, excessive inventories, high costs and poor customer service. For example, if a customer orders a product that requires a manufacturer to acquire 20 part numbers to assemble a product and then, only 19 of the 20 part numbers are available, you have nineteen part numbers which are excess inventory.

Worse, the product can't be shipped to create revenue and the customer is not serviced. Think for a moment about the complexities of making products that require hundreds and maybe thousands of part numbers to be available in the right quantity, at the right place and at the right time to make products to satisfy customer orders. It is a complex network to control and a set of inventory management tasks that must be performed with precision.

## INVENTORY TURNOVER RATIO

Inventory turnover ratio is one of the Accounting turnover ratios, a financial ratio. This ratio measures the number of times, on average, the inventory is sold during the period. Its purpose is to measure the liquidity of the inventory. A popular variant of the Inventory turnover ratio is to convert it into an average days to sell the inventory in terms of days.

*Remember that the Inventory turnover ratio is figured as "turnover times" and the average days to sell the inventory is in "days":*

- Inventory turnover ratio = Cost of goods sold/ Average inventory
- Average days to sell the inventory = 365/ Inventory Turnover Ratio

## JUST IN CASE

Traditional manufacturing is sometimes referred to as Just-In-Case manufacturing by Manufacturing engineers. In JIC, manufacturers need to maintain large inventories of supplies, parts, warehousing resources, and extra workers to meet production contingencies. These contingencies, more common in less industrialized countries, can be poor transportation, poor quality control, other suppliers production problems, and environmental. This can lead to inefficiencies because a manufacturer has to have excess inventory and backups of "fragile" stages of production which can get out of sync and cause delays for other manufacturers.

## JUST-IN-TIME (BUSINESS)

Just-in-time (JIT) is an inventory strategy that strives to improve a business's return on investment by reducing in-process inventory and associated carrying costs. To meet JIT objectives, the process relies on signals or Kanban between different points in the process, which tell production when to make the next part. Kanban are usually 'tickets' but can be simple visual signals, such as the presence or absence of a part on a shelf. Implemented correctly, JIT can improve a manufacturing organization's return on investment, quality, and efficiency. Quick notice that stock depletion requires personnel to order new stock is critical to the inventory reduction at the centre of JIT. This saves warehouse space and costs. However, the complete mechanism for making this work is often misunderstood.

For instance, its effective application cannot be independent of other key components of a lean manufacturing system or it can "...end up with the opposite of the desired result.". In recent years manufacturers have continued to try to hone forecasting methods, however, some research demonstrates that basing JIT on the presumption of stability is inherently flawed.

## LIFO (COMPUTING)

LIFO is an acronym which stands for last in, first out. In computer science and queueing theory this refers to the way items stored in some types of data structures are processed. By definition, in a LIFO structured linear list, elements can be added or taken off from only one end, called the "*top*". A LIFO structure can be emphasised with the example of a stack of trays. The last tray to be placed on top is also the first to be taken off the top.

The term in computing generally refers to the abstract principles of list processing and temporary storage, particularly when there is a need to access the data in limited amounts, and in a certain order. LIFO is most used in cases where the last data added to the structure must be the first data to be removed or evaluated. A useful analogy is of the office worker: a person can only handle one page at a time, so the top piece of paper added to a pile is the first off; parallel to limitations such as data bus width and the fact that one can only manipulate a single binary data address in a computer at a time.

The abstract LIFO mechanism, when applied to computing inevitably devolves to the real data structures implemented as stacks whose eponymous relation to the "stack of paper", "stack of plates" should be obvious. Other names for the device are "Push down list" and "piles" The term FILO can be used synonymously, as the term emphasizes that early additions to the list need to wait until they rise to the LIFO structure "top" to be accessed. The difference between a generalized list, an array, queue, or stack, is defined by the rules enforced and used to access the mechanism. In any event, a LIFO structure is accessed in opposite order to a queue: "There are certain frequent situations in computer science when one wants to restrict insertions and deletions so that they can only take place at the beginning or end of the list, not in the middle. Two of the data structures useful in such situations are *stacks* and *queues*."

## LOWER OF COST OR MARKET

Lower of Cost or Market (LCM) is an approach to valuing and reporting inventory. Normally ending inventory is stated at historical cost but there are times when the original cost of the ending inventory is greater than the cost of replacement thus the inventory has lost value. If the inventory has decreased in value below historical cost then its carrying value is reduced and reported on the balance sheet. The criterion for reporting this is the lesser of the value of the original cost or the market value. Any loss resulting from the decline in the value of inventory is charged to Cost of Goods Sold if non-material, or Loss on the reduction of inventory to LCM if material.

## NEW OLD STOCK

New old stock are old parts for obsolete equipment that have never been sold at retail. The term refers to merchandise being offered for sale which was manufactured long ago but that has never been used. Such merchandise may not be produced anymore, and the new old stock may represent the only market source of a particular item at the present time.

Although not an officially recognized accounting term, it is in common use in the auction and retail industries. For example, owners of antique vehicles seek NOS parts from specialized vendors that are needed to keep their automobiles, motorcycles, or trucks operational or in factory-original condition. eBay uses the term on their auction website.

Another example is a business catering to vacuum tube enthusiasts that defines NOS as, any stocked item which is either A: out of production; B: discontinued from the current line of product; C: has been sitting on a stockroom or warehouse shelf for some time; or D: any combination of the above. While damage to the original packaging is common, damage to its contents is generally not acceptable in determining if an item is NOS, as it should be presentable in the same form as when new.

Some people refer to such merchandise as new obsolete stock to further indicate that the parts have not been manufactured for several years. This describes parts that are used in obsolete equipment or the like.

Other people refer to new original stock meaning that they are original equipment parts that remained in inventory for a use that never came. Automobile dealers and parts companies often sell such slow moving stock at a discount. Other specialty parts vendors then market these NOS parts that may either decline or increase in value depending on their type and desirability.

## ORDER FULFILLMENT

Order fulfillment is in the most general sense the complete process from point of sales inquiry to delivery of a product to the customer. Sometimes Order fulfillment is used to describe the more narrow act of distribution or the logistics function, however, in the broader sense it refers to the way firms respond to customer orders.

The first research towards defining order fulfillment strategies was published by Mather and his discussion of the P:D ratio, whereby P is defined as the production lead-time, i.e. how long it takes to manufacture a product, and D is the demand lead-time, i.e. how long customers are willing to wait for the order to be completed.

*Based on comparing P and D, a firm has several basic strategic order fulfillment options*:

- Engineer-to-Order - Here, the product is designed and built to customer specifications; this approach is most common for large construction projects and one-off products, such as Formula 1 cars
- Build-to-Order -Here, the product is based on a standard design, but component production and manufacture of the final product is linked to the order placed by the final customer's specifications; this strategy is typical for high-end motor vehicles and aircraft
- Assemble-to-Order -Here, the product is built to customer specifications from a stock of existing components. This assumes a modular product architecture that allows for the final product to be configured in this way; a typical example for this approach is Dell's approach to customizing its computers.
- Make-to-Stock -Here, the product is built against a sales forecast, and sold to the customer from finished goods stock; this approach is common in the grocery and retail sectors.
- Digital Copy -Where products are digital assets and inventory is maintained with a single digital master. Copies are created on-demand, downloaded and saved on customers' storage devices.

*In its broadest definition the possible steps in the process are*:

- *Product Inquiry*:Initial inquiry about offerings, visit to the web-site, catalog request
- *Sales Quote*:Budgetary or availability quote
- *Order Configuration*-Where ordered items need selection of options or order lines need to be compatible with each other
- *Order Booking*:The formal order placement or closing of the deal

- *Order Acknowledgment/ Confirmation*: Confirmation that the order is booked and/or received
- *Invoicing/ Billing*: The presentment of the commercial invoice/ bill to the customer
- *Order Sourcing/ Planning*: Determining the source/ location of item(s) to be shipped
- *Order Changes:* Changes to orders, if needed
- *Order Processing*: Process step where the distribution centre or warehouse is responsible to fill order.
- *Shipment*: The shipment and transportation of the goods
- *Delivery* - The delivery of the goods to the consignee/ customer
- *Settlement*: The payment of the charges for goods/ services/ delivery
- *Returns*: In case the goods are unacceptable/ not required

The order fulfillment strategy also determines the de-coupling point in the supply chain, which describes the point in the system where the"push" and"pull" elements of the supply chain meet. The decoupling point always is an inventory buffer that is needed to cater for the discrepancy between the sales forecast and the actual demand. It has become increasing necessary to move the de-coupling point in the supply chain to minimize the dependence on forecast and to maximize the reactionary or demand-driven supply chain elements. This initiative in the distribution elements of the supply chain corresponds to the Just-in-time initiatives pioneered by automobile manufacturers in the 1970s.

The order fulfillment strategy has also strong implications on how firms customise their products and deal with product variety. Strategies that can used to mitigate the impact of product variety include modularity, option bundling, late configuration, and build to order strategies-all of which are generally referred as mass customization strategies.

## PERIODIC INVENTORY

Periodic inventory is a system of inventory in which

updates are made on a periodic basis. This differs from perpetual inventory systems, where updates are made as seen fit. In Periodic Inventory System no effort is made to keep up-to-date records of either the inventory or the cost of goods sold. Instead, these amounts are determined only periodically-usually at the end of each year.

As the inventory records are not updated as transactions occur, there is no need of *Inventory Subsidiary Ledger*. The foundation of the periodic inventory system is the taking of a complete physical inventory at year-end. This physical count determines the amount of inventory appearing in the balance sheet. The cost of goods sold for the entire year then is determined by a Short Computation.

## PERPETUAL INVENTORY

In business and accounting/accountancy, perpetual inventory or continuous inventory describes systems of inventory where information on inventory quantity and availability is updated on a continuous basis as a function of doing business. Generally this is accomplished by connecting the inventory system with order entry and in retail the point of sale system. In this case, book inventory would be exactly the same as, or almost the same, as the real inventory.

In earlier periods, non-continuous, or periodic inventory systems were more prevalent. Starting in the 1970's digital computers made possible the ability to implement a perpetual inventory system. This has been facilitated by bar coding and lately radio frequency identification labeling which allows computer systems to quickly read and process inventory information as part of transaction processing.

Perpetual inventory systems can still be vulnerable to errors due to overstatements or understatements that can occur as a result of theft, breakage, scanning errors or untracked inventory movements, leading to systematic errors in replenishment.

# CASH MANAGEMENT

Cash management, or treasury management, is a

marketing term for certain services offered primarily to larger business customers. It may be used to describe all bank accounts provided to businesses of a certain size, but it is more often used to describe specific services such as *cash concentration, zero balance accounting,* and *automated clearing house* facilities. Sometimes, private banking customers are given cash management services.

## CASH MANAGEMENT SERVICES GENERALLY OFFERED

*The following is a list of services generally offered by banks and utilised by larger businesses and corporations*:

- *Account Reconcilement Services*: Balancing a checkbook can be a difficult process for a very large business, since it issues so many checks it can take a lot of human monitoring to understand which checks have not cleared and therefore what the company's true balance is. To address this, banks have developed a system which allows companies to upload a list of all the checks that they issue on a daily basis, so that at the end of the month the bank statement will show not only which checks have cleared, but also which have not. More recently, banks have used this system to prevent checks from being fraudulently cashed if they are not on the list, a process known as positive pay.
- *Advanced Web Services*: Most banks have an Internet-based system which is more advanced than the one available to consumers. This enables managers to create and authorize special internal logon credentials, allowing employees to send wires and access other cash management features normally not found on the consumer web site.
- *Armored Car Services*: Large retailers who collect a great deal of cash may have the bank pick this cash up via an armored car company, instead of asking its employees to deposit the cash.
- *Automated Clearing House*: services are usually offered by the cash management division of a bank. The

Automated Clearing House is an electronic system used to transfer funds between banks. Companies use this to pay others, especially employees. Certain companies also use it to collect funds from customers. This system is criticized by some consumer advocacy groups, because under this system banks assume that the company initiating the debit is correct until proven otherwise.

- *Balance Reporting Services*: Corporate clients who actively manage their cash balances usually subscribe to secure web-based reporting of their account and transaction information at their lead bank. These sophisticated compilations of banking activity may include balances in foreign currencies, as well as those at other banks. They include information on cash positions as well as'float'. Finally, they offer transaction-specific details on all forms of payment activity, including deposits, checks, wire transfers in and out, ACH, investments, etc.
- *Cash Concentration Services*: Large or national chain retailers often are in areas where their primary bank does not have branches. Therefore, they open bank accounts at various local banks in the area. To prevent funds in these accounts from being idle and not earning sufficient interest, many of these companies have an agreement set with their primary bank, whereby their primary bank uses the Automated Clearing House to electronically"pull" the money from these banks into a single interest-bearing bank account.
- *Lockbox - Retail services*: Often companies which receive a large number of payments via checks in the mail have the bank set up a post office box for them, open their mail, and deposit any checks found. This is referred to as a"lockbox" service.
- *Lockbox - Wholesale*: services: are for companies with small numbers of payments, sometimes with detailed requirements for processing. This might be a

company like a dentist's office or small manufacturing company.

- *Positive Pay*: Positive pay is a service whereby the company electronically shares its check register of all written checks with the bank. The bank therefore will only pay checks listed in that register, with exactly the same specifications as listed in the register. This system dramatically reduces check fraud.
- *Reverse Positive Pay*: Reverse positive pay is similar to positive pay, but the process is reversed, with the company, not the bank, maintaining the list of checks issued. When checks are presented for payment and clear through the Federal Reserve System, the Federal Reserve prepares a file of the checks' account numbers, serial numbers, and dollar amounts and sends the file to the bank. In reverse positive pay, the bank sends that file to the company, where the company compares the information .to its internal records. The company lets the bank know which checks match its internal information, and the bank pays those items. The bank then researches the checks that do not match, corrects any misreads or encoding errors, and determines if any items are fraudulent. The bank pays only"true" exceptions, that is, those that can be reconciled with the company's files.
- *Sweep accounts*: are typically offered by the cash management division of a bank. Under this system, excess funds from a company's bank accounts are automatically moved into a money market mutual fund overnight, and then moved back the next morning. This allows them to earn interest overnight. This is the primary use of money market mutual funds.
- *Zero Balance Accounting*: can be thought of as somewhat of a hack. Companies with large numbers of stores or locations can very often be confused if all those stores are depositing into a single bank account. Traditionally, it would be impossible to

know which deposits were from which stores without seeking to view images of those deposits. To help correct this problem, banks developed a system where each store is given their own bank account, but all the money deposited into the individual store accounts are automatically moved or swept into the company's main bank account. This allows the company to look at individual statements for each store. U.S. banks are almost all converting their systems so that companies can tell which store made a particular deposit, even if these deposits are all deposited into a single account. Therefore, zero balance accounting is being used less frequently.

- *Wire Transfer*: A wire transfer is an electronic transfer of funds. Wire transfers can be done by a simple bank account transfer, or by a transfer of cash at a cash office. Bank wire transfers are often the most expedient method for transferring funds between bank accounts. A bank wire transfer is a message to the receiving bank requesting them to effect payment in accordance with the instructions given. The message also includes settlement instructions. The actual wire transfer itself is virtually instantaneous, requiring no longer for transmission than a telephone call.
- *Controlled Disbursement*: This is another product offered by banks under Cash Management Services. The bank provides a daily report, typically early in the day, that provides the amount of disbursements that will be charged to the customer's account. This early knowledge of daily funds requirement allows the customer to invest any surplus in intraday investment opportunities, typically money market investments. This is different from delayed disbursements, where payments are issued through a remote branch of a bank and customer is able to delay the payment due to increased float time.

In the past, other services have been offered the usefulness of which has diminished with the rise of the Internet. For example, companies could have daily faxes of their most recent transactions or be sent CD-ROMs of images of their cashed checks.

Cash management services can be costly but usually the cost to a company is outweighed by the benefits: cost savings, accuracy, efficiencies, etc.

# Index